# THE
# COMPLETE
# GUIDE
# TO

# DIGITAL
# GRAPHIC
# DESIGN

# THE COMPLETE GUIDE TO >>

# DIGITAL GRAPHIC DESIGN

Consultant Editors
Bob Gordon and Maggie Gordon

With 531 illustrations

 **Thames & Hudson**

First published in the United Kingdom in 2002 by
THAMES & HUDSON LTD
181A High Holborn
London WC1V 7QX

This book was conceived,
designed and produced by
THE ILEX PRESS LIMITED
Cambridge
England

Art Director: Alastair Campbell
Designer: Jonathan Raimes
Design Manager: Tony Seddon
Editorial Director: Steve Luck
Project Editor: Lachlan McLaine
Technical Editor: Keith Martin
Picture Research: Heather Vickers

Contributors
Design Basics: Maggie Gordon
Design For Print: Jonathan Raimes
Advertising: Paul Springer
Packaging: Richard Gooch
Signage: Ian Chilvers
Exhibition: Sue Perks
Internet & Multimedia: Phil Taylor
Games: Jonathan Smith
Type Colour Image: Bob Gordon

British Library Cataloguing-in-Publication Data
A catalogue record for this book is available from
the British Library

ISBN 0-500-28315-X

Printed and bound in China

For further information on this title refer to:
www.cggraphicdesign.com

**00**

# CONTENTS

**01** **02** **02** **03** **04**

# INTRODUCTION

# INTRODUCTION

## 00

'Digital', 'graphic' and 'design' have become three very potent words in our vocabulary. There can be few people living in the developed world whose life has not been touched or influenced by information and design technology. Personal computers and the ubiquitous silicon chip have found their way into the homes and workplaces of millions of people irrespective of background, age or culture.

One of the most common words bandied about as an all-encompassing descriptor is 'digital'. This is almost inevitable, since computers depend on streams of electronically generated 'digits' to function. So we have digital telephone lines, digital printing, digital radio and digital television, amongst the many areas connected with information, communication and design. Virtually all data, whether it is in the form of words, numbers, images, sound or movement, can be digitized and transmitted using a range of technologies.

Digitization has created a common method of recording and transmitting data, allowing a high level of interactivity across many forms of media. This interactivity allows the full range of creative elements to work together in a single context, and has radically changed designers' working methods by providing access to the vast storehouse of knowledge on the Internet and corporate Intranets, and enabling them to send and receive media electronically via email from their own computers.

Digital data transmission speeds are constrained by the size of files, the medium through which data flows and the speed at which computer processors can handle the information, but every day sees an improvement in all of these areas: files can be compressed more efficiently, fibre optics, allowing speed of light transmission, are being used more and more, and processor speeds are getting faster and faster. Together with increases in transmission speeds there is a growing convergence of media transmission which is bringing about a merging of personal computing, television, radio, telephone, publishing, games, web, email and ecommerce technologies. Flat screen technology is now fast replacing CRT monitors and computers, together with other peripheral devices, are getting smaller. These developments take us into an era where the quality of visual content is going to play an increasingly important role in the way we communicate to a wider range of audiences. The quality of visually received information is the responsibility of the digital graphic designer.

Design finds its way into every aspect of daily life, from the look of clothes, buildings and consumer goods, to reading matter, interior and exterior environments, communication and graphic design plays an important part in all these visual experiences. It is almost impossible to avoid being bombarded by visual messages in the environment to which the graphic designer's role is so often to bring order and clarity. Much of what is published in print or on screen has a tendency to be visually discordant or jumbled, but in a world that is so information- or message-orientated, it is increasingly important for the digital graphic designer to strive for higher visual standards. Understanding how audiences react to visual material is key to the problem-solving process for the graphic designer. Equally important is an understanding of how eye and brain work together in scanning and understanding the 'written' or typeset word.

So, while the earliest scribes perhaps could be described as the first 'graphic designers' – text, whether scratched in clay, carved in stone or inked onto vellum, needed to be arranged in a logical and efficient way – it was the invention of printing, with its inherent potential for producing a multiple, and thus commercial, product that formed the bedrock for graphic design as a recognizable trade.

The invention of moveable type in the mid-15th century (widely attributed to Johann Gutenberg), although originally intended as a means of replicating the written word, radically changed the design of letter shapes, standardizing them as well as introducing different styles to emphasize meaning. Thus, while the handwriting of the scribe had evolved slowly and gently over centuries – emphasis being placed as much on style and embellishments as on letter forms – it was the invention of moveable type that saw the birth of conscious type design. Graphic design continued to develop over the years as a hybrid activity, owing as much to mathematics, engineering and psychology (providing inspiration for problem solving) as to the fine arts (providing aesthetic and emotional stimulation). Changes in art, fashion and taste, and dramatic developments in printing technology had massive influences on the development of graphic design, along with the contributions of innumerable artists, typographers, designers and stylists. However, the overwhelming message conveyed by the more influential 'graphic designers' is that few drew on history for inspiration. Indeed, following the First World War the members of the Bauhaus School saw history as dead convention and preferred instead to redefine those conventions by

first-class tools for exploring, extending and realizing ideas in flexible, faster and more cost-effective ways.

Many features of the reprographic processes have remained essentially the same over the last few decades, albeit enhanced through computerized devices. Computerization has, however, made a significant contribution to the decline in the number of specialist crafts and trades people, and the considerable increase in the responsibility of the digital graphic designer as control of more production functions is transferred to the computer desktop.

Printing had for many years dominated the way in which graphic designers worked – packaging, exhibition design and advertising

## Digital developments have given designers a range of first-class tools for exploring, extending and realizing ideas in flexible, faster and more cost-effective ways

rejecting them. All avant-garde thinking – a major component of graphic design – is driven by the need to escape from the past in order to explore the future.

The emphasis of this book, however, is on *digital* graphic design, and more influential even than desktop computers, was the concept of the 'graphical user interface' (GUI) – the means by which graphic symbols enable the user to control, or interface with, a computer. The Macintosh, by using graphics for its interface, allowed the concept of graphic display to be exploited – and thus digital graphic design was born.

The digital revolution overtook traditional graphic design working practices with extraordinary speed. Designers now need to be fully conversant with the fundamentals of computer-driven processes, be able to learn new skills rapidly and, in a field that is constantly expanding, can expect to be continually developing these skills.

There are, however, several aspects of graphic design that remain relatively unaffected by technology. These include generating and developing ideas and concepts, design and typographic principles and creative problem solving – all attributes that distinguish graphic design from other professions. Happily, digital developments have given designers a range of

are all related to printing processes. Traditional printing methods have undergone rapid revolutions. During the 1960s, offset lithography took over from the labour intensive letterpress (or relief) printing and within a decade had become the most common form of reproduction. This major change was followed closely by computerized typesetting which was subsequently absorbed into the digital technology of the personal computer.

Through the concentration of design and production features into software applications, the digital designer now has unprecedented control and responsibility for design realization and production. For instance, a file containing all the information necessary for output can be either handed over or digitally transmitted to the printer. The printer's equipment then makes films and plates exactly as directed by the electronic file and the job can be printed with little other human intervention. Naturally, professional designers and printers would normally meet to discuss a complex job although the fact remains that a high proportion of the decision-making and graphic assembly control is embedded in the digital file produced by the designer: hence the meticulous care that needs to be taken in its preparation.

Some say that the digital revolution, has reached maturity, and many young designers of today are probably puzzled as to why those of a certain age think that the digital age is so 'cool'. But it is essential that we all have one eye on the future otherwise a great deal of time will be spent lamenting the hours wasted learning all about Web design when, in all likelihood, the Web, in future, will in fact be... what, exactly? Difficult even to second guess since, as the saying goes, 'If we can see into the future, then we're not looking far enough ahead.'

# THE ROLE OF THE DIGITAL GRAPHIC DESIGNER

associated with repetitive design or editing tasks have been reduced considerably by automated features built into most applications, such as 'search and replace', 'auto-spell-check', 'auto-image-import', 'style sheets', 'actions', to name just a few. If you can't find a feature that automates a repetitive task, you can be sure it will be included in the next upgrade.

Paradoxically, in an era that has seen many industries and professions having to specialize in order to survive, the digital graphic designer has been required to diversify. The most significant growth is in the explosion of the Internet and multimedia industry. Many graphic designers are fully engaged in Web page design involving typography, imagery, animation, movies and even sound. The computerization of graphic design work, with the development of numerous, disparate, yet often overlapping, software programs has

As graphic designers can work across so many fields, they need to be familiar with a wide range of different production and manufacturing processes and related support professions and skills. This may often include photographers, illustrators, musicians, writers and film makers. Digitization of sound, image, animation, movies and production processes has enabled professionals to collaborate and work across an increasingly wide spectrum.

The emergence of the personal computer and desktop publishing programs, together with their wide availability to non-designers, could have signalled the beginning of the end for the practising graphic designer. Photography, as a profession, could also have died out as automated and high-

## Professional graphic design will continue to thrive because ideas and innovation, good composition and a creative eye cannot be 'packaged'

greatly increased the range of work in which they can be involved. In addition to the rich creative elements of many programs, including sound and animation, there are many built-in productivity and labour-saving features. Previously specialist areas of graphic design now share similar software programs for image and text origination.

The digital power readily available to the designer is now immense. Every aspect of graphic design can be created and finished to a high professional level on a single PC or Apple Macintosh workstation. Not only has the creation of actual projects been made easier, but the way in which they can be previewed by both designer and client has transformed the way in which creative people work – from technologies such as PDF files for wide distribution, to walk-through software for three-dimensional designs, packaging software that folds and makes up packs from flat designs, to slide shows and movies that can be used for 'real life' presentations. Many of the chores

quality cameras became accessible and easy to use for anybody and everybody. However, like professional photography, professional graphic design will continue to thrive because ideas and innovation, good composition and a creative eye cannot be 'packaged'.

Graphic design is an immensely exciting and vibrant activity in which to be involved and, as such, is a rewarding profession to follow. But it requires vision, stamina, creativity and good humour combined with analytical and methodical ways of working. Designers need a working knowledge of budgets, manufacturing and reproduction processes. Successful graphic designers aim to devise inventive solutions to visual communication problems in response to clients' needs and, in order to do so, often work with clients in formulating a brief and working strategy prior to starting any visual work. A good understanding of human nature and the cultural environment as well as the ability to lead or be a team player is what, together with a keen eye for detail, distinguishes the truly excellent designer from the average.

Good design is the product of the creative intellect supported by innovative use of sophisticated digital tools and cannot be bought 'off the shelf'.

# THE COMPLETE GUIDE TO DIGITAL GRAPHIC DESIGN

The aim of this book is both to inspire and inform the reader by exploring a wide range of visual communication and graphic design contexts while introducing essential design methodology and concepts on which to build. It explores the diversity of graphic design and showcases the work of inventive and talented designers using digital media for the development, realization and production of projects.

*The Complete Guide to Digital Graphic Design* demonstrates different facets of digital graphic design and seeks to demystify some of the technical jargon that is often associated with computing and the design world.

The introductory pages show examples of work from a wide range of visual communication contexts, setting the scene for further in-depth exploration within individual sections.

**Part One**, Design Basics, explores some of the fundamental principles that underpin good and efficient graphic design. This section is, in essence, 'away from the screen' as it involves thinking and creative processes related to idea generation and informed design decision-making. It includes an appreciation of the 'building blocks' essential to good graphic design, shape and form, spatial awareness, what type is and how to work with it. The emotive use of colour and how colour can work for the digital designer is also looked at, as a powerful tool rather than just decoration.

**Part Two** consists of sub-sections that explore defined areas of surface graphic design. These include Design for Print, Packaging, Signage, Advertising, and Exhibition and Display Design.

**Part Three** looks at design for the Internet, Intranets and multimedia. This part is particularly useful for those who may feel somewhat swamped by the terminology in this area. It shows clearly how designers have to respond and adapt to a fluidity of display by different Web browsers and computer platforms, and compares this with the more stable environment of a multimedia project.

Leading practitioners from each field take an in-depth look at their specialist areas. Where equipment or software, additional to the core list introducing these sections, is considered important, this is highlighted. Specialist processes, which include four-colour offset lithographic printing, are discussed together with related creative and support professionals mentioned as appropriate. At the end of each section, a case history is explored and the critical and key creative and production stages involved in arriving at the final design are explained.

**Part Four** takes a focussed look at the technical intricacies of Colour, Type and Image Making.

The use of colour is discussed in the Design Basics section but it is essential for the practising graphic designer to understand how colour is created and why, for instance, different sets of primary colours are used for discussing monitor displays (RGB) from those used in printing (CMYK). As mixing, controlling and adjusting colour plays such an important role in graphic design, the attributes and terminology of colour and how it works are looked at closely.

Digital type, too, has a language of its own. The Design Basics section covers working with type from an aesthetic and functional point of view, but on a technical level the graphic designer has to appreciate how type is handled by the computer. What are bitmap or outline fonts, for example? Why might we need Adobe ATM as essential software for use with type? Typefaces and font files, managing fonts, font libraries, buying fonts and font copyright are also explained.

Computer programs have made retouching, montaging and technical and fine art image-making readily accessible to the designer and artist. The essential way in which bitmap programs work compared to the very different vector-based programs is made clear. The creation of special effects, the use of painting programs or drawing programs and how they interact with each other is also discussed and explained.

**lucy bullivant:** musing on the contemporary museum >When museums outgrow their institutional facilities, they don't necessarily have to marry old and new by extending on one site. The satellite idea creates a complex field of activity less bound by place. Architecture grounds each one in a context – it's down to the staff to design the field. Everyone is an architect in this business nowadays. >The term museum implies the facilities of collection, endowment, preservation and curatorial pedigree. It doesn't automatically signify retailing elements. Is the term 'hybrid' architecture a simplification of the need to create a dynamic relationship, in formal and programmatic terms, that endures in a climate of change? >Contemporary museum design pitfalls: gratuitous and not so revelatory form-making [every museum architect should reveal as well as display], and seduction by the myths of flexibility. If neutrality is an illusion, flexibility is an illusion's holy grail. >Curators have to be very flexible, even de-curate the architecture, but everyone works better with parameters. >Museum design now bridges the physical and the virtual worlds. How do we describe such an architecture, and how does it change the way we see museums? Improvisational tactics in lieu of physical facilities: the virtual friends' room [how far can you go with the museum without walls'? One mouse for every friend, perhaps, which is also a camera into all the other spaces, or is that another typology altogether]? >The contents and ambience of a museum [whether more masculine or more feminine] are frequently disturbingly various: the architecture cannot afford to be, but nor should it entirely lose the mystery of the gathering place, of chosen, untouched objects from the underworld. In this distillation, there is no other kind of secular solace. >The Centre Pompidou – that quintessential expression of the democratizing of knowledge and culture, a child of its time [1977]. But, [referring to the new renovation], how do you update utopia when it's lost its original meaning, its ethos of cultural democracy? Now, with the new pay to enter policy, you can't see one of its best exhibits, the views of the city of Paris, for free any more. >Don't forget take away museum experiences. Where tv is going [consumer choice], museums are following: at Frank Gehry's soon to be completed Pop Music Museum in Seattle visitors make their own customised disk from a sound bank to play later. >We have a museological climate where retailing elements frequently impinge on cultural pleasure, as harmlessly diverting as a form of museum downtime as they usually are. 'The ace caff with the museum attached' allows us to carry out more of our personal lives in these spaces. The museum community is interested in civic values in a place they want to feel is theirs too. After all, the fortunes of outdoor public space have waned, and perhaps the museum is a better, more rainproof place anyway in which to renew the idea of the civic agora. >Museums in the city: the relatively rare building of a new street smart metropolitan museum or its extension redefines the local urban fabric, causing its value as real estate to soar. >We need 'trickle down' on occasion to work more slowly [yes, developers], not to upset context into a total face lift that excludes the locals. On the other hand, if museums don't get above themselves, something else is bound to fill the space. >Cultural multiplex at one end of the spectrum, single theme museums at the other: you can't generalise. Isn't it reassuring that museum architecture as a subject and as a response is too rich and too layered to be conveyed in a rhetorical, 'talking to your one circulation choice walk', acoustiguide recording? >Lucy Bullivant is an architectural writer and curator, Archis and Domus correspondent, and director of >enter, her international exhibition/events consultancy.

**herbert girardet/urban futures:** rethinking the city >At the start of the new millennium cities and their resource use dominate life on earth. In the last 100 years, human numbers have grown fourfold, whilst both the world economy and urban populations have grown about 15 fold. Today, half of us live in cities while most of the rest depends on urban markets for their economic survival. One species now uses about half of nature's entire annual production, and we are increasingly undermining the integrity of the global environment. We have to rethink how we run our urban economies, energy, transport and waste systems, and the way we construct our buildings. If sustainability was the main frame of reference for the way we plan urban spaces, structures and processes – how would things change? >Given the vast scale of urbanisation today, cities would be well advised to model their functioning on natural ecosystems. These are generally systems of permanence, whereas currently man-made systems are defined by high levels of entropy. Cities have a linear metabolism, consisting of the flow of resources and products through the urban system. Nature's own ecosystems have an essentially circular metabolism in which every output by an organism is also an input which renews the whole living environment of which it is a part. The web of life hangs together in a 'chain of mutual benefit'. To be sustainable, cities have to develop a circular metabolism, minimising waste discharges, and using and re-using resources as efficiently as possible. >Thinking differently is an important starting point in the process of remodelling our cities. The real challenge however is to act differently. People all over the world are working on how to make their cities more sustainable, in both environmental and social terms. This exhibition is intended to enhance that process in the city that started it all: London. It is, at present, a city of vast global dependencies. Its ecological footprint extends to an area the size of the UK, about 125 times its own surface area. If all the world's cities demanded such vast surface areas to supply themselves three planets would be needed rather than the one we have. >It makes sense for people to live in cities. They have the potential for great resource efficiency through closed-loop economies, diversity and mutuality. In the past, economic growth has meant automatic growth in the consumption of resources and services of all kinds. Sustainable development, in contrast, requires new solutions to ensure that economic well-being is founded on efficient use of resources, minimising pollution and waste. New energy systems can supplant technologies we inherited from the past. It is clear that many new local jobs can be created on the way. In the exhibition the main focus is on these areas where the potential for change is greatest. These sections form an agenda for constructing the future sustainable city. >The quest for sustainability requires a strengthening of local democratic processes. Methods such as neighbourhood forums, action planning and consensus-building should be widely used, because they usually lead to better decision making. Community groups, local and central governments are increasingly aware that efforts to improve the living environment must focus on cities and urban lifestyles. Eco-friendly urban development could well become the greatest challenge of the twenty-first century, not only for human self-interest, but also for the sake of a sustainable relationship between cities and the biosphere on which humanity ultimately depends.

Cities, occupying 2% of the world's land surface, consume 75% of the world's resources and discharge 75% of the world's waste

London's total ecological footprint extends to around 125 times its surface area

act differently/living city

**Living City events**

**Mayoral Candidates Interviews**
14 April to 04 May
decide who to vote for by viewing videos of the candidates policies on sustainability
RIBA Architecture Gallery

**Living City Forum**
Tuesday 09 May
6.30pm
with Herbert Girardet, Patrick Bellew of Atelier Ten, Robin Murray of Ecologika and Dickon Robinson of Peabody Trust. Chaired by Paul Finch, Publishing Editor, emap, the event will outline practical steps to take forward possible outcomes of the Living City initiative.

**Education Sustainability Forum**
Tuesday 16 May
2.30pm to 5.30pm
Event for technology and design teachers in architecture.
Contact: Pamela Edwards, RIBA Education

**Green Kids Workshop**
Saturday 10 June
11am
Bring the children to the Architecture Week family day at RIBA. This workshop, run by the Centre for Sustainability, is free

Left: **A double-page spread for the Royal Institute of British Architects' Annual Report. Such multipage book work relies on a strong underpinning grid structure and clear typographic signposting to guide the reader and maintain interest.**
Design by Studio Myerscough, UK

Above: **DPICT**, a creative photography magazine, was able to take advantage of IBM's Infoprint Colour 100 printer to print 560 different, personalized covers for its launch edition. This would have been completely uneconomic in the past. The computerized selection, delivery and output of discreet text and imagery is beginning to alter our perception of volume publishing as new printing technology is exploited.
Design by DPICT, UK

Right: The Providian 2000 Annual Report focussed on the financial services company's employees and the cities where they lived and worked. In doing so, the report humanized what might otherwise seem a faceless corporation. The sensitive and creative imagery and interesting assembly of disparate typographic elements is facilitated by the flexible tools of the page layout application.
Design by Cahan and Associates, USA

# DESIGN FOR ADVERTISING

Pre May 12th.

Post May 12th.

The Economist
Now in colour.

Left and above: A series of British Airways posters by M & C Saatchi displayed in London Underground stations. Digital printing allows for customized, large format posters in small quantities, providing advertisers with opportunities for focussing on specific target audiences.
Design by M & C Saachi , UK

Top: Double-page spread advertisement for *The Economist* magazine, 'Now in Colour'. A simple photographic image to make a powerful point.
Design by Abbott Meade Vickers, UK

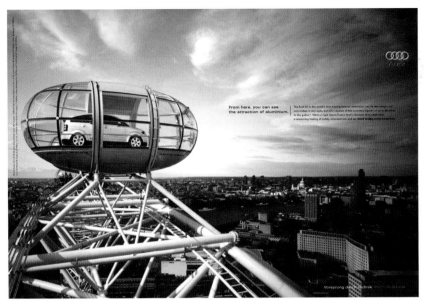

Left: This advertisement works by association: the slick engineering used to produce London's Millennium Wheel with that of the Audi. In advertising this is called 'borrowed interest'. In visualising the composition, the image would have been mocked up either as a Photoshop collage or as a 'moodboard' (usually rendered in marker and pencil). Note the treatment of the sky (the negative space), flattened in tone and colour to make the body text legible.
Design by Bartle Bogle Hegarty, UK

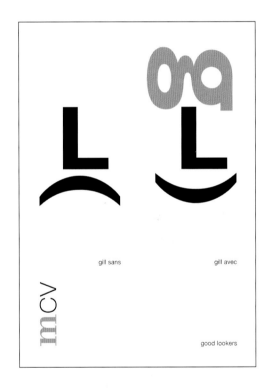

Left: Claimed to be the world's largest building graphic at over 150 metres high, this promotion for the Dutch national football team, was produced by large format digital printers VgL who printed 4500 panels covering 10,000 square metres. Printed on 3M Perforated Window Marking Film (PWMF), the graphics do not stop people being able to look out through the building's windows.
Design by Wieden and Kennedy, Netherlands

Above: This full page magazine advertisement for the recruitment consultants MCV, aimed at creative professionals proves the power of simplicity and wit.
Design by Peter Stimpson, UK

# DESIGN FOR PACKAGING

Left: The catalogue for an exhibition of fashion design by Jill Ritblat was wittily designed to be carried as a handbag.
Designed by Area, UK

Right: When packing becomes an invitation. For the opening ceremony of Zeum, an interactive arts centre in San Francisco, invitees received a velvet drawstring bag containing a brick of modelling clay elegantly wrapped in the invitation itself.
Design by Cahan and Associates, USA

Above: Wrapping paper is highly flexible and, ultimately, the simplest form of packaging. This example, designed by Summa for a Spanish supermarket, uses colour coding to identify delicatessen items, meats, vegetables, fish and bread products.
Design by Summa, Spain

Right: Making a virtue out of simplicity, this entirely typographic solution by Simon and Lars for a small bakery reflects the fresh, uncomplicated yet upmarket product.
Design by Simon and Lars, UK

Right: The Veuve Clicquot champagne laminated cardboard 'Magic Box' unfolds to create a strong, insulated and perfectly watertight ice bucket.
Design by Veuve Clicquot, France

# DESIGN FOR SIGNAGE

Left: **Taking digital design quite literally, the interior and exterior graphics for Apple Computer's research and development campus borrows pixellated imagery from the company's distinctive graphical user interface.** Design by Sussman/Prejza &Co, USA

Below: Signage has sometimes to be subtle and understated in order to fit into interior environments. Choice of materials and scale of presentation is all important, as can be seen here in the elegant freestanding lobby sign
Design by Sussman/Prejza & Co., USA

Right: These signage icons for varuious sporting activities installed in the Nishi Kasai district, Tokyo, are integrated into street furniture which minimises their intrusion without compromising their effectiveness.
Design by Edogawa Ward, Japan

Left: This signage system reflects the strong colours used for the Georges Pompidou Centre in Paris and creates a special energy for a building devoted to the promotion of the visual arts.
Design by Integral Ruedi Bauer & Associés, France

Below: Signs are not always explicitly designed as such. This decorative element on a Swiss school has become a familiar landmark and works much as a purpose-built sign would.
Design by Niklaus Troxler, Switzerland

# DESIGN FOR EXHIBITIONS

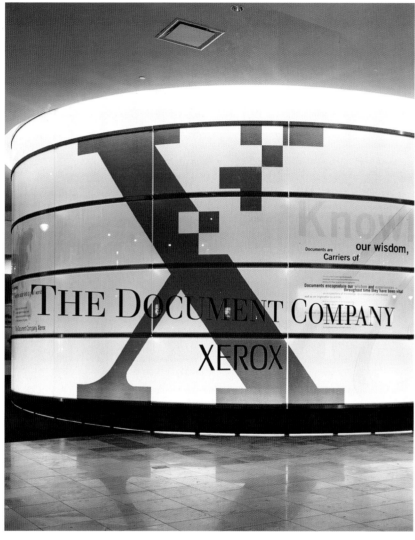

Above: **The Newseum, located in Washington D.C., deals with all aspects of news gathering and reporting. The exhibition design incorporates the Illuminated front pages of newspapers and a video newswall as well as computer stations for interactive learning. The visually dynamic space reflects the constant flow of information, news and data in the modern world.** Design by Ralph Applebaum Associates, USA

Above: **The design of the Xerox trade stand is dominated by a 10-metre-high example of the memorable, partly pixelated, capital X that represents Xerox everywhere.** Design by IDEO, USA

Left: This curving wall, created for a University of Rochester exhibition, demonstrates how design for exhibition can be a liberating pursuit – unconstrained as it is by paper size formats or the ubiquitous rectangle of the computer monitor.
Design by Poulin & Morris, USA

Above: The 'Power of Maps' exhibition at the Cooper Hewitt National Design Museum in New York incorporates exhibition panels that reflect the folding nature of maps and how they are used.
Design by Pentagram, USA

# DESIGN FOR THE INTERNET

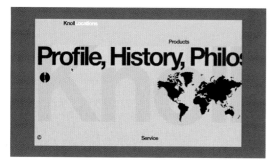

Above: www.knoll.com
A refreshingly direct, strong and uncluttered website created for Knoll, a furniture design company. The site's simplicity ensures that it loads quickly and is easy to navigate.
Design by NB:Studio, UK

Left: www.yes-indeed.net
French graphic designer, Donna DiStefano, has used strong imagery and a clean-cut interface to create this site as a showcase for her many design talents.
Design by Donna DiStefano, France

Above and top: www.designers-drug.de
This site contains urban photographs taken by the German designer Daniel Althausen. Pictures are displayed by category: city, people, traffic and abstract. Subject matter ranges from Amsterdam station at sunrise to passengers travelling on a train. It has a lean yet lively interface making navigation easy and interesting.
Design by Daniel Althausen, Germany

ART
DESIGN
FASHION
LIFESTYLE

DESIGN **MEMPHIS** approaches this area of cultural work through the pressing role that design has in shaping the world in which we live, the critical role of design/designer in culture. From this perspective, **MEMPHIS** engages both the work of individual designers, with special attention to its relationship to the field of design, and recent trends in the field at large. **MEMPHIS** hopes not only to provide co-mmentary and coverage, but to establish a forum for the development of current issues facing design.

features

Above: **www.memphisnotebook.com**
Memphis Notebook is an online magazine dedicated to art and design. The site is laid out like a print publication with predominantly textual content. However, the use of large photographic images mixed with unusual typography ensures it is far from boring.
Design by Memphis, USA

Right: **www.guinnessstorehouse.com**
A well planned and highly animated site designed with Flash. Lots of interactivity and added music make the tour a lively experience.
Design by Imagination, UK

# DESIGN FOR MULTIMEDIA / DESIGN FOR GAMES

Above: **Multimedia can be used to produce effective educational tools for many specialist professions. These screens are a sample from an interactive multimedia project which explains the use of technical imaging equipment for medical diagnosis.** Design by Maddalene Beltrami and the Ospedale Maggiore di Milano, Italy

Below: **InterStitch created this motion graphics video for the San Francisco chapter of the American Institute of Graphic Arts (AIGA) to promote a lecture series. The video was a hybrid of analog and digital design. Digital video was shot and composited in Adobe AfterEffects with animated graphics and 3D modelled elements. The lecture series discussed the topic of truth in beauty. The video addressed this by presenting the dissection and construction of its own form.** Design by InterStitch, USA

Below: This animation formed
part of a winning bid for a
project development
competition. Created in Adobe
Premiere it was presented on a
laptop and via a LCD projector.
Design by RTKL

Top: The Settlers IV
Computer game design is an arena
where digital graphic design is
often pushed to its technical limits.
Very much a team exercise, the
graphic designer will typically only
have reponsibility for a small part
of the overall look of a game.
Design by Blue Byte, Germany

Above: EA Sports NHL 2002
Even the most advanced 3D games
require some 2D interface design
and this is where the skills of the
multimedia designer come to the
fore. The challenge for the
designer is to present information
and choices with perfect clarity
while maintaining the mood and
overall look of the game.
Design by EA Sports, USA

# DESIGN BASICS

Basic design principles are the building blocks of graphic communication. To appreciate their value and relevance it is best to begin by looking at their particular characteristics away from an applied context.

Graphic designers find themselves working at large and small scales across increasingly varied areas at local, national and international levels. The flexible, innovative perspectives they need must be underpinned by basic principles if they are to make informed design decisions and aesthetic judgements. These principles are common to all design disciplines and provide a valuable constant in the midst of the continually developing opportunities with which the graphic designer is presented.

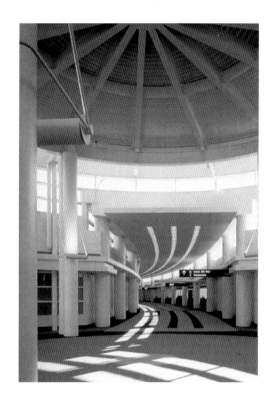

**PART 0I. DESIGN BASICS**

**CHAPTER ONE**

# THE VALUE OF DESIGN BASICS

Left: **Promotional brochure for the Museo de Arte Contemporaneo (MARCO) de Monterey in Mexico. The square, derived from the shape of the building, forms the basis of the museum's logo and overall visual identity.**
Design by Lance Wyman, USA

Above: **Circular architectural forms soften the large ticketing area in Chicago airport and offer an organic-looking background to the starkly contrasting rectangular information panels, ensuring that the latter stand out.**
Design by Carol Naughton & Associates, USA

**PRIMARY SHAPES** The familiar shapes – square, circle and triangle – together with their three-dimensional derivatives – cube, sphere and pyramid – underpin all the structures seen around us. There is very little that will not break down into, or visually relate to, some form of primary shape.

The square, like the cube, is a wholly static, form with no directional pull. It can be used to frame, exclude, include, attract, define area or for modular division, and it will sit comfortably in almost any arrangement of multiples. Even when rotated and in a more dynamic, diamond form, it retains its inherent, fixed quality. Minor modification to a linear square will, however, begin to direct the eye and also create associations. For example, if the corners are opened, or if a side is removed or tilted, the eye will move into the shape and associations of exit or entrance will be made. An extended square, or rectangle, directs the eye along, up or down its length and beyond, making the eye look for common alignments.

The circle has two main attributes – it provides a powerful focus for the eye and at the same time invites it to take a journey round either itself or a circular layout of any kinds of element. By contrast, a series of circles suggests self-contained units and so makes the eye 'jump' from one unit to the other, quickly tiring it. Although circles do not easily fit together, the eye can be made to spin across the surface by physically linking a series of circles. The pace of the spin is controlled by the size of circle.

The triangle is a balanced and completely stable form in both two- and three-dimensional forms, but also suggests a dynamic energy, even when equilateral. Unlike the circle or square, the proportions of a triangle can be radically altered to give it directional force without affecting its basic shape. The eye finds this directional force difficult to ignore.

It is important to understand the significant influence that these key forms have on the viewer's perception. Such an understanding will enable the designer to confidently organise the form and content of a design to communicate a visual message.

Kieler Woche     1997

21.- 29. Juni

Above: **The primary shapes and bright colours that underly the concept of this 3D, giant-sized children's hospital sign are familiar things with which a child can comfortably identify, even in unfamiliar surroundings. Variations on the playful and cheerful signage theme are used throughout the system.** Design by Emery Vincent Design, Australia

Left: **This poster for a sailing regatta uses a simple, primary shape inspired by both sails and small directional flags used in the regattas. Overlapped and cropped, the shapes evoke a sense of activity and celebration.** Design by Niklaus Troxler, Switzerland

**POINT, LINE AND AREA** are the basic elements used in all graphic design and, as with primary shapes, the way in which they are used will affect the overall perception of any communication. Most basic visual design decisions involve some representative combination of these shapes and elements. These may be used explicitly or implicitly, and with varying levels of complexity.

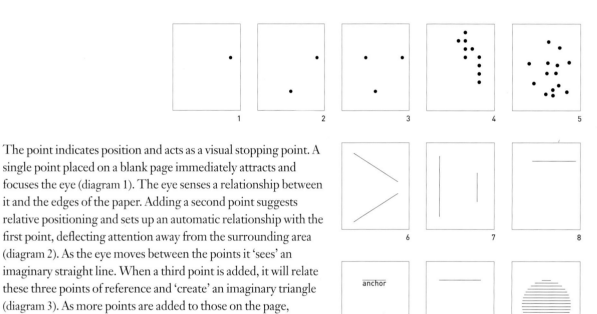

1  2  3  4  5

6  7  8

anchor

9  10  11

Diagrams:
1. A point of focus.
2. Points suggesting a line.
3. Points suggesting a shape.
4. Organised grouping of points leading the eye from start to finish in an ordered way.
5. Random grouping of points. This causes the eye to scan the area constantly looking for starting and finishing points.
6 & 7. Lines creating an illusion of depth.
8. Placing a line closer to one edge of an area will direct the eye along it.
9. Centring a line on a page closer to either the top or bottom will visually anchor it.
10. Lines may be used to direct the eye to a given area.
11. Rules of different lengths build an image. Lines of type can produce the same effect.

The point indicates position and acts as a visual stopping point. A single point placed on a blank page immediately attracts and focuses the eye (diagram 1). The eye senses a relationship between it and the edges of the paper. Adding a second point suggests relative positioning and sets up an automatic relationship with the first point, deflecting attention away from the surrounding area (diagram 2). As the eye moves between the points it 'sees' an imaginary straight line. When a third point is added, it will relate these three points of reference and 'create' an imaginary triangle (diagram 3). As more points are added to those on the page, grouping and subgrouping patterns will occur. The positioning of these groupings, relative to each other, determines the viewing sequence and levels of importance (see diagrams 4, 5).

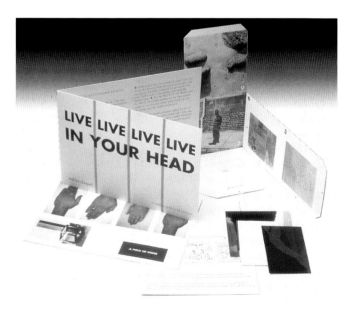

Line essentially indicates direction and so leads the eye. It will also encourage the eye to continue beyond its length. It may be either implied through the juxtaposition of two elements, as with a point, or actual, as in a drawn line, a line of text, a typographic rule or set of images or other elements. The strategic placement of several lines can create an illusion of depth (linear perspective) (diagrams 6, 7). Lines may also be used to suggest form, delineate, enclose or divide, emphasize and act as a visual marker (diagrams 8, 9, 10, 11).

 Area is a defined surface or plane, and it acts as a visual container, drawing attention to its content or edges. Graphic designers are concerned with area as a means of defining format and proportion and as a way of pacing

Left: With the competition of both Web and CD-ROM, designers of brochures, catalogues and promotional print are having to reconsider the possibilities of size, format, content and surface quality. This inventive exhibition 'catalogue' mixes techniques and materials to produce a pack that works as a visual and tactile experience that informs and entertains
Design by Jo Stockham, UK

Right: Creating an axis through proportional division of space can be an effective way of visually coordinating radically different sized elements within a single design concept, such as an exhibition or display.

the viewing within a design at any scale. It is easy to be distracted by disparate elements on the surface without realizing that area is also a powerful element in its own right – 'empty' areas can create energy within a design – and can be used to direct the eye from one place to another. This energy is known as dynamic white space.

Choice of format (rectangular or otherwise) may be dictated by either job content or production practicalities or both. There are some time-tested formats that have proved to be particularly suited to a wide range of uses. Print, for example, makes frequent use of the international standard series of A and B paper sizes, which are based on a rectangle having sides in the ratio of 1:1.414, the latter remarkable number being the square root of 2. Repeated folding parallel to the short side allows paper in this

Above: **In this poster for a jazz concert, simple lines, strategically placed, symbolize saxophonist, dancer and trumpet player. Their dynamic positioning is designed to capture individual movements which combine to create a harmonious performance as a trio.** Design by Niklaus Troxler, Switzerland

proportion to be halved into further rectangles – all in the same 1:1.414 proportion – giving the designer a flexible range of proportionally related sizes with which to work.

Although screen design formats generally follow the maximum allowable vertical and horizontal dimensions, there is no reason why this must be rigidly adhered to.

Equal division of an area conveys a static feel, whereas contrasting division communicates greater dynamism. The golden section has been used for centuries as a formula for creating harmony. In this formula, the relationship of the smaller area to the larger area is equal to the relationship of the larger area to the whole – approximately 8:13.

**DYNAMICS, EMPHASIS AND CONTRAST** Visual emphasis is a means of specifically directing the viewer, ordering complex information by creating a visual hierarchy and highlighting elements. Four basic ways of creating visual emphasis are through the use of size, weight, colour and disposition (placement).

# Headline

Dos espacios que se aman, que se besan, pour una puerta que no se sabe si separa o une. Aquí todo tiene la suficente claridad y la deliciosa oscuridad de la armoniá. No nos sabemos dentro hasta que unos pasos más allá de la primera puerta, nos encontramos fuera del edificio; nunca sabemos qué es demasiado. Todo recuerdo de este viaje será el instante en que abandonamos esa sensación de recogimiento, memoria irrecuperable de un espacio inmenso, inmensamente fugaz.

Small print following definition of a man was written by R Buckminster-Fuller in 1938 "A self-balancing, 28 jointed adapter-based biped; an electrochemical reduction plant, integral with segregated stowages of special energy extract in storage batteries for subsequent actuation of thousands of hydraulic and pneumatic pumps with motors attached; 62,000 miles of capillaries...

Left: Typesize is generally used to rank text into levels of importance – in this case headline, body text and small print. Drop caps (the large 'D') are used to indicate the start of a new section of text.

I paddled as fast as I could, my board started to draw back on itself as the wave sucked me into it's stomach.

wave
speed
fear

Above: **The contrasting type size and positioning of the headlines in this book spread, together with the diagonal, inward direction of the image bring the reader directly into the experience. Using lowercase letters at a large scale, tightly kerning them and reducing the scale of the surfer to match the letters, accentuates the emotion and drama.** Design by Barney Pickard, UK

Right:
Diagram 1: The exact central placement of an element within an area will produce a fixed appearance.
Diagram 2: Placing an element close to the top edge of an area will encourage the eye to travel upwards beyond it.
Diagram 3: Placement to the left and a third of the way down will draws the eye downwards.

The skilled use of emphasis is essential to communicating with clarity and pace, and works to focus and progressively direct the viewer through or around a design. Emphasis, like all other design basics, should always be considered in relation to the design as a whole. Many examples of size, weight, colour and disposition used as emphasis can be seen in newspapers and magazines where the visual pace is broken down into small parcels of information. These are identified (or emphasized) in many different ways, for example, by a heading (size), bold introductory text (weight), a coloured rule or tonal change in text setting (colour), placement or discrete arrangement of elements (disposition).

Size creates emphasis through contrast in proportions of format, type, image, relationship of elements, dimension (length and height) and volume (area and depth). Reducing an element to a small size on a large format can be just as powerful as enlarging it to fill the area, if not more so.

Weight suggests visual substance and mass, which can range from heavy or bold to light. It is often used in conjunction with size but works successfully when used across uniformly sized elements. Contrast in weight alone between individual words or lines can be effective in large amounts of text. Changes of weight between elements or blocks of continuous or display

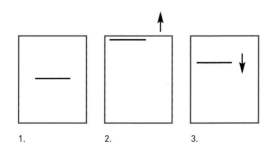

1.          2.          3.

Below: The Trocadero complex in London makes use of the latest technology to create an ambience of energy, excitement and power within the seven storey space. Natural light is excluded in favour of vibrant colour lighting. With more than a hundred different, independently controlled light sources, rotating billboards, video wall, TV screens, sound, animatronics, lasers and smoke machines, the Trocadero is a prime example of a digital entertainment destination.
Design: RTKL and Jonathan Spiers & Associates, UK

La puerta con dos casas es lo permanente, inacesible. Esta casa de alforja se encuentra en el territorio de los acontecimientos simultáneos. Dos espacios que se aman, que se besan, pour una puerta que no se sabe si separa o une. Aquí todo tiene la suficente claridad y la deliciosa oscuridad de la armoniá. No nos sabemos dentro hasta que unos pasos más allá de la primera puerta, nos encontramos fuera del edificio; nunca sabemos qué es demasiado. Todo recuerdo de este viaje será el instante en que abandonamos esa sensación de recogimiento, memoria irrecuperable de un espacio inmenso, inmensamente fugaz.

La puerta con dos casas es lo permanente, inacesible. Esta casa de alforja se encuentra en el territorio de los acontecimientos simultáneos. Dos espacios que se aman, que se besan, pour una puerta que no se sabe si separa o une. Aquí todo tiene la suficente claridad y la deliciosa oscuridad de la armoniá. No nos sabemos dentro hasta que unos pasos más allá de la primera puerta, nos encontramos fuera del edificio; nunca sabemos qué es demasiado. Todo recuerdo de este viaje será el instante en que abandonamos esa sensación de recogimiento, memoria irrecuperable de un espacio inmenso, inmensamente fugaz.

Above: Text set in three different weights of the same typeface – light, regular and bold. These variants can be effectively used to create a visual hierarchy with continuous text as well as to lend tone and texture (typographic colour) to text.

**La puerta con dos casas es lo permanente, inacesible. Esta casa de alforja se encuentra en el territorio de los acontecimientos simultáneos. Dos espacios que se aman, que se besan, pour una puerta que no se sabe si separa o une. Aquí todo tiene la suficente claridad y la deliciosa oscuridad de la armoniá. No nos sabemos dentro hasta que unos pasos más allá de la primera puerta, nos encontramos fuera del edificio; nunca sabemos qué es demasiado. Todo recuerdo de este viaje será el instante en que abandonamos esa sensación de recogimiento, memoria irrecuperable de un espacio inmenso, inmensamente fugaz.**

Left: The signage system developed for this hospital site uses distinctive colours and shapes directly influenced by the idiosyncratic design of the hospital building. The building has a strong identity of its own and the signs have to be very distinctive in themselves, yet visually link with it. This sign picks up the strong colour and quirky shape of a nearby red wall and is illuminated internally at night.
Design by by Tom Graboski Associates, USA

text will set up different spatial planes and can influence the viewing and reading order. Degrees of density and openness in text and the tonal value of images can be used to increase or decrease levels of emphasis.

The use of colour not only highlights, but also adds depth to every aspect of emphasis through association, mood, temperature and emotion. Appropriate colour choice can be based on any one or combination of these areas. Random choice or personal preference in the use of colour can wrongly emphasize or detract from the content or message. Interaction and / or contrast between individual colours together with the level of saturation (intensity) and brightness (tone) will significantly modify the degree and volume of emphasis (see Designing with Colour). Typographic 'colour' created by weight change from one body of text to another can also be used as a means of subtle emphasis or contrast.

Disposition, like colour, interfaces with every aspect of emphasis. It is so integral to visual communication that its potential is often undervalued. Disposition is inextricably linked to area and is concerned with the strategic placement of elements. It can subtly or dynamically draw attention to elements within the overall design area. For example, the small folio sitting on its own at the bottom or top of a page does not shout but is instantly found by the reader through its unique positioning. Similarly an indent (the placement or disposition

# ONE
# STEP
## CONTACT
### LENS SOLUTION

PEROXIDE SYSTEM

DISINFECTS & NEUTRALISES

FOR ALL TYPES OF CONTACT LENSES

superdrug

Right: One of a series of posters in which the capital letter 'A' was used as the key design feature. In this example the size, angle and distortion of the letter plays with the idea of a shaft of light contrasting with the predominantly black space.
Design by Pentagram, UK

Left: This contact lens solution packaging makes a clever play on the opticians' eye chart and uses the varying type sizes as a way of ordering and highlighting elements of the product.
Design by Williams Murray Hamm, UK

1.    2.

Left: 1. Asymmetrical placement works best if the elements are informally grouped with the space in between and around used to lead the eye though them. 2. Diagonal arrangements need careful consideration in structuring in order to avoid causing the eye to dart from element to element. Setting up basic directional lines can help avoid this.

of the first word in sequences of paragraphs) quietly creates pace for the reader. It is surprising how successfully judicious use of disposition can work without recourse to other methods of emphasis. However, poorly considered placement of elements on a page can set up confusing dynamics that may hinder the reader.

Contrast is used to create and sustain visual interest, in the same way that tone and intonation add interest to speech. Without contrast, graphic communication would become dull and flat, with little to attract attention or sustain interest. Contrast draws on visual opposites or dissimilarity to emphasize, differentiate, set up competition, attract and change the reading pace. It can be both quantitative and qualitative, obvious or subtle. Its use should always be considered in direct relation to the concept and the design as a whole. As there is little limit to the areas in which contrast may be used, it can be helpful to initially look for potential within the main emphasis groups – size, colour, weight and disposition.

Everyday visual opposites (loud and quiet, warm and cool, balance and motion) can also be a source of inspiration for graphic contrast. To be effective, contrast needs to be appropriate to the concept and be closely linked to emphasis. Overuse may result in a lack of focus in the design, with elements fighting for the viewer's attention and the eye being pulled in different directions.

Sept 13   Carlos Jimenez

Sept 20   Peter Wilson Bolles+Wilson

Oct 04   Mark Robbins

Oct 11   Craig Dykers Snøhetta

Nov 01   Alberto Kalach

Nov 08   Tod Williams+Billie Tsien

**1999 AIA SFMOMA**
**Architecture Lecture Series**

## moreModern

Left: This poster uses dramatic yet subtle contrasts in size, weight, colour, disposition and proportion to communicate a sense of architectural modernity.
Design by: Tenazas Design, USA

Below left: This poster for an unusual theatre piece with a theme of food and love, based around a refrigerator, combines disposition and colour to highlight the key elements of the play. The subtle use of line to depict the refrigerator prevents its comparative size from overpowering them.
Design by Niklaus Troxler, Switzerland

Below: The colour palette created for this book was designed to underline the zen quality of tea. The palette was given to the photographer to help in selecting props so that some element of the colour chosen for the chapter openings would appear in the photograph.
Design by Chronicle Books, USA

Theatergesellschaft Willisau

Regie: Henrique König
Musik: Daniel Steffen, Stefan Bolzern

Kulturwerkstatt Beutler-Hallen

LIEBE AUF EIS GELEGT

Fr   3. Nov.
So   5. Nov.
Mi   8. Nov.
Fr   10. Nov.
Sa   11. Nov.
So   12. Nov.
Fr   17. Nov.
Sa   18. Nov.
So   19. Nov.
Fr   24. Nov.
Sa   25. Nov.
Fr   1. Dez.
Sa   2. Dez.

werktags
20 Uhr
sonntags
17 Uhr

Vorverkauf:
Papeterie Imhof, Tel. 041-970 14 34

## SPICY BLACK BEAN SOUP
### SERVES 4 TO 6

**196**

There are many versions of this soup, but this is one of the best to serve on a midwinter day. Purée it in the food processor until it's the consistency you prefer—chunky or smooth. Offer a choice of toppings in small bowls.

Canned beans are used in this soup for convenience and quick preparation, but with the same good flavor.

## QUICK BLACK BEAN SOUP
### SERVES 4 TO 6

**197**

Above: The idea of 'bigness' was the key concept for the design of this cookery book. Over-sized numerals are used to emphasize the large number of recipes in the book. These shift vertically and horizontally, bleeding off the page, using disposition and cropping to reinforce the message.
Design by Chronicle Books, USA

**THE MECHANICS OF TYPE** The designer needs to understand how type is constructed and assembled as well as having an aesthetic appreciation of it. Letters of the alphabet are made up of complex combinations of straight lines and curves that give them their individual character.

Far right and below: **Comparison of the variation in cap and x-height between four typefaces of the same point size.**

All letters have common, notional points of reference in their physical make-up, regardless of the typeface design, style or size. These notional points are the baseline (the line on which all letters sit), the x-height (the height of the lowercase letters), the ascender line (the extent of the vertical upstrokes of lowercase letters), and the descender line (the extent of the downstrokes of lowercase letters).

The terms used to identify the different parts and structures of letterforms within this notional framework help to ensure accurate recognition and reference (see diagram above). Some characters have detailing unique both to

themselves and to the typeface, for example the ear of lowercase g or the tail of uppercase Q. However, although letterforms are recognized by these specific characteristics, the overall shape of the characters and the counter-shapes (enclosed areas) also contribute to the character of a typeface. Although there is considerable individuality

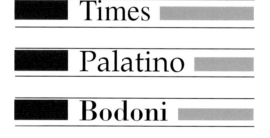

within the different characters of a typeface, typefaces are designed to form a cohesive whole and give a global colour and texture when typeset. Appreciating the physical make-up of type helps the designer to identify points to look for and so facilitates typeface choice for different purposes.

Although the size of type is described by a common system (usually in points), you need to be aware that different typefaces at, say, 10 pt, may look quite different in size (see examples above). This happens because of the relative proportions of the characters. Helvetica, for instance, has a large x-height and comparatively short ascenders and descenders, whereas some Garamonds have a

## Times

La puerta con dos casas es lo permanente, inacesible. Esta casa de alforja se encuentra en el territorio de los acontecimientos simultáneos. Dos espacios que se aman, que se besan, pour una puerta que no se sabe si separa o une. Aquí todo tiene la suficente claridad y la deliciosa oscuridad de la armoniá. No nos sabemos dentro hasta que unos pasos más allá de la primera puerta, nos encontramos fuera del edificio; nunca sabemos qué es demasiado. Todo recuerdo de este viaje será el instante en que abandonamos esa sensación de recogimiento, memoria irrecuperable de un espacio inmenso, inmensamente fugaz.

## Palatino

La puerta con dos casas es lo permanente, inacesible. Esta casa de alforja se encuentra en el territorio de los acontecimientos simultáneos. Dos espacios que se aman, que se besan, pour una puerta que no se sabe si separa o une. Aquí todo tiene la suficente claridad y la deliciosa oscuridad de la armoniá. No nos sabemos dentro hasta que unos pasos más allá de la primera puerta, nos encontramos fuera del edificio; nunca sabemos qué es demasiado. Todo recuerdo de este viaje será el instante en que abandonamos esa sensación de recogimiento, memoria irrecuperable de un espacio inmenso, inmensa-mente fugaz.

## Bodoni

La puerta con dos casas es lo permanente, inacesible. Esta casa de alforja se encuentra en el territorio de los acontecimientos simultáneos. Dos espacios que se aman, que se besan, pour una puerta que no se sabe si separa o une. Aquí todo tiene la suficente claridad y la deliciosa oscuridad de la armoniá. No nos sabemos dentro hasta que unos pasos más allá de la primera puerta, nos encontramos fuera del edificio; nunca sabemos qué es demasiado. Todo recuerdo de este viaje será el instante en que abandonamos esa sensación de recogimiento, memoria irrecuperable de un espacio inmenso, inmensamente fugaz.

## Garamond

La puerta con dos casas es lo permanente, inacesible. Esta casa de alforja se encuentra en el territorio de los acontecimientos simultáneos. Dos espacios que se aman, que se besan, pour una puerta que no se sabe si separa o une. Aquí todo tiene la suficente claridad y la deliciosa oscuridad de la armoniá. No nos sabemos dentro hasta que unos pasos más allá de la primera puerta, nos encontramos fuera del edificio; nunca sabemos qué es demasiado. Todo recuerdo de este viaje será el instante en que abandonamos esa sensación de recogimiento, memoria irrecuperable de un espacio inmenso, inmensamente fugaz.

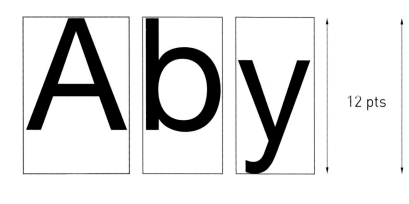

12 pts

one Pica EM

12 pts

relatively small x-height and longer ascenders and descenders. These differences in proportion result in different typographic colour when text is set – the bigger the x-height, the more open the texture and colour, making it essential to look at different sample settings. For the same reason, the number of characters that will fit on a given line length varies between typefaces at the same size. Even if this makes little difference to small amounts of copy, it can make a considerable difference to many pages of text.

## THE POINT SYSTEM

Digital processing allows designers to work on screen in a range of interchangeable measurement systems, to their own choice. However, when dealing with type, most people find it more practical to work with a common system that allows everyone to grasp and quickly appreciate the values being talked about. The point system used for measuring type – unique to the printing industry – has, surprisingly, remained the same since the days of metal type. In the days of phototypesetting, an attempt was made to use millimetres as a basic unit for type measurement, but it was never taken up.

Type size, as shown in the diagram, is determined by the size of the type body (which, in the past, was a piece of moveable metal) rather than by the actual letter. Nowadays, the body can be considered as the distance between the top of the highest part of the letterform (usually an ascender) to the bottom of the lowest (a descender), plus a notional amount of clearance, which varies from typeface to typeface.

The typographer's point is approximately 0.3 mm or 1/72 inch. Such a very small unit is necessary when describing very small sizes of type. However, attempting to express large measurement in points is cumbersome, so a larger unit of 12 pt, the pica em, is used. In many programs, it is possible to select pica ems or picas as a unit of measurement, for example, horizontal measurement for setting column widths. In practice, digital graphic designers will probably find themselves working in several measurement systems – points

for type, millimetres for area or page size, and inches for scanning resolutions (dpi).

The em (without the pica) is a measurement notionally based on the width of a capital M. Therefore, the value of the em is the same as the point size being used. All units of digital letter spacing and character construction are based on dividing the em of the given type size (be it 8.9 pt or 24 pt) into thousandths – infinitely more subtle than in earlier times.

**DESIGNING WITH TYPE** When working with type, the graphic designer automatically draws upon the influence of centuries of development. Typeface design evolved as printing technology developed but, given the flexibility of digital technology, recent typeface design has had few constraints. Radically different and new letterforms, often challenging typographic convention, have emerged alongside the redrawing and digitization of many classic typeface families, which were originally designed for hot metal.

Digital flexibility has enabled the new concept of the Multiple Masters font, in which the user can manipulate a typeface family into many variant forms by controlling properties such as width, weight and optical scale without distorting the essential characteristics of the letterforms.

Many of the huge range of typefaces available fall broadly into one the following groups: serif, sans serif, glyphic, decorative and display, script, blackletter and contemporary. (The more recent, innovative digital typeface designs follow their own rules and do not fit easily into these groups.) The terms used describe the overall character derived from basic characteristics such as whether or not the letters have serifs, the shape of any serif, the contrast between thick and thin strokes, and the angle of stress or axis of the letters. These characteristics combine to give a typeface its unique character, typographic colour and rhythm. They should be carefully considered when you choose a typeface. Trying out different text settings is always useful in assessing the typographic colour and rhythm in a particular context (see The Mechanics of Type).

It is blinkered to consider type as a limited graphic medium because it can equally well be used in its own right as 'image'.

**Zapf Chancery**

*ABCDEFGHIJKLMNOPQRSTUVWXYZ*
*abcdefghijklmnopqrstuvwxyz*

**Vag Rounded**

ABCDEFGHIJKLMNOPQRSTUVWXYZ
abcdefghijklmnopqrstuvwxyz

**Gridnik**

ABCDEFGHIJKLMNOPQRSTUVWXYZ
abcdefghijklmnopqrstuvwxyz

**Serpentine**

ABCDEFGHIJKLMNOPQRSTUVWXYZ
abcdefghijklmnopqrstuvwxyz

**Reactor**

ABCDEFGHIJKLMNAOPQRSTUVWXYZ
ABCDEFGHIJKLMNOPQRSTUVWXYZ

Left: Variants in weight and proportion are shown in this example of a Multiple Master font which maintains the intrinsic character of the letter style. Multiple Master fonts are extremely useful where a broad typographic hierarchy is required without any loss of character.
Design by Adobe, USA

Above: Recent innovative typeface designs (commonly produced digitally) follow their own rules and do not fit easily into the standard typographical family groups.

1- Old Face: marked axis inclined to the left, subtle change from thick to thin in the letter strokes, bracketed serifs which are angled on the ascenders and an 'e' with a horizontal bar. Capital letters are sometimes shorter than ascenders.

2- Transitional: axis that is slightly inclined to the left (can also be vertical), bracketed serifs which are angled on the ascenders.

3- Modern Face: vertical axis, abrupt contrast between thick and thin letter strokes, unbracketed (or minimally bracketed) hairline serifs.

4- Geometric Sans Serif: normally monoline letterstrokes, based on simple geometric shapes. Often with a single storey lowercase 'a'.

5- Humanist Sans Serif: some contrast in the letterstrokes, based on inscriptional letterforms, with two storey lowercase 'a' and 'g'.

6- Slab Serif: monoline or with minimal contrast in the letter strokes. Unbracketed, heavy serifs.

In a context where pictorial images are inappropriate or do not exist, a heading, single word or letterform can be inventively used as a graphic focal point to create interest, evoke mood or set the scene for the rest of the design scheme. Visual onomatopoeia, in which type is made to suggest the meaning of the word visually and 'talk' to the viewer, is also an engaging way of getting the message across.

## DECIDING ON A TYPEFACE

Typefaces are the voices of words and determine the visual tone of the text. The success of typographic communication depends as much on the choice of typeface as on the use of space and layout. Deciding on one typeface over another is a matter of visual judgement, fitness for purpose and style. A close look at the basic characteristics of different typefaces within the broad groups will help to make the choice more manageable. A typeface can be specifically chosen to reflect, or contrast with, the content and mood of the text in relation to feel of the overall design, but care should be taken to ensure that this does not conflict with the message or overpower the look of the text. Identifying the purpose and

Above: **The giant type on these signs at the Melbourne Exhibition Centre work as a powerful graphic element. Although cropped and placed at odd angles, the type still retains its legibility. This dynamic typographic signage is integral to the building, adding to its unique and unmistakable character.**
Design by Emery Vincent Design, Australia

context of the text – advertising, signage, packaging, print, web or multimedia, the audience and the location in which it will be read – will all help to inform the choice of size, weight and style of typeface.

Type is used for informing, entertaining, providing reference, instructing, directing, or otherwise involving the reader in some way. Each of these contexts will require a different level of concentration and reading pace, and both concentration and reading pace are relevant to the choice of typeface. For example, road signage has to be instantly recognizable: using a decorative face for a directional road sign might dangerously distract the driver's attention from the road while he deciphers the information. Reading may be sustained (as for a book), intermittent (as for a magazine, on a website, package or exhibition panel) or focused (as for a set of instructions or reference source). Text may need to be read under compulsion (as for a warning), or as an option (as for a disclaimer). The choice of size, weight and style of the typeface, as well as the typeface itself, should be linked to the reading pace. For example, it would be inappropriate to set instructional text in small, closely spaced, bold type: the difficulty in reading and understanding would be reflected in the reader's attitude to the task.

It is generally felt that serif, rather than sans serif, typefaces are easier on the eye and less tiring to read over lengthy continuous text, but there is no hard-and-fast rule. It is, however, worth reflecting that complete novels are not often set in a sans serif face. Discussion over the relative merits of serif and sans serif text faces will inevitably continue.

Interstate Light Compressed
**Interstate Compressed**
**Interstate Bold Compressed**
**Interstate Black Compressed**
Interstate Light Condensed
*Interstate Light Condensed Italic*
**Interstate Condensed**
*Interstate Condensed Italic*
**Interstate Bold Condensed**
*Interstate Bold Condensed Italic*
**Interstate Black Condensed**
Interstate Light
*Interstate Light Italic*
Interstate Regular
*Interstate Italic*
**Interstate Bold**
*Interstate Bold Italic*
**Interstate Black**
*Interstate Black Italic*

Below: Lively, characterful letterforms, symbolising the past, present and future of the New York Public Library, combine to celebrate the start of the Library's second century. The widely varying

Left: A selection of typefaces from the extensive Interstate family. Using related typefaces within a document will help to ensure a professional-looking result.

Right: Variants in weight and proportion are shown in this example of a MultipleMaster font which maintains the intrinsic character of the letter style. MultipleMaster fonts are very useful where a broad typographic hierarchy is required without loss of character.
Design by Adobe Systems, USA

Below right: This office space and facade for Gensler Design, San Fransico, reflects the company's own design approach. Innovative graphics are used throughout the interior, where individual workstations are mixed with shared work areas. Giant dingbats above the entrance make for unusual typographic imagery. The only sign identifying the company is very small and can be seen on the lower right hand side.
Design by Gensler, USA

Below: The stark contrast in size gives this CD cover a range of levels of interest in type as image and information. Individual letterforms were enlarged and the resulting abstracted shapes layered using PhotoShop. The typeface (developed specially for the project) creates a visual tension between the heavy rounded letterforms and the crisp arrow-shaped countershapes.
Design by Swifty Typografix, UK

styles and sizes of letterforms are strong and interesting enough to work both individually or together in monochrome or colour at very different scales making them highly flexible and suitable for merchandising and packaging.
Design by Chermayeff & Geismar, USA

Right: Exaggerated kerning and a degree of baseline shift transform a simple word into a powerful typographic impasse in this spread from the book 'Just One More'. The size and scale of the letters in relation to the page, together with the sharply contrasting text sizes reinforce the message.
Design by Barney Pickard, UK

Modernism, as we have know it, has served as the aesthetic, spiritual and moral conscience of our time. It embodies the essentially democratic idea of the creative artist as the inventor of a personal style, a unique vision of the world.

Modernism, as we have know it, has served as the aesthetic, spiritual and moral conscience of our time. It embodies the essentially democratic idea of the creative artist as the inventor of a personal style, a unique vision of the world. Modernism fosters a dynamic

Display faces are specifically designed for use with only a few words, as the term suggests. They are not normally suitable for continuous text. Gimmicky or quirky typefaces are usually best used for display work only. Text types can be enlarged to display sizes, but doing so may create letters with distorted proportions, which will affect the type's appearance and may affect legibility.

Most typefaces are designed with a basic roman (upright) and true italic (or oblique) style and perhaps one or two other weights (light, bold, etc.). Other types have extensive families of weights ranging from extra-light to ultra-bold and of styles ranging from condensed to expanded. Using a classic extensive type family such as Univers (which has twenty-two variants) can be useful when complex information needs different levels of emphasis; it will ensure that changes of type will work well together stylistically.

### TYPE FOR SCREEN DISPLAY

Text for monitor display should be set at sizes larger than for print since small letterforms cannot be formed accurately by the restricted number of pixels on screen, so making them difficult to read. Similarly, typefaces with fine serifs are unsuited to screen display – fine detailing is lost in the screen rendering. However some type companies, notably Agfa Monotype, have produced fonts called ESQ (Enhanced Screen Quality) that have been enhanced for on-screen viewing.

The colour of both background and type needs extra consideration, since monitors can be bright and harsh to the eye. Coloured or dark backgrounds can help to ease monitor glare.

Above: Minus leading between the three words of this book title creates a simple, typographic image that echoes the image of a perfect ride, on the perfect wave, on the perfect day. The full bleed used with the image is designed to give readers a sense of being on the board themselves, inside the gigantic curl.
Design by Regina Frank / SDA Creative, USA

### SPACING TYPE

Type is spaced both horizontally and vertically. Vertical spacing, referred to as 'leading', is the space between each line of type and is measured in points from the baseline of one line of type to the baseline of the preceding line. Increasing the leading can sometimes help to improve legibility.

Horizontally, type is spaced in proportion to each character, using units as small as one-thousandth of an em (that is, the em of the type size in use). Designers of the best digital typefaces program special adjustments to the spacing of difficult pairs of characters such as AV, Te, ll and li into their fonts. This information forms part of the font metrics and is applied automatically when type is set. Some page layout programs allow the graphic designer to modify these pairs, but this is something recommended only for experienced typographers who have good reasons for doing so.

Space can be added or subtracted between a range of characters (for example across several words or lines) by tracking. Word spacing can be similarly adjusted. The space between individual pairs of letters can be kerned (increased or decreased) to make them sit more comfortably together.

The space between lines of type is known as leading

Word
Kerned

Word
Unkerned

Logo

Colours

Air Freshener

Agency / Wink
Client / Sky Wash Detial and Lube
Date / Summer 2000
Art Direction, Design / Erik Torstensson
Photography / Sesse Lind
Icons / 500 GLS

Typeface

# Neue Helvetica 35

## Neue Helvetica 55

Business Card and Compliment Slip

Letterhead

Service Menu

Icons

Complimentary Wash Card

### Complimentary Wash

The world's most luxurious car-care facility

Posters

Thank You Card

### Thank You!

### Save 15% next time

**Above: A company logo is very often only the first step in creating a corporate identity. This range of elements from a corporate identity design for Skywash – a car wash company based in Atlanta –** illustrates how a whole range of graphics can be developed by cleverly picking up on key elements of the logo.

Design by Wink Design, USA

**THE DESIGN PROCESS** Design is normally carried out in response to a need and inevitably involves a certain amount of planning. The parameters may not always be clear in the first instance, as clients can have difficulty in pinpointing their exact requirements. Graphic designers are normally employed to bring their individual creative ability and practical understanding to solving a particular problem.

Acquiring an insight into the clients' businesses is an important part of informing the creative process. This can often be done simply by listening to and learning from clients, who usually know their own businesses intimately. Sometimes a client may be convinced that a particular medium or context is the best way to promote a product or service but, after careful analysis of the brief by the designer, an entirely different medium or approach may emerge as more suited to the actual, rather than the perceived, needs of the client.

The designer needs to make a reasonably accurate assessment of the size and complexity of the job and level of budget allocation. It is, for instance, unwise to embark on a corporate identity design without first agreeing which specific elements are going to need design consideration – is it a logo or letterhead, or will there also be a requirement to look at packaging, vehicle livery and uniforms, a signage system, website and design standards manual? Even a small-scale design can involve unexpected work, such as having to include,

Above: **This poster formed part of an in-store campaign for a department store that aimed to move away from clichés and express the real spirit of Mother's Day – a lie-in or a half-hour to herself will mean more than just tokens of appreciation.**
Design by Williams Murray Hamm, UK

Above left: **The idea for this classic poster grew out of the designer setting his own parameters in response to a wide open brief for Designer's Saturday in London. The event combined business and fun as the inventive and witty transformation of the primary shapes suggests.**
Design by Alan Fletcher, UK/USA

or rework a highly complicated diagram. Preliminary enquiries have to be made as to the feasibility and timescale of any reprographic and production processes from the completion of digital artwork before a realistic timetable can be worked out and agreed with the client. These initial planning stages are all essential to the design process. The only real drawback to digital design is that it allows designers to explore endless variations of ideas and colourways in a process where time is usually at a premium and decisions have to be made quickly.

When it comes to the creative element of the design process, there is little doubt that paper, pencil and digital software can work well in partnership. Paper and pencil are valuable basic tools for the digital graphic designer – much creative inspiration can come from doodling and note-making both on- and off-screen. Whichever starting point you use, your creative approach should always be informed by the brief. Basic guidelines for possible approaches can be set up by identifying from within the brief the answers to four simple questions. This exercise will also help you to clarify your intentions for the design.

The questions are:

| | |
|---|---|
| **What** | – is the message to be communicated? |
| | – is the reason for the brief? |
| | – is the problem to be solved? |
| **Why** | – does the client want to communicate the message? |
| **Where** | – is the message going to communicate, and under what conditions? |
| **Who** | – is the intended audience or market? |

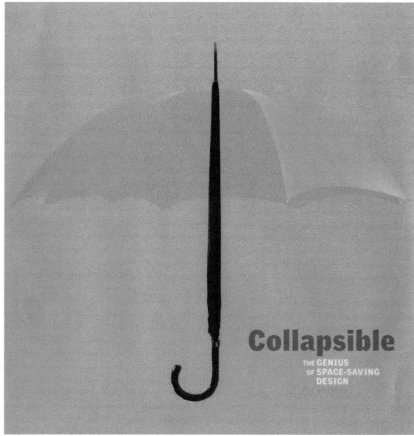

Working out and evaluating the answers to these questions should give you a springboard for idea generation that will help you maintain a reasoned link between the brief and even the most lateral approaches. One or more key words, images or points should emerge from the analysis. These can be used as the basis of short but intensive visual brainstorming sessions on paper or screen to help start ideas and associations flowing.

Drawing need not be restricted to paper for these sessions, as many designers find working with a digital tablet creates a natural progression from hand to screen. But, whichever method you use, the value of drawing as a tool for visual thinking and exploration is important to recognize. Thinking through drawing focuses the mind and, as it rarely throws up 'finished' or resolved ideas, its flexible immediacy can suggest alternative routes for exploration, allowing for 'happy discoveries' along the way. For this reason, put down every response that comes to mind, whether or not the relevance is immediately clear – often, it is not! Wit and humour can also play an important part in graphic communication, and they often make for entertaining, informative and memorable designs.

When working in a three-dimensional field, any initial two-dimensional creative thinking can be developed through the making process with small-scale maquettes and mock-ups or by using a three dimensional modelling program.

Drawn or doodled ideas, whether on paper or screen, should be stored, and those with potential should be researched and developed further without imposing too many constraints. Although ideas are generated by the creative intellect, they normally need some form of reference to underpin them, as the imagination cannot always be relied on for accuracy. Access to the Internet is extremely useful for this purpose – the World Wide Web offers a vast storehouse of knowledge and visual references that can both inform and

Above left: **This masculine indentity, designed for the re-launch of 'Nutters', the London clothiers founded by maverick tailor, Tommy Nutter in 1969, whose trademark look was created through dramatic and humorous twists on classic English style.** Design by Bryn Jones, UK

Above: **This double-layered book jacket features an outer layer printed on heavyweight tracing paper, designed to play with the book's theme visually and to physically involve the reader as the book is opened.** Design by Chronicle Books, USA

stimulate the design-making process. Digital image libraries offer downloading facilities, and it is possible to download royalty-free images. Ideas should always be thoroughly explored until they are fully resolved, and all research should be kept as it can sometimes throw up different ideas worth following.

When an idea seems right, the designer should assess how it can be realistically applied to all the components of the job. Decisions as to choice and use of type, images, and colour then need to be made. If you do not have the typeface you feel is suitable, font manufacturers have many browsable websites where it may be possible to find a face that fits your particular requirements. To assess colours and make choices, alternative colourways can be set up and viewed in most graphic art software packages. Images and graphics may either be supplied by the client or may need to be commissioned by the designer. They in turn may also help to generate ideas and influence the final design (see Image Selection and Image Creation).

Above: A page of ideas, notes, visual thinking, and thought exploration – an essential part of the design process, helping to generate and develop ideas as well as clarify intentions. Finding a 'story' that will lend itself to visual interpretation is often a challenge to the designer. For this report for Cadence Design Systems, the aim

was to conceptually show the unique role of the company and the irony that difficult situations in a complex industry creates growth opportunities. In the completed report, the headline and velour cover inventively encapsulate the aim with the images reflecting the global and everyday use of Cadence technology.
Design by Cahan & Associates, USA

Pulling the creative and informative strands of your design together and fine-tuning it can be done using drawing, image-manipulation, page-layout or three dimensional modelling programs, as the job demands. These programs can produce superficially seductive results, so you should always make sure that your design concept has 'substance'.

Most clients will have computing set-ups that allow you to communicate by email and to send visuals in a digitally viewable form. The graphic designer should be in a position to make PDF files, which can be viewed on any computer, and should also have a commonly used compression program. Once initial ideas have been approved or modifications agreed, the detailed design for each and every component of the job can be finalized before work can be prepared for production.

Every production process demands varying amounts of execution from the designer, but it will inevitably involve a digital file being prepared in a graphic arts program. The designer's file may be used directly to drive a printing device or a process with little or no intervention from the printer or anyone else. This raises two very important points. First, the content of your digital files must be correct in every aspect, with type and image information appropriately supplied. Second, it is extremely valuable to develop a good working relationship with your supplier, and ensure that there is a clear indication and understanding of responsibilities. Never assume that everything created digitally is going to be perfect – it is absolutely essential to have proofs for all print work, regardless of how small or big the job may be. Never rely on output from your studio printer being identical to that of the printer's or bureau's device.

FEELS DIFFERENT,
DOESN'T IT?

Left & right: Initial ideas sheet for sculptural light towers designed to define and frame entrances to the new scheme for Pincipe Pio, one of Madrid's main rail station and metro interchanges. The design combines ideas of movement, destination and connection with angled signage elements that further enhance the idea of dynamic movement. Bold colour reflects the modernity and elegance of the space. Design development and refinement for presentation visuals were done in Illustrator 9.0. Rendering effects were applied in PhotoShop 6.
Design by RTKL

V
E
R
T
I
C
A
L

# HORIZONTAL

## LEGIBILITY VERSUS READABILITY

Continuous text needs special attention, as it contains large amounts of detailed information that need to be easily understood. Readability is concerned with the speed and ease with which the reader can assimilate and retain information printed on the page or screen. Although individual components (letters) may be legible, this does not automatically mean that reading is easy. Readers perceive words not simply as sequences of letters, but as groups of letters and words. These letter and word groupings facilitate speedy recognition as the eye scans the text. Anything that contributes to the breaking up or the slowing down of this scanning process makes for harder and more tiring reading. For example, exaggerated tracking (character and word spacing) will disrupt the normal shape of words (recognizable letter groupings) causing strain to the eye and brain.

Character and word recognition are more easily achieved with upper- and lowercase letters, since they create a greater range of word-icon shapes and individuality than uppercase alone. Capital letters all appear to occupy equal spaces when set in a line of text, so the words they form are more difficult to discern at a normal reading speed. The relative weight of type can also affect legibility. Medium weights are easiest to read because of the visual balance between the counter-shapes and letter strokes. Extreme weights of both light and bold type are more difficult and tiring to read as the contrast between the letter strokes and counter-shapes is distracting.

Modernism, as we have known it, has served as the aesthetic, spiritual and moral conscience of our time. It embodies the essentially democratic idea of the creative artist as the

Modernism, as we have known it, has served as the aesthetic, spiritual and moral conscience of our time. It embodies the essentially democratic idea of the creative artist as the inventor of a personal style, a unique vision of the world.

Modernism, as we have known it, has served as the aesthetic, spiritual and moral conscience of our time. It embodies the essentially democratic idea of the creative artist as the inventor of a personal style, a unique vision of the world.

Modernism, as we have known it, has served as the aesthetic, spiritual and moral conscience of our time. It embodies the essentially democratic idea of the creative artist as the inventor of a personal style, a unique vision of the world.

Although these disturbances will have little effect over a few lines, they will tire the eye over large amounts of text. As a rough guide to line length, an average line of text in the English language reads comfortably with approximately sixty-three to sixty-five characters (counting word spaces as characters).

Digital technology enables both display and text type to be very flexibly set into shapes. Running text round images is also easily done. However, in working with either, care has to be taken to maintain coherent, readable text by controlling each individual line break.

Display type is normally restricted to a few words and presents fewer problems to the reader due to its size, weight and dominant position in the design area or on the page. The designer should, however, look carefully at the spaces between characters and words in larger type sizes. Pairs of letters may need individual kerning to aid readability. Where several words are involved, one or more word spaces may need to be optically balanced – adjusted by kerning or tracking – to counteract the effects produced by the shapes of the last and first letters of the words at either side, which may be exaggerated at display sizes.

The style of text setting – justified, flush left or right, centred or asymmetric – together with line length, also has an effect on the readability of text. In reading any length of text, the eye is generally more comfortable in returning to a straight left-hand edge. However small groupings of text can normally be read in most of the setting styles. Justified setting (text that is aligned at both sides) is not suitable for very small blocks of text where ugly word spacing will occur. Justification can also sometimes create difficulties with hyphenation and word spacing in longer, continuous text unless this is carefully controlled. Hyphenation at line ends can sometimes create an unnecessarily 'spotty' look and should be avoided where possible.

Line length also affects how text is read. If lines of text are too long, the eye has difficulty in returning to the start of the next line. Conversely, if lines of text are too narrowly set, the eye is made to progress too quickly from line to line and may skip lines, interrupting the flow of comprehension.

Garamond Alternate ligatures  Garamond Alternate italic  Garamond Alternate regular

Adobe Caslon Alternate ligatures  Garamond Regular/Garamond Alternate terminal letters

Bembo roman accents

Lining numerals  1 2 3 4 5 6 7 8 9 10

Non-lining numerals  1 2 3 4 5 6 7 8 9 10

## EXTENDED OR EXPERT SETS

Many digital typefaces have extensive ranges of characters well in excess of the basic set of letters, numerals, punctuation marks and symbols included as standard in most fonts. Some font formats allow such additional characters to be included within a single font file; these fonts are referred to as having extended character sets. More commonly, additional characters for a typeface design are supplied as a separate font, known as an expert set. In either case, the serious typographer is provided with a range of alternate and supplementary letterforms that share the inherent form and structure of the basic typeface.

One example of an alternate character is the swash character, a decorative version of a letter with an exaggerated sweeping entrance or exit stroke that may even extend beyond the normal width of the normal character (i.e. the stroke overlaps the preceding or following character). Many swash characters are meant to add a flourish to either the start or the end of a word, so there can be more than one version of any individual letter. Capitals are common, but some designs include swash initial, terminal and even medial lowercase letters (see above).

Non-lining (or old style) numerals make for more fluent reading than lining numerals and can be useful for softening large quantities of numerical information, particularly when set in the body of text. Expert sets may also include alternative small capitals, which are generally matched to the typeface's x-height and weight, unlike reduced size capitals.

Above left: **Expert font set showing the range of alternative characters available. Most expert sets include 'old style' or non-aligning numerals in which some numerals rise above and below the x-height and baselines. This style of numeral works well within text as they are less disruptive to the visual continuation than aligned numerals. They can also be softer to read in tabular form.**

Above: **This page from a brochure for Entec, creates a precise yet complex typographic 'sound image' which reflects the nature of the product: high-fidelity speakers. The three-dimensional, broad ranging nature of sound is suggested through strong contrast in size, weight, colour and type style and semi-abstraction of parts of the letterforms.**
Design by Mauk Design, USA

**LAYOUT** The design area or page format and margins are the basic components of layout, which – like everything else in the design process – should always be informed by the content of the job and the creative approach. How and where the end-product is to be used or viewed must be taken into consideration in deciding a suitable size and format.

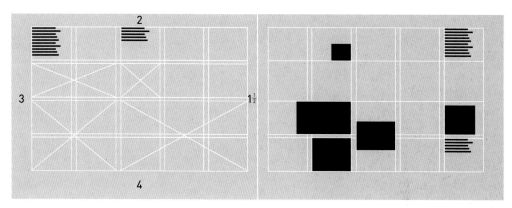

Size and format can range from pocket to wall-size, in both two and three dimensions. When designing for the Web or multimedia, where the overall maximum area is predetermined, consideration should still be given to the page proportions.

In almost every design context, the graphic designer will need to set up an appropriate page or design area structure (see above). This is normally done in a page-layout program, and it initially involves making a series of interrelated design decisions: width of the top, foot and side margins (essentially there for handling purposes and for leading the eye), the number of columns for text and image organization and, where appropriate, the number of pages or surfaces that may be involved. Once these

Above left: Structuring the design area across a series of pages or surfaces so as to give maximum flexibility without losing continuity is important to holding the viewer's attention. This can easily be achieved using master pages.
Above: Margin proportions will vary depending on the design context as in the diagram above, but as a guideline, the foot margin is normally double the head margin and the foredge margin double the width of the back margin.

decisions have been made, the page structure can be set up as single or facing pages in templates (or master pages in desktop publishing programs) to allow automatic repetition of the original structure across numerous pages.

Multipage surface design benefits from adding a further underpinning structure or grid to the basic page. This is done by subdividing the basic page structure into sets and subsets of equal vertical column widths. The greater the number of divisions or columns, the greater the flexibility. The modularity that is created can be used invisibly to structure the relationship of quite disparate elements, with some running across several or all of the columns. If the complexity of the job requires additional underpinning, a horizontal grid can be constructed in a similar way. A grid system can be particularly useful in helping to keep a sense of continuity across a range of different pages, sizes, scales or formats. Corporate identities, exhibitions, advertising campaigns and multimedia can all benefit from the controlling influence of a grid system.

Diagonal layouts can be very powerful but need to be kept simple as they may hinder the reader if too many elements are involved.

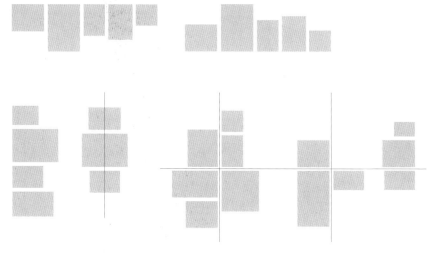

Left: Most graphic design work involves a number of different sized and proportioned elements which have to be coordinated within a given area. This diagram shows 'hanging', 'sitting', vertical and centred alignments together with combined horizontal and vertical axes around which different clusters of elements can be grouped cohesively.

**DOCUMENT SIGNPOSTING** Most graphic design includes working with some element of text or copy. Most copy needs ordered presentation, so before any design work starts the designer should work through it to establish some basic organization or hierarchy.

Breaking the copy down into digestible passages, if only by white space, will automatically pace the reader. Controlling the space between elements will determine the reading sequence. Hierarchical conventions will direct and signpost the reader through, for example, a book, via the title page, the contents page, the page numbers (folios), chapter headings, subheadings, paragraphs and footnotes.

Designing a website will often involve developing an ordered, functional and user-friendly navigation process to take the viewer through the various pages. In advertising, the hierarchy of information may be as simple as a main heading and strapline, whereas an instruction manual may contain many layers of information. Developing a visual hierarchy will order information and make it easily accessible. The exercise will normally include typeface and style together with varying levels of emphasis for other elements through the use of size, weight, colour and disposition. Even the structuring of the basic paragraph needs many decisions about detailing (see diagram).

Bullet points (circular, square or triangular) and selected dingbats (for example, Wingdings) can be used to highlight and draw attention to listings, instructions or blocks of text, but the level of emphasis should be compatible with the rest of the text and overall context. The size, weight or colour of bullets and dingbats should complement, rather than

compete with, the other elements in the design, and should direct the reader to and through the points in a relevant sequence.

Frames and rules are devices that can help to isolate, contain, formalize, contrast and draw attention to text, image or area. The weight, style and colour of the line used to make a frame will control the level and intensity of focus, but the design and proportion of the frame should be integrated with the main context. Framed text or other elements often appear within a main body of text, but they should still be capable of being read independently. To achieve this, the framed text needs to be set to a narrower width than the main text to allow for the thickness of the frame and a reasonable space

Column width

Type face — La puerta con dos casas es lo permanente, inacesible. Esta casa de alforja se encuentra en el territorio de los acontecimientos simultáneos. Dos espacios que se aman, que se besan, pour una puerta que no se sabe si separa o une.

Indents — Aquí todo tiene la suficente claridad y la deliciosa oscuridad de la armoniá. No nos sabemos dentro hasta que unos pasos más allá de la primera puerta, nos encontramos fuera del edificio; nunca sabemos qué es demasiado.

Alignments

Type size — Todo recuerdo de este viaje será el instante en que abandonamos esa sensación de recogimiento, memoria irrecuperable de un espacio inmenso, inmensamente.

Type style — *La puerta con dos casas es lo permanente, inacesible. Esta casa de alforja se encuentra en el territorio de los*

Leading — *acontecimientos simultáneos. Dos espacios que se aman,*

Inter paragraph spacing

Case — AQUÍ TODO TIENE la suficente claridad y la deliciosa oscuridad de la armoniá. No nos sabemos dentro hasta que

Tracking — unos pasos más allá de la primera puerta, fuera del edificio; nunca sabemos qué

Below: **Where it is essential that the viewer reads the design in a particular sequence, subtle grouping through the use of white space – one and a half to two times the spacing between the individual elements in a group – will naturally guide the eye through the grouping sequentially. When elements are butted up to each other, the eye will read the surface as an entity in itself.**

**part 01. design basics**

Below: Size, type style, icon, disposition and typographic devices are combined to visually pinpoint key locations in the wayfinding system for the American Museum of Natural History in New York. Clarity in the design is essential in preventing visitors from getting lost in the huge building.
Design by Lance Wyman, USA

Right: Examples of conventions which are used to make sense of copy and so guide the reader through documents.

**HEADINGS**
Chapters
Sections
Major topic
Headings
Subheads
Sub subheads

**CAPTIONING**
Illustrations
Photographs
Charts
Diagrams
Tables

**NUMBERING**
Pages
Paragraphs
Foot notes
Cross referencing

**INDEXING**
Index
Table of contents
Glossaries
Appendices
Bibliographies

**QUOTATIONS**
Speech
Extracts

**PUNCTUATION**
Pace
Sense

between it and the text. Surrounding white space can suggest a frame (as with margins on a page) through the placing of single element within a large area. Decorative frames should be used sparingly as they can easily distract attention from the content.

Desktop publishing programs make a distinction between rules that can be placed before or after paragraphs and underlining, which is a feature of the type style (character underlining or word underlining).

Typographic rules have considerable potential in their own right as design elements and need not be restricted to being used in conjunction with paragraphs. They can direct and arrest the eye, physically divide areas or separate elements, pace the viewer and be a facilitating device in leading the eye along the horizontal, vertical or diagonal direction. When placed above, below or to the side of an element, a rule has an anchoring effect on it. The level of focus and emphasis created in this way can be accentuated or diminished by modifying the relative size, colour, texture or weight of either the rule or the element. If different weights of rule are used in the same design area, they should be distinctly contrasting – if they are too similar in weight, they may look like a mistake or be indistinguishable from each other. Whichever type of frame or weight of rule is used, it is generally better to keep the scheme simple.

Above right: The impenetrable nature of the Berlin Wall is graphically conveyed in this exhibition display through the use of heavy typographic rules carrying tightly contained, reversed out type.
Design by Ruedi Bauer and Pippo Lionni, Germany/France

Right top: A contrasting rule will anchor text to it. This device can be continued within the same design with different column widths to give an overall visual structure. A further rule placed after space below text or images will help to contain them.
Middle: Within a design that uses marginal headings or two different column widths, a combination of vertical fine and bold rules can help to determine the reading hierarchy.
Bottom: Rules can be a useful device for both separating and coordinating different elements within a design.

**IMAGE SELECTION** The client may provide the designer with a set of images that are integral to a particular job, which leaves the designer with no say in the content or design of the image and little say in the selection. However, the designer does have control over how the images are used and, when selecting from a range of existing images, he or she should ensure that the selection 'tells the story' appropriately.

Right: **The paintings used in this Corporate Membership Program for the National Gallery in London were all selected from the Gallery's vast collection of new and old works. The repeated use of strip images plays on the title and human nature – the reader's desire to see more.**
Design by Agenda, UK

Above: **Strong images and a bold message were used in this Maxygen annual report to illustrate how the company's new technology, molecular breeding –** which imitates the natural process of classical breeding to achieve desired genetic characteristics – is not worlds away from farming.
Design by Cahan & Associates, USA

Initial impact may be of prime importance, but drawing the viewer in through secondary and tertiary levels of interest should also be considered. There are, however, some occasions when it is better to invest in a completely new set of images. The designer can then advise on them or be involved in selecting them or commissioning them from a photographer or illustrator. As coordinator of all the elements in a design and manager of the process, the designer has a responsibility to prepare a focused brief outlining the aims, purpose, format and context of the image-making. This should be agreed with the client and photographer or illustrator, and supplemented with detailed instructions concerning appropriate file formats and resolution values (see Image Creation).

Every aspect of an image should contribute in some degree to the overall message and mood of the design. Images may clarify, contrast, enhance, and partner text or other elements, but they should never be used as gratuitous 'add-ons'. Scaling and cropping images and deciding on a presentation method (colour, black and white, duotone, cutout, squared-up) need considerable care and attention, and should also bear a direct relevance to the overall design. Judicious cropping can substantially affect the visual impact and balance of the image itself, as well as influencing the message and other design elements.

Below: The nature of the high-tech company, Geron which develops treatments for age-related diseases, is humanized in this annual report companion design with its dramatically contrasting images and scales captioned with the subjects' small handwritten text. It is an approach with which readers can easily identify.
Design by Cahan & Associates, USA

Bottom: In this book spread the image is used to inform the typography in which the horizontal lines and colour are picked out and continued through onto the facing page.
Design by Chronicle Books, USA

## Chapter 8 : THE END of the RAINBOW

J. A. Bauer Pottery Co.,
Los Angeles
Plainware mixing bowls (left)
c. 1930.
Meyers Pottery, Vernon
California Rainbow mixing
bowls (center), c. 1935.
Japan Cactus salt and pepper
shakers, unmarked, c. 1930s.
Meyers Pottery, Vernon
California Rainbow low bowls
(right) unmarked, c. 1935.
California Rainbow casserole
(lower center).
J. A. Bauer Pottery Co.,
Los Angeles
Cyclinder vase (foreground),
c. 1950.

If ever a Golden Age was misnamed, it was California Pottery's. Except for some gilt trim from Sascha Brastoff, the treasures of that period are of little intrinsic value. They're just some molded earth sealed with a few nonprecious minerals. Although pottery is currently enjoying a collector/decorator revival, the worth of these once insignificant objects is best measured in terms of the pleasure they give to those who use, collect, or simply admire them. The fact that after all this time they are being used, collected and remade confirms their relevance to the way we live now.

For years collectors had been baffled: despite their best efforts they had been unable to learn anything about the creator of the pottery signed "Barbara Willis" that some of them prized. Then, in 1995, a woman in her seventies wearing a straw hat over bright red hair pointed to a vase at a Los Angeles flea market and said: "That's mine. I'm Barbara Willis. I made that." It turned out that Ms. Willis had closed her North Hollywood pottery in 1958 and was living happily in Malibu. After her "discovery" she began producing again, hand-thrown pieces this time, but in the same signature combination of intense glazes and exposed

**DESIGNING WITH COLOUR** Colour is the element that brings an added, almost magical dimension to visual communication. It reflects the everyday world and human experience, giving the designer a strong common language with which to express mood, emotion and significance.

Far left: Colour has been used to great effect in this initial lively sketch for the final, dynamic jazz poster. A simple, brilliant colour 'sings' from a rich, dark background evoking the mood and rhythm of the music.
Design by Niklaus Troxler, Switzerland

Left: This inventive annual report for the Linear Technology Corporation is made up of two contrasting books – 'Digital' and 'Linear' – packaged in this bright sleeve. The 'Digital' book is monochrome and only contains indecipherable streaming ascii code. The 'Linear' book dramatically makes the point that 'digital means nothing without Linear' through pages of brilliant digital colour and succinct, accessible black text on pure white.
Design by Cahan & Associates, USA

The digital graphic designer has an almost limitless colour palette with which to work and evoke specific responses in the viewer. Colour can be used as appeal, inspiration, entertainment, a focus or an identifying marker.

Colour is always relative and never works in isolation. The viewer responds to colour within a context and in association with other colours and graphic elements. Environmental and lighting conditions affect the way colour is perceived, which is a particular consideration when choosing colours for packaging, signage, and exhibitions.

Colour can be used as a means of identification and coding, as in pie and bar charts, where a range of different elements of equal importance need to be identified. In such contexts, care should be taken to mix colours (hues) of similar tones (brightness) and intensity (saturation) to avoid giving undue emphasis to any one element. In a situation where it is necessary to create levels of relative importance, a change in colour intensity or brightness or both can be used as a hierarchical device.

Combining complementary colours (true opposites on the colour wheel) will set up a natural vibrancy if a sense of excitement and energy is needed. To use colour emotively, it is essential to have an understanding of the design subject matter and the audience to which it is directed, so that colour choice can be appropriately related. Colours can be considered as warm or cool, soft or hard, light or dark, passive or active – all of which characteristics can be used individually or in association with each other. Mood is greatly affected by colour temperature.

Colour association forms an important part of colour language in all areas of graphic design. This can be seen in the way that greens are used for freshness, blues and whites for hygiene, red for danger and purple for richness. There are many examples of colour combinations that are associated with politics, nationality, sport, religion or cultural and social conventions. The designer has to be aware of all of them, in order to avoid creating confused messages. For example, red and green are recognized across the world as symbolizing 'stop' and 'go'.

S+U-Bahn-Netz　　Tarifbereich Berlin Ⓐ Ⓑ Ⓒ　　Ⓐ Ⓑ Bahnhöfe in Berlin Ⓒ Bahnhöfe in Brand...

Left: Colour coding in diagrammatic maps ensures a clarity of communication and quick recognition that can be flexibly applied to related graphics and signage.
Design by MetaDesign, Germany

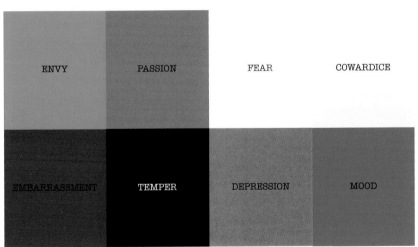

| ENVY | PASSION | FEAR | COWARDICE |
| EMBARRASSMENT | TEMPER | DEPRESSION | MOOD |

Above: Colour and meaning varies widely in different cultures. For example, in much of Asia white is associated with death whereas in the West it is associated with purity. These associations and differences can be useful in making unusual connections or changing perceptions depending on the design context.
Design by Alan Fletcher, UK/USA

Below: The distinctive colour choice and minimalist packaging design for Apollo Lager deliberately breaks away from traditional beer packaging to coolly reflect the product name and the associated space travel theme in a memorable, understated way.
Design by Cahan & Associates, USA

| L | 0 | 2 | 9 | 16 | 23 | 30 |
| M | 0 | 3 | 10 | 17 | 24 | G |
| M | 0 | 4 | 11 | 18 | 25 | 1 |
| G | 0 | 5 | 12 | 19 | 26 | U |
| V | 0 | 6 | 13 | 20 | 27 | G |
| S | 0 | 7 | 14 | 21 | 28 | N |
| D | 1 | 8 | 15 | 22 | 29 | 0 |

It is impossible to provide a set of rules for particular harmonious colour combinations since these change according to different environments, fashions and culture. The designer may consider setting up disharmonies as a way of creating shock or provocation, which may be a perfectly legitimate way of communicating a message.

Graphic art software provides tools for selecting and mixing colours in a variety of models. These give the designer unprecedented control over colour creation and usage (see Colour). The hue, saturation and brightness (HSB) model is particularly useful as it enables the creation either of different hues of the same brightness and intensity or of varying intensities or brightnesses of the same hue.

Designers should be aware that their colour perception can be affected if they set strong background colours for their monitors. Large areas of colour and poor lighting in the working environment will have a similar effect on perception. It is advisable, therefore, to set the monitor to a neutral grey when working intensively with colour, and to paint design studios in neutral colours.

Left: The combination of green background and fluorescent ink used to print the tiny numbers on the June page of this Olivetti calendar, was so dazzling that the Italian printer wore sunglasses whilst working with the job! The powerful colour combination that suggests red flowers in a green field is primary and the information secondary. This emphasis is used to bring feel of summer into the office environment.
Design by Alan Fletcher, UK/USA

## TYPE AND COLOUR

All the uses of colour to express mood, emotion or significance can be equally well applied to type. Colour may be used to modify the way in which type works: bold type can be softened, hierarchies can be developed without recourse to change of size or weight, text can be enlivened and typographic emphasis can be subtly enhanced.

When designing with coloured type on a coloured background, the designer must consider the choice of colour combination carefully in order to ensure legibility. In general, type and background need to be significantly contrasting. Dark type on a pale

Right: These unusual curved vertical signs for a drycleaning and laundromat business mimic laundry drying on a line. The freely drawn imagery combines with crisp type and fresh colours for this new concept in clean clothes' – the idea being that doing the laundry should be more fun than a chore. The colours are carried through the clean lines of the interior and branded merchandise.
Design by Ashdown Wood Design, Australia

Left: Colour and type reflect the 'straight-talking' policy of TKB Solicitors, enlivening and humanising the traditional, rather formal, perception of the legal profession.
Design by the The Partners, UK

Left: Black was an unusual but distinctive choice for a coordinating element in the new, Suma supermarket identity in Barcelona. Together with special lighting, it is used as a means of focussing the eye on the many different colours of their merchandise. The graphics on these staff aprons show colour used as coding for fish, meat and vegetables.
Design by Summa, Spain

Right: Subject areas are grouped together into discrete gallery displays in the Tate Modern, London. Each is identified in the plan (or on the website) by a unique colour used in both the titles and floor plan, facilitating visit planning and wayfinding through the vast building.
Design by Halmes Wood, UK

background, rather than on a white background, will result in less glare (particularly with screen-based designs, for example on Web pages). Type and backgrounds of equal brightness (tone) will reduce legibility considerably. Colour can be used with type to create a sense of progression and recession, to enhance spatial quality and suggest depth and perspective. The reading pace and sequence of text and display type can be further controlled through the use of colour.

Setting type in dark colours may be unsuccessful if the letters have a small surface area with which to carry colour; the result may appear to be a poor version of black. Type, particularly text type, has little surface area compared to the background surface on which it appears, so dark-coloured type generally appears darker and light-coloured type generally appears lighter. A heavier weight of type can be used to compensate for this phenomenon.

Interestingly, the millions of easily accessible digital colours have also brought a revived energy to the use of black and white that should not be underestimated.

# SURFACE DESIGN

The roots of graphic design lie in our desire to communicate information – more especially by the arrangement of type and pictures on a printed page. Although the development of digital technology has made the possibilities virtually limitless, graphic design and print remain inextricably linked.

Graphic design for the medium of print embraces an extensive and varied range of products. These include promotional applications such as brochures, leaflets, flyers, direct mail, catalogues and posters. Business communication tools include stationery, newsletters, training manuals, reports or menus. The publishing industry, producing magazines, books and newspapers, is still one of the largest sectors employing graphic designers.

With ever-increasing market and client pressure to create eye-catching, innovative ways of presenting printed information, there are jobs that call for more specialized print processes. The use of materials other than paper – plastic, metal or even fabric – is also becoming more prevalent.

The processes that take the concept to the printed product affect many design decisions made at concept stage. The choice of paper or other media, or the size of the print run, will dictate not only the type of print technology used but also the way the production files are created – including the appropriate choice of type and the size of the halftone dot.

The computer has shaped not only conceptual design, by encouraging freedom of layout and the breaking of typographic conventions, but also the linear process of transferring the design from screen to printed page. The traditional boundaries of the design-for-print process have been blurred. The designer equipped with a PC, or more commonly an Apple Macintosh, linked to a desktop scanner, a colour output device and a modem can take conceptual ideas through to press, although the final stage is still invariably an analog process.

There is a huge range of software available to realize this workflow. It is now possible for the designer to prepare the digital files required to make printing plates directly, virtually eliminating any intermediate reproduction stages.

**PART 02. SURFACE DESIGN.**

**CHAPTER ONE**

# DESIGN FOR PRINT

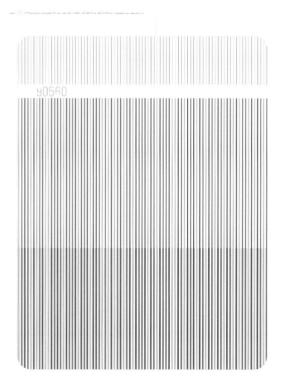

Left: **Visual identity for Yosho.com. The design uses a series of stripes printed as 'spot' colours. The colours were chosen to translate accurately into four colour process tints when incorporated into other printed elements, such as a brochure that contains photographic imagery.** Design by Segura, USA

Far left: **Effective use of colour, type and imagery for the cover of Frieze Magazine. The choice of colour for large, flat areas is very important as some hues are less intense when printed as process separations rather than as specific PANTONE inks.** Design by Harry Crumb, UK

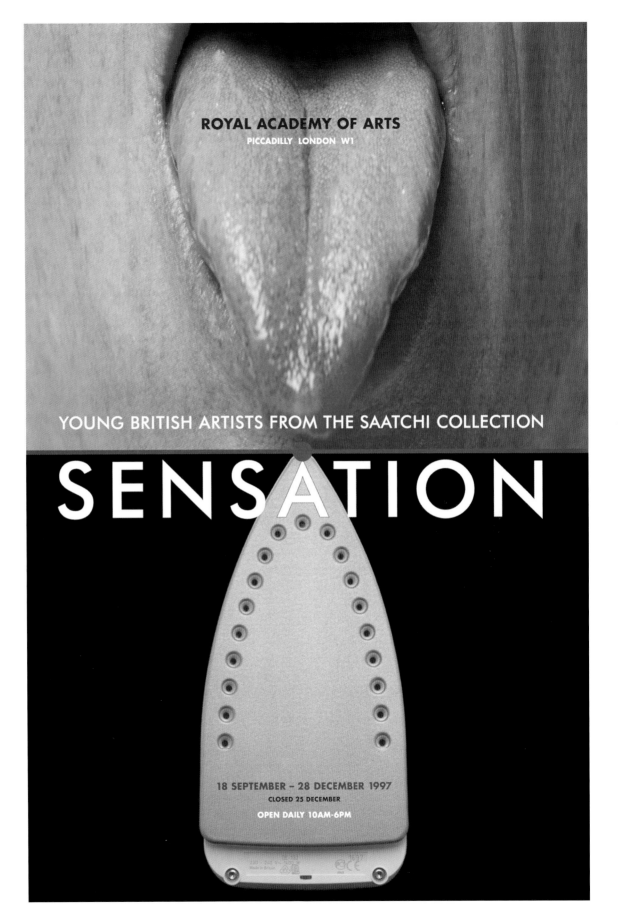

Right: Cleverly chosen imagery creates a powerful visual pun in this poster for an exhibition of British contemporary art.
Design by Why Not Associates, UK

**THE SOFTWARE** Over the past few years, there have been significant developments in software dedicated to both design and production, providing more streamlined digitally driven systems that take design directly to print. As a result, the definition of 'publishing' has been greatly extended.

## DESKTOP PUBLISHING (DTP)

Desktop publishing (DTP) software has evolved from the fundamentals of word processing into fully fledged design tools, streamlining the creation of very accurate 'artwork' in which all text and pictures can be infinitely manipulated, and the construction and management of long documents simplified. Text can be imported and then styled to the designer's requirements. There are virtually limitless attributes that can be applied in addition to the font style and weight. H&Js (hyphenation and justification), horizontal and vertical scaling, leading, kerning and tracking can all be finely tuned.

Although there are far more Windows PCs than there are Apple Macintoshes, the design world is still dominated by the Mac. Because of this and although almost all of the most important applications are available in both Macintosh and Windows formats, if you're serious about design you should use a Mac. The only exceptions are if you need to work with specific specialist tools such as CAD (computer aided drawing), where some of the key software is made for Windows only.

The key players in the DTP software market – QuarkXPress (regarded as the professional industry standard) and Adobe PageMaker (both vector based applications, see page 208) – led the boom in desktop publishing in the late 1980s. These two old rivals have been joined by InDesign, Adobe's latest, advanced, desktop publishing software, aimed at both designers and prepress professionals. This benefits from excellent typographic controls and full 'drag and drop' support, where graphic elements can be dragged into layouts directly from other applications.

Common to these DTP applications is the use of frames. Picture and text frames can have their exact position defined on the page (aided by the use of snap-to guides) and can be pre-formatted with type, paragraph or run-around specifications, allowing the designer to lay out documents with fixed structures that are independent of content.

Frame tools include rectangle, circle and polygon shapes. To make a frame, you simply draw the shape on screen using the text or picture tool chosen from the toolbox. Using text frames

also means that text can be placed inside virtually any shape and be justified. Picture frames can be given a run-around value to control the flow of text around an image. Frames can be layered, locked, stepped and repeated by designated increments, or placed on master pages. They can also be converted to multiple text columns. Text frames can be linked, allowing text to flow automatically through the document.

Flexibility is further enhanced by the use of layers, which until recently have only been associated with graphics programs. Layers can be on or off, locked or unlocked, and in view or out of view. They can also be exported and printed independently. Multiple-document layers are useful in a number of instances: for example, you may need to create several versions of your document using different languages, or you may need to add notes and comments to a document for

Opposite and this page: **The three most commonly used page layout programs utilize similar toolboxes and on-screen dialog boxes to modify elements on the page and show accurate measurements. Pagemaker (opposite) QuarkXPress (above and left) and InDesign (right)**

production and prepress purposes. You could also use the layers feature to develop documents for both online and print purposes. Low-resolution images could be placed on one layer for Web pages, while higher-resolution images could be placed on another for print.

New colour technologies that, only a few years ago, were the preserve of the high-end prepress market have been brought to the desktop. The latest DTP software now makes it easy for the designer to produce digital documents that have a high degree of colour fidelity and accuracy, making colour publishing cheaper and more accurate for desktop prepress systems. Colours can be set up as spot colours or specials, using a recognized PANTONE or Focoltone number, or can be converted to four-colour process.

DTP software now has built-in abilities to draw freeform shapes with Bézier tools although, in common with other graphic disciplines, designing for print still makes extensive use of vector drawing applications such as Illustrator and FreeHand. The designer also needs to be conversant with Photoshop for image manipulation and for correcting colour, resolution and file type.

When it comes to sending the final job to the next stage of production, DTP software has a 'Collect for Output'

Left: **A typical QuarkXPress desktop showing an activated text box. The box can be resized using the six 'handles' and the position accurately adjusted in the measurements dialog box situated at the bottom left of the window.**

Left: **The floating palettes in action. The document layout indicates the current page. By clicking in a text or picture box, and then making a selection from the colours palette, any element on the page can be colour modified – individual letters, words, blocks of text, rules, or even the boxes themselves. Note the use of the master page guides (in blue) and the individual positioning guides (in green).**

facility that places all required files in one folder. A number of independent prepress 'collection' programs have also been specifically designed for this purpose. PreFlight Pro, for example, simplifies job preparation by not only collecting but also itemizing all files necessary to process the job correctly. Designers muct comply with font copyright when sending files to printers.

## PRODUCTIVITY FUNCTIONS

Design productivity and document consistency have been greatly improved in DTP applications through features such as style sheets and master pages. Paragraph and character style sheets can be created to expedite the styling of text. Headings, sub-heads, introduction text, body text and captions can all be assigned a style sheet and accompanying keyboard short cut. If a font or style subsequently needs to be changed, the change can be made globally simply by amending the relevant style sheet. In some software, character styles can be applied to text within paragraphs without affecting the overall paragraph style.

Production can be further streamlined by using master pages, which might contain text, picture boxes and grids arranged with the help of precise vertical and horizontal guides. Some applications feature multiple master pages, allowing several layouts to be managed within the one document. Pages

Above: **Some of Quark's productivity features: The style sheet set-up dialog boxes can be used to record individual text styles once the designer is satisfied with the layout. These can be appended to any other document. The find/change feature can change individual words, punctuation, font and size throughout the document with a single click.**
'Collect for output' places all required files into one allocated folder in order to send them to the printer or output house. The 'measurements' bar shows all the attributes of the selected box.

can be set up singly or in 'facing' spreads, depending on the type of document, with automatic control of page numbers. Style sheets, colours and hyphenation values can be selectively appended from one document to another, which is useful in magazine production when spreads with similar design attributes need to be created individually. Text alignment can be standardized by 'locking' text to the baseline grid which is particularly useful for long documents and book design.

Although each new version of DTP software seems to incorporate more and more specialized and sophisticated tasks, many third-party 'plug-ins' or 'extensions' are available to increase productivity further by automating specialist tasks. For example, printer's sections can be created automatically, entire pages or groups of elements can be scaled, and text can be treated with effects such as drop shadows. It becomes almost possible to perform every drawing, image or prepress function within one application.

## OPI AND FPO

Open Press Interface is an electronic imaging workflow standard that makes the on-screen design process quicker and the 'live' files smaller. Images are pre-scanned and the designer is supplied with low-resolution positional guides, known as FPOs (for position only), to prepare the layout. Use of 'low-res' images speeds up scrolling, screen rewriting and rough proofing. The high-resolution versions are substituted before running film or plates by the OPI system.

**SCREEN TO PROOF 1** Once the creative process is complete and both designer and the client are satisfied with the design, the more practical side of production takes over. Preparing the page layouts for trouble-free output is essential.

## PREPRESS

Much printing still involves producing film separations of each colour to prepare printing plates, so it is likely that the designer will need to use the services of a bureau or the printer's own reprographic department. Although desktop scanning devices have greatly improved in quality, specialists continue to offer a higher quality scanning service, using high-resolution scanners. Even if the workflow is totally digital, they can sometimes handle the conversion of files to Acrobat PDF format (see page 70).

It is important to have a good working relationship with your chosen bureau: you will need to discuss problems openly and know exactly what they expect from your files. The bureau will be able to advise on how to prepare the final file composition to speed up production, keep costs to a minimum and make sure that the end-result will print without mishap. If colour or images 'bleed' off the page, for example, the bleed specifications (usually 3–5 mm) need to be agreed with the printer and set up accordingly in the document, to ensure that any irregularity in guillotine register does not result in an unprinted gap at the edge of the page.

One of the most common problems when passing a job over to the bureau is the compatibility of fonts. Never use the type style functions in your layout software to artificially italicize or embolden fonts, as the RIP (see page 70) may not recognize them. Use PostScript fonts, and, when the job is sent, include a comprehensive list of fonts itemizing the various weights and styles. To output a file to film correctly, the bureau must have fonts identical with those used in the document, not just some that appear to have the same name. Strictly speaking, you should not send the fonts with the file, as this constitutes a copyright infringement: the bureau will need to have its own licensed copies (see Font Copyright, page 186). A possible work-round is to send PDF files with the fonts 'embedded'; however, without the font on its system, the bureau will be unable to make last-minute text corrections.

Above: **A high-resolution drum scanner is a big investment. Machines like this need a high throughput of work to be cost effective and so remain in the domain of the bureau.**
Below: **When two screens are superimposed and are not quite aligned the result can be an unsightly moiré pattern.**

The bureau can manage other issues the designer may not wish, or necessarily need, to be involved with. Trapping is the function of overprinting edges of colour areas to compensate for poor registration on the printing press. Colours or black can be set to overprint or 'knock out' showing the colour behind it, and special inks may require special treatment for trapping. Even if you have set trapping preferences in QuarkXPress the imagesetting RIPs may override them. Again, the printer will advise the bureau on the best trapping method for the intended press. The percentage spread of a dot of ink when printed on a particular paper is known as dot gain. To correct for this, the printer will supply values that enable the bureau to adjust the dot size of the output film. To avoid the unwanted moiré pattern or 'screen clash' sometimes apparent on a colour halftone, the bureau will need to assign certain unique angles to the halftone screen dots.

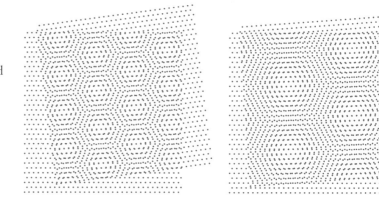

Right: Imposition for a typical sixteen page section. Eight pages are printed on one side, the paper is then turned and printed on the other side.

## IMPOSITION

A document of more than two pages will normally be viewed on screen as a series of double-page spreads. When a multi-page document is printed, however, the pages will be arranged on a larger sheet to be cut and folded into one or more sections. A page has two sides: a single fold creates four sides; fold again and you have eight sides; and so on. Binders' sections are, therefore, made up of multiples of four. The commonest section size is sixteen pages and, as large litho presses can print more than 32 pages per side, there may be several sections on one sheet. The planning of the pagination is called imposition.

Imposition will normally be carried out by the bureau, before running the film, or by the printer prior to platemaking. The designer should be aware of the most economical use of

Above: One side of a section ready to be trimmed, folded, and assembled, the result will be sixteen consecutive pages. The imposition is generally left for the repro house, bureau, or printer.

paper and the relationship between machine size and final trimmed size, and plan the page count accordingly. The best way to be certain of the structure of a long document is to draw a flat plan, a miniature page plan indicating the content and position of each numbered page in the section.

If the design of the spread incorporates an image that crosses over the gutter, it should be remembered that the two halves will be separated into two different areas of the printed section, or even onto different sheets. When finally bound, they may well misalign or colour variation may be apparent.

If the document has fewer than sixteen pages, both sides of the section can be put on the same plate. In this method, known as 'work-and-turn', all the pages are printed on one large sheet, which is then turned over and run through the press again. After the sheet is cut in two, the two identical piles of short sections are folded and trimmed.

## COLOUR MANAGEMENT

Whether you use four-colour process or spot colours, the final file should contain only the colours you want to print. Delete all unused colours (using the colour-editing menu in the DTP software) to avoid the creation of more plates than intended. If the design uses spot colours, ensure they adhere to the naming conventions of the ink libraries, such as PANTONE, in all the applications that went into the creation of the document.

If you use PANTONE colours in process printing, the PANTONE must be converted to CMYK separations prior to film output to avoid the extra cost of five or six colour printing. If you define a PANTONE colour to allow separations, the software will use a look-up table to create the substitute recommended percentages of the four process colours to produce the closest equivalent CMYK colour. Certain PANTONE colours cannot be reproduced accurately by the four-colour process. To avoid any surprises during

Above and left: **QuarkXPress offers comprehensive colour management.** Conversion can be made from one of the proprietory spot colour system palettes to CMYK, ready for four colour print output. A floating on-screen dialog box shows the selected colour at a glance.

production, it is a good idea to check when you make colour selections. Pantone Inc. produces colour swatch books that show how the process versions compare to the true colour.

Transmitted light from computer monitors produces more vibrant or intence colours than can be printed, making some colour matching unpredictable. A safer method of improving the predictability of the printed colours is to use a colour management system such as ColorSync in your DTP and graphic programs. This provides input, display and output device profiles and will be recognized by both the colour proofing device and the printer's press and so help preserve consistency.

When printing a solid black, a denser colour can be achieved either by printing the black twice, known as 'double hitting', or by first printing a tint, or 'shiner' colour such as cyan under the black (see Colour).

Below: **For four-colour process printing,** the colour bar is used by printers to assess the performance of the press, giving information such as dot gain and poor registration. Printed away from the image, it is later trimmed off.

## RIPS

Most page layouts, supplied either as a DTP document or as a PDF, are output to an imagesetter through a Raster Image Processor or RIP (pronounced 'rip'). This device changes the outlines of the type and drawings from PostScript (the standard language used by computers to communicate with printers or imagesetters) into a bitmap (an array of dots) that the imagesetter can print out. RIPs are essentially dedicated computers with vast amounts of RAM linked directly to the imagesetter. The RIP will also process all the screening of halftones.

It would be very time-consuming to do all the 'ripping' on the designer's computer. In a faster version of the process, only the text and non-scanned vector graphics are sent to the RIP, along with low-resolution, position-and-crop guide files for the high-resolution images, which are then replaced. This process is known as Automatic Picture Replacement (APR). Late binding is a term used to describe last-minute changes made within PostScript files while they are in the RIP, such as adding trapping and imposition information.

Files that are 'RIP friendly' will be processed faster, keeping reprographic charges to a minimum. For instance, it is best to optimize layouts for imagesetting by using Photoshop to prepare bitmaps of the correct finished size and orientation, rather than scaling and rotating bitmaps in your DTP software.

Imagesetters can now handle most file formats, but the format of any included images will affect the speed of the imagesetting process. The best format will depend on the bureau's equipment, but will usually be EPS (encapsulated PostScript) or TIFF. JPEG, a 'lossy' format used in online and multimedia design, should be avoided in documents destined for print. It is worth remembering that a compressed TIFF file will take longer to output than an uncompressed version and so may be less economical. If you intend to include a mixture of high-resolution bureau scans and some created in-house, then check to find out the minimum and maximum

resolutions required for the particular job. Attention should also be paid to the width of lines or rules, whether drawn in a vector illustration or in a DTP document. Hairlines, of 0.25 pt or less, will RIP to film but may break up or even disappear when on press, as may very fine tints of colour.

## DELIVERING THE GOODS

The designer must decide on the most productive and cost-effective way to deliver the job to the bureau or printer. If either is located nearby, manual delivery on disk (CD, DVD, Jaz or Zip) may be a cheaper option. For more distant output locations, ISDN, ADSL (high-speed telephone connection) or a dedicated prepress delivery service such as Wham!Net can be used.

To speed the transmission process, the files should be compressed into the smallest possible package. A number of compression utilities are available, the most common being those that write the zip format (not to be confused with Zip disks) and Aladdin's Stuffit. These utilities allow single files or folders containing all the relevant files to be compressed to approximately half their actual size, resulting in half the transmission time.

Below: **The designer's computer can act as the front end to the system at the repro house. Flat artwork and transparencies are sent to the repro house where high and low resolution scans are made. The low-res scans are returned to the designer, who places them in the document. They are replaced later by the high-res versions prior to running film or plates.**

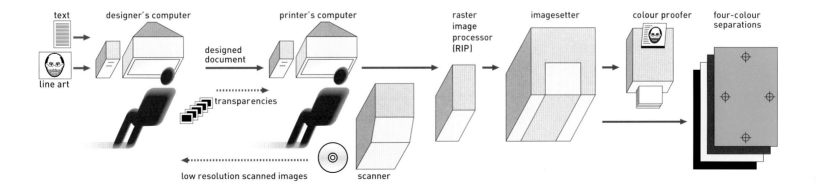

text    designer's computer    printer's computer    raster image processor (RIP)    imagesetter    colour proofer    four-colour separations

line art    designed document    transparencies

low resolution scanned images    scanner

**SCREEN TO PROOF 2** Adobe introduced the PDF (Portable Document Format) as a universal file type for transmitting and printing business documents. It is now the standard format for distributing cross-platform manuals, technical drawings, marketing information and proofs. PDF has been heralded as the key to the future of prepress, eliminating film, plates and repro bureaux.

## THE FUTURE OF DIGITAL WORKFLOW

PDF is a secondary file format, created from other files. Instead of sending separate page layout, font and image files to the filmsetter, designers are able to use all these files to create a single PDF document file. These files are small enough to be transmitted on-line and can be output to any proofing device and eventually run on any printing press.

However, there are hazards that currently inhibit this perfect scenario. It is easy, for example, to let unconverted RGB images slip through to the final file, resulting in a mono image when the printer RIPs the file. Designers may neglect to embed all the necessary fonts, and the options for automatically converting images to CMYK can also produce unpredictable results. Image compression options are inflexible and images placed at inadequate resolution may not be detected. Trapping is not handled at all. As with DTP files, it is a good idea to run a 'preflight' check on PDF files such as Enfocus' PitStop.

In an attempt to avoid PDF pitfalls – and to maintain their foothold in the prepress industry – many repro houses are encouraging designers to supply them with native files,

Above: **Adobe applications, vector, image and DTP, support direct conversion to PDF. Independent software such as QuarkXPress requires the file to go through Acrobat Distiller, although this process can be facilitated by third-party plug-ins. The distilling process takes only a few seconds and settings – the file compression, for example, or the colour output format – can be customized.**

which they, in turn, output to PDF instead of film. This would seem to negate the benefit of using the format, but it does bring certain cost benefits. For example, 'soft' proofs (viewed on screen) supplied in PDF format vastly speed up the production process (although traditional checking of film is still regarded as the only failsafe method), and plates are run directly from the file, removing labour-intensive film make-up. For publishers producing weeklies or products requiring a fast turnaround this can provide a competitive edge.

Ultimately, an industry-wide adoption of the PDF format would seem to benefit everyone. Repro houses could dispense with costly imagesetters while still offering high-resolution scanning and final composition. Printers could accept jobs directly from designers as well as bureaux.

Currently the process is not quite the hoped-for simple, universal solution to prepress needs, but it is getting there.

**PROOFING** Only the designer knows how he or she expects the final printed product to look. The proof is the last opportunity to check for text, alignment and colour errors, and it is ultimately the designer's responsibility to clear it.

Probably the most widely used prepress proofing is done photographically using plastic laminate systems such as Matchprint or Cromalin – often called dry proofs. Coloured powders or pre-coated sheets matching the process colours are exposed using filters and subsequently laminated together onto white paper.

It is important to remember that prepress or dry proofs are only an approximation of the finished result, although they usually give an adequate guide to the colour balance. The only true method of seeing the final job, albeit the most costly, is to run a wet proof on a flatbed proofing press on the correct stock. Wet proofing usually includes a set of 'progressives' (see below).

Do not be afraid to question the colour reproduction if you are not satisfied. It is far better to correct at proof stage, because although limited colour adjustments can be made on press, they tend to be less localized and will affect the balance of a larger area than may be desired.

For a single colour, film is usually proofed as a positive dyeline or diazo print, known as an ozalid, brownline, blueprint or blue. Halftone images are proofed either all together as a 'scatter proof' or correctly positioned as 'page proofs'. Full-colour page proofs can be output digitally from the designer's file as laser, inkjet, dye-sublimation, or thermal-transfer prints. There are many affordable colour output devices on the market, but choose carefully. For serious proofing it is important to have proper PostScript-based printing. Most personal inkjet printers do not include PostScript, which means prints from QuarkXPress and Adobe InDesign will not match the final result. Fortunately, additional PostScript RIP software can remedy this.

Above: Wet proofing typically includes a full set of progressives, colour proofs printed in the same order as the process colours on the final press. Each colour printing is shown separately and also overprinted with the other colours.

**Proofing systems compared** (**** = excellent  *** = good  ** = average  * = poor)

| System | speed | quality | cost |
|---|---|---|---|
| Matchprint | * | *** | ££££ |
| Cromalin | * | **** | ££££ |
| Iris | ** | ** | ££££ |
| Inkjet | **** | ** | ££ |
| Wet proof | *** | **** | £££££ |
| Ozalid (monochome) | *** | * | £ |
| Digital | **** | **** | £££ |

# THE PRINTING PROCESS 1
The halftone plays a fundamental role in the printing process. To understand it, the designer specializing in print must first grasp the basic principles of colour separation and screening technology.

## COLOUR AND THE HALFTONE

Whether you use spot colour or CMYK process colour in your design depends entirely on the job. Spot colour will generally give better specific colour matching and can result in brighter, more vibrant flat colours, but CMYK is the preferred process for photographic reproduction. Sometimes adding a spot colour to a CMYK job is necessary, but this means additional printing impressions, which in turn will drive the printing costs up (see Colour).

There are two forms of primary colour; the red, yellow and blue we all learned about in school, and the red, green and blue of all computer and television displays, referred to as RGB. RGB is colour created by combining light (hence, additive colour), while all forms of print rely on reflection from pigment (subtractive colour). A modified form of the red, yellow and blue primary colour set – magenta, **y**ellow and **c**yan – is used for most forms of colour printing. Because the three colours do not actually form a true black when mixed together, black is used as the fourth ink to increase contrast and add depth. C, M and Y are used as printers' inks to produce full-colour work, and are known as the process colours. Black is referred to as the key (K), so the system is known as CMYK.

When artwork, a photographic print or a transparency is scanned, a beam of light is used to pick up the three colour components in a series of horizontal lines. The split beams are digitized and a laser writes the dots of the screened separations to paper, film or disk.

Brighter, more stable colours can be achieved by using a technique called GCR (grey component replacement). With GCR, the black replaces the grey areas created in shadows by the process-colour mix. It is then possible to run the process colours at different densities to increase colour saturation without creating a 'muddy' shadow.

A less widely used, but more sophisticated system known as Hexachrome, uses six colours, adding vivid orange and green to a tuned CMYK spectrum. This method produces an excellent quality of colour reproduction, with subtle variations and greater range, but requires a specialized printing press, though Hexachrome is now starting to be used in desktop printers.

Prior to printing, the 'continuous tone' images that result from scanning need to be screened to convert them to halftone dots. Digital imagesetters can write halftone screens of almost any shape, although the square dot is commonly used in four-colour process separations. The fineness or frequency of the screen is measured in lpi or dpi – lines or dots per inch (per cm in Europe), and the optimum frequency is determined by the paper stock and the type of printing press. Coarse, soft material such as newspaper will use a coarse screen, such as 55 or 65lpi, to compensate for the spread of ink and prevent the dots from merging, whereas a good-quality art paper would use a 170-lpi screen.

Below: The colour halftone screens must be applied at different angles to prevent unwanted moiré patterns. Black is rotated to 45° as this is the easiest on the eye; 90° is the most difficult to guarantee, so this is reserved for the yellow; cyan and magenta are rotated at approximately 105° and 75°. Black and white photographs are normally converted to a monochrome (single-colour) greyscale, but a designer may sometimes prefer to increase the tonal range of a monochrome image by printing in two or three inks as a duotone or tritone. The conversion can easily be performed in Photoshop by superimposing a contrasting black halftone over a single-colour halftone made from the highlights and mid-tones of the same image. This effectively adds depth to what may otherwise be a flat image, while also adding a coloured tint.

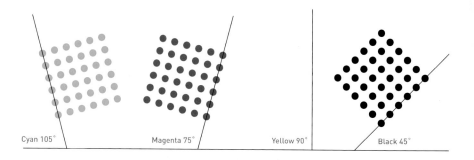

Cyan 105°    Magenta 75°    Yellow 90°    Black 45°

Above: **An image separated for four colour process printing and enlarged (by approximately x 300,000) creates a 'rosette' pattern clearly showing the angles of the individual colour screens.**

Right: **An enlargement of a conventional mono halftone image reveals the dot pattern. A regular array of different sized dots arranged according to the screen and screen angle being used. Smaller dots represent the lighter tones.**

## THE PRINTING PROCESS 2
The design-to-print workflow can now be executed totally digitally. However, the final step – the printing press – is still predominantly analog. This is also the stage over which the graphic designer has least influence. Knowing how the finished product will look and feel is an essential part of the design process, so the designer must have a basic knowledge of the various printing techniques available to achieve the desired result.

### LITHOGRAPHY

Lithography is by far the most common form of printing today. Originally devised more than 200 years ago, its success is based on a simple principle: oil and water do not mix.

In offset lithography the image is printed from a rubber coated roller (blanket) to which the ink is transferred from the plate. The image is firstly created on a printing plate either photographically or by using a CTP (computer-to-plate) digital system. (CTP systems are not yet the standard, but this method is set to dominate within the next few years.) When the photopolymer resin coating of the plate is exposed to ultraviolet light exposed areas are hardened. The unexposed areas are subsequently washed off during processing. Stopping solution is then applied to the surface to make the non-image areas water-receptive and grease- repellent (ink-repellent). Plates can either be negative or positive working. Negative-working plates are much less expensive and are generally used for single-colour work. The same process applies to negative-working plates but in reverse, it is the exposed areas that become unstable leaving the unexposed areas to print.

The thin metal, plastic or paper plate is then wrapped around the plate cylinder of the press. As the cylinder rotates, it makes contact with rollers dampened either with water or another dampening solution and rollers conveying ink. The dampening solution prevents ink adhering to the non-printing areas of the plate. The inked image areas are then transferred to a rubber covered blanket cylinder, finally offsetting the image onto the paper as it passes between the blanket and impression cylinders.

The latest litho presses can be connected directly to the digital output source, eliminating both film and the platemaking stage, making the press another link in the digital chain, though at present this system is only economical for shorter runs. There are also some uniquely digital problems that may occur, such as ghosting and mottling.

Lithography is well suited to the four-colour printing process, since larger presses can print the four colours consecutively in a single pass. Indeed, modern commercial litho presses can print up to eight colours. Smaller presses are sheet-fed, but longer print runs such as books and magazines are offset onto paper fed from large rolls on a so-called web press.

The size of the halftone screen and the surface of the paper stock will determine the amount of ink required in the litho process. Uncoated paper is more absorbent and will soak up more ink; to compensate for this, the dot size can be reduced in film production. Positive-working plates produce less dot gain and are generally preferred for web-offset magazine printing.

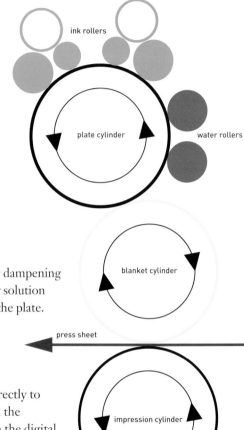

Above: Thick, viscous printing ink is forced through a system of rollers, making it semi-liquid. A thin layer is distributed over the plate. A fountain solution moistens the plate's non-image areas so that ink adheres only to the image areas. The plate cylinder revolves into contact with the blanket cylinder depositing an inked, reversed image. Paper passes between the blanket and impression cylinders, offsetting a right-reading image.

# DREAMT IN HEAVEN. FORGED IN HELL. MADE IN LAS VEGAS.

TEXT BY STEPHEN BARRETT  PHOTOGRAPHY BY GLENDA STUART

Throughout history great cities and civilizations have risen and fallen. Meccas like Babylon, ancient Egypt, Rome, Paris, and New York have shaped and defined the most dominant eras in the history of the world. The ideals and visions of these civilizations can be found in its art, architecture and ruins of their cities, with stories buried deep within their walls. But what of American civilization? The definitive American city must embody the American Dream — that concept which always seems to be just beyond the grasp of definition. God only knows what the American Dream is. It has not been defined, but it has been pursued. The American Dream, perhaps no longer deemed enough, seems to be ever expanding, taking on global proportions. There is one city, one American city that seems up to the task of offering its citizens and visitors the world and everything in it — even if this city's vision of the world is a bit skewed. Only one city can deliver all the world has to offer, be it Rome in the guise of Caesar's palace, New York's Empire State Building and Statue of Liberty, Paris's Eiffel Tower, or the great pyramids of Egypt cleverly camouflaged as the Luxor Hotel and Casino. It is the world brought to your feet. Plastic. Prefab. American. Las Vegas.

The American Dream is exactly that: a dream. It is both a vision and a quest. The Las Vegas version of that dream began in the mind of Ben Siegel with the planning and opening of the Flamingo in 1946 on a desolate stretch of Highway 91 in the Nevada desert. Writer Nick Tosches said in *Dino* his biography of Dean Martin, that "It was Siegel who believed that the desert town in the middle of nowhere could become the air-conditioned Eden of every dirty dream." This was it. To hell with the idea of owning a little bungalow in middletown America; that's no dream. The real fantasy is fast women and fast money cruising the Vegas strip. And by the 1960s Las Vegas was the mecca for a decadent American lifestyle.

Left and Below: In a typical web-offset system, the paper is printed on both sides in one pass. A web press consists of up to eight consecutive units like this, one for each colour.

Above: A spread from the Canadian magazine Coupe, printed in four-colour process on a web-offset press. Magazines are commonly printed in sixteen page sections. Colour can be adjusted on the press electronically by increasing or decreasing the deposit of any of the four process inks to sections of the printing plates. However, once on press, localized colour changes to individual images are not possible.
Design by The Bang, Canada

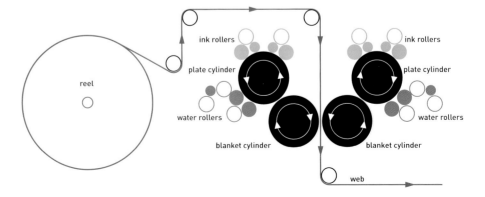

reel

ink rollers

plate cylinder

water rollers

blanket cylinder

ink rollers

plate cylinder

water rollers

blanket cylinder

web

# THE PRINTING PROCESS 3

The print industry is not limited to lithography, and the designer may choose to employ another printing process, perhaps one capable of printing on a wider variety of materials to create more interesting, tactile effects.

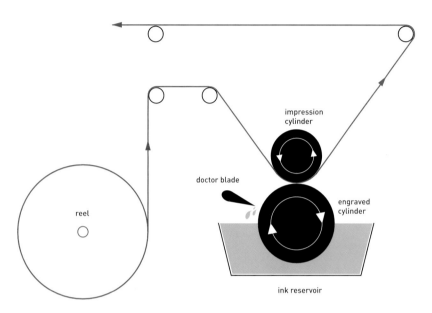

## GRAVURE

Possibly the biggest rival to web-offset is gravure. This process is used to print everything from postage stamps and banknotes to wallpaper and wrapping paper. Gravure is a comparatively recent adaptation of the ancient etching method of producing print with tone. Gravure presses print from 'cells' of different depths engraved into the surface of the cylinder, deeper cells holding and subsequently depositing more ink, rendering a darker image. As the ink from neighbouring cells tends to merge, this produces an almost screenless image.

Gravure is commonly printed onto a web of paper. The process is digitally prepared – diamond styli in the engraving heads that cut the printing cells are fed digital information directly from the prepress source. An engraved cylinder revolves in a reservoir of thin, solvent-based ink, flooding the surface. A flexible steel blade (the 'doctor blade') wipes the cylinder clean as it revolves, leaving ink only in the image areas. Finally, a rubber-covered impression cylinder presses the paper onto the engraved surface.

The drawback with gravure is type, which may appear less sharp than in lithography.

Above: A typical gravure press is web-fed. The engraved gravure cylinder rotates through an ink reservoir, and the surplus ink is wiped from the surface by a 'doctor' blade. The printed image is made by pressure between the plate cylinder and the impression cylinder.
Below: On a letterpress press the paper is placed face down on an inked block, or 'forme'. Pressure is applied by screw or lever.

## LETTERPRESS

Once the most popular printing process, letterpress is now only used for specialized jobs or limited edition (short-run) books. The use of hot-metal typesetting really survives only to produce a proof that can then be scanned and printed by offset litho to reproduce the traditional effect.

Letterpress machines have largely been converted to or replaced by flexography, in which the metal type trays of letterpress are replaced by a flexible rubber or polymer plate. Generally used by the packaging industry, flexographic (or 'flexo') presses are similar to gravure, using a series of rotating cylinders to collect ink from a reservoir and transfer it onto a web-fed printing material via plate and impression cylinders. Flexo presses can print on materials unsuitable for offset litho, such as cardboard, plastic bags or waxed paper.

Right: *O* by Frederico d'Orazio, PlaatsMaken. This plastic 'book' can be unfolded and blown-up into a human sized inflatable mattress. Text and graphics are screenprinted onto the plastic.
Design by Frederico d'Orazio, Italy/Netherlands

squeegee/flo-coater carriage

hinged frame

ink

screen

paper

vacuum base

## SCREENPRINTING

Often associated with poster and art print reproduction, the silkscreen or screenprinting process gets its name from what was originally a stretched silk cloth used to hold a stencil. This versatile printing process can produce thick, opaque deposits of ink in brilliant colours, and can be used to print on virtually any material, including shop windows and the sides of vans, or even curved or uneven surfaces such as bottles, T-shirts and printed circuit boards.

Above: A common hand-operated screenprinting press. The rubber bladed squeegee is pulled over the surface of the screen, forcing the ink through the mesh onto the paper or material held in position on a vacuum bed.

Modern screens are made from a fine polyester mesh, stretched on a metal or wooden frame. A simple line stencil is cut using a digitally controlled pen plotter that manipulates a knife. More complex stencils and halftones can be made using a film positive as in lithography. The screen is coated on both sides with a light-sensitive polymer emulsion and exposed through the film with ultraviolet light, after which the image areas are washed away with water. The screen is mounted on the press and a rubber-edged squeegee forces the ink through the mesh, passing only through the 'open' image areas. Though fine screens are available, screenprinting is not recommended for close registration or work involving very small type sizes.

## DIGITAL PRINTING

Digital presses are increasing in popularity for economic short-run, full-colour work. Running at high speeds of up to 2000 copies an hour, these presses can create a different image on every sheet of paper if necessary (see page 13, DPICT magazine cover), allowing considerable scope for printing personalized documents from, for example, mailing databases. The absence of prepress processes and materials, such as film and platemaking, makes short-run work as economical as high-volume printing. An important application of this technology is Print-on-Demand publishing.

**FINISHING** Once the job has been printed, there is one final stage before delivering the finished product. These entirely mechanical processes, which may involve trimming, folding, collating or binding, must be considered early in the design process because they will affect the way the document is constructed and therefore the production budget.

Finishing can also include print-related operations such as die-stamping, embossing, varnishing and laminating. Die-stamping and embossing use a metal die (engraved by a digitally controlled machine tool) to 'stamp' or press a relief image into paper or board. The image can be impressed with or without ink, to create subtle effects. Frequently seen on paperback book jackets, a metal foil can be combined with the raised impression, using a heated die. Die-cutting physically cuts out sections of the paper. Digitally controlled laser die-cutting is used to cut fine detail such as company logos in business stationery.

There are a number of ways to protect the printed page and make it scuff-resistant. Varnishes can be printed on the litho press to give varying degrees of gloss or matt finish. To add extra strength, a film lamination, again in matt or gloss,

Above: **Some of the varied ways of folding. Left to right: Single fold four-page sheet. Accordion eight-page fold, Gatefold eight-page fold, Rollover eight-page fold.**

Left: **Folding, binding and trimming in progress . Folded and collated 'signatures' move along a conveyor of saddles in the shape of inverted 'V's. Wire staples are inserted along the fold of the spine. The three remaining edges are then trimmed by a series of guillotine blades prior to packing.**

can be glued to the stock under pressure through a heated roller. Interesting design effects can be created by mixing spot areas of gloss and matt varnishes or by adding a varnish after the lamination is applied.

### FOLDING AND BINDING
Once the print finishes have been applied, the stock is ready to be folded. Folding is accomplished using a buckle, knife or combination folding machine. There is no limit to the number of folds employed, and interesting visual effects can be created by using a single sheet designed to fold into several smaller sections. After folding, multi-page jobs have to be gathered, bundled and collated (put in order), prior to binding and guillotining. Other operations that may need to be considered are perforating or tipping-in (adding a single page to a multi-page publication).

guillotine

guillotine

delivery

face trimmed

head and foot trimmed

Right: Perfect binding. The sections are collated and the spines then trimmed off. The edges are roughened and glue is applied to attatch the wrap around covers.

Binding may be performed by several methods. Booklets, and magazines up to a maximum of 96 pages, are commonly bound by saddle-stitching (stapling) or perfect binding. Unsewn binding is known as perfect binding: the gathered and collated sections are placed in the binding machine, spine down, and the edge is roughened and an adhesive applied. The cover is folded, scored and wrapped around the pages. The adhesive is cured by heat and the pages are trimmed. The designer must remember that in perfect-bound books with lots of pages, text and pictures may disappear into the gutter as the spine on these books is less flexible than sewn titles and some fold is lost in trimming.

Case-bound or hardback books have a separately made case. The page sections are sewn through the spine with thread and gathered together to form a 'book-block'. The cover and book-block are assembled with tipped-in endpapers, usually of a heavier stock, before collating and sewing. Finally a separate 'dust' jacket is wrapped around the cased book.

Above: Multi-folded concertina brochure commissioned by Photo '98: Year of Photography and Electronic image.
Design by Eg.G, UK

Right: Promotional Brochure for 'The Lightbox' property development. By using a plastic cover and ring-binding mechanism, this brochure could be economically updated by inserting or removing pages as the project progressed.
Design by Foundation, UK

Above: Kenneth Grange Design Identity. A monochromatic two-dimensional logo has been given a three-dimensional quality with thoughtful use of embossing.
Design by Lippa Pearce Design, UK

Right: Case-bound books are assembled with a 'book block' made up of sewn sections or 'signatures', endpapers and a heavy board cover or 'case'.

**CHOOSING PAPER** The choice of paper is the foundation of a successful print job. The designer must consider carefully what the finished item is trying to achieve and select a stock that will not only convey the right message but also fit within the print budget.

A huge range of papers and boards is available – machine-made, handmade and recycled. For some jobs, the type of paper will be determined by the method of printing employed. Offset litho presses require papers with good surface strength and dimensional stability, preferably with a low water content. The finish is a less important factor, as offset ink will adhere both to glossy coated and to matt uncoated surfaces. For gravure, the paper must be smooth but absorbent enough to collect the ink.

The paper must fit the brief for the job, and the finish should also be appropriate to the content. If you are looking for good-quality colour halftone reproduction, a coated stock (made with mineral fillers to create a very smooth surface) would normally be used, although some very fine uncoated papers can now boast excellent colour quality. The weight of paper is classified in grams per square metre (gsm or gm$^2$), a standard sheet of photocopying stock weighing 90 gsm. The impact of a prestigious catalogue could be increased by using 150 or 200 gsm paper. Generally heavier papers or artboards are thicker than light ones, but the density and type of fibre will have an effect on thickness (bulk). Glossy art paper can sometimes feel thinner than an uncoated stock of the same weight, so it may be necessary to increase the weight when choosing a gloss finish. If a brochure needs to be mailed, the weight of the stock will affect the cost of the postage. Be careful of ink showing through from the reverse side of some lightweight papers.

Budget may also limit the choice of paper. Your design might look wonderful printed on a specialist or handmade stock, but the cost might well be beyond the reach of the print budget. When deciding on the size and format in the early stages of the design, take into account the size of paper the job will print on, so that costly wastage can be avoided.

Paper is manufactured in sizes known as A or B (an international standard based on the ratio 1:$\sqrt{2}$ – sheets maintain this ratio when folded in half), and if possible, the document or section should be designed to fit one of the standard sizes, without creating too much wastage. Remember to consult the printer and allow for any bleeds and for sufficient free 'gripper' edge as required by the press. The brief might call for a special finish, such as varnish or lamination, in which case the printer will give advice as to the best stock to use. Do not overspecify: it is not necessary to use a gloss stock if you are adding a gloss varnish. Types of binding and printing will be influenced by direction of grain (the way the fibres lie), so prior consultation is important.

The printer will often be able to supply designers with sample books produced by paper merchants and mills showing all the weights and finishes of their branded stock. It is a good idea to build a library of sample books, some are inspirational works of design in their own right.

Right: **Paper sample books such as this one for Monadnock Paper will usually include all the weights and colours available from a manufacturer and extend to such items as envelopes if they are available.**

Design by Pollard & Van der Water Golden, USA

Above: **Paper sample books can be interesting design projects in their own right. Modo Paper Mills Inc, USA strive to stimulate their target audience – the designers who will specify their product – with strong, colourful photographic imagery and unusual binding.**

Design by SEA, UK

Right: **Rolland Motif Paper Promotional Calendar. Innovative use of print techniques, dye cutting and binding, cleverly demonstrate the versatility of the paper samples.**

Design by Époxy, Canada

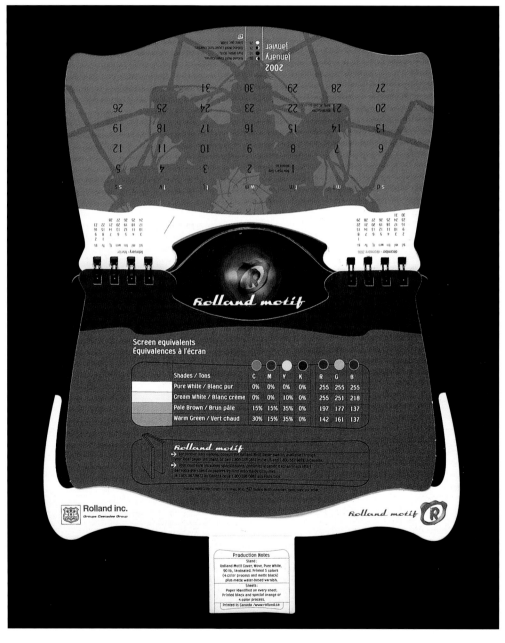

# CASE HISTORY    LIVING IN THE CITY

An exhibition to display the results of an international architectural competition organised by the Architecture Foundation in London, to promote the regeneration of derelict inner city sites, and develop innovative models of future urban accommodation. The exhibition was held at the Design Museum in London.

The Architecture Foundation and the Design Museum required a number of printed graphic elements to both promote the exhibition and explain the architectural concepts proposed by the winning entries.

The designer was briefed to produce the exhibition graphics accompanied by a promotional poster, advertising and various invitations to openings and private views. The initial brief also included a catalogue. However, as the results of the competition arrived from the international architectural practices, it became apparent that a more substantial publication would be required, and a book was proposed.

Although the exhibition was funded through sponsorship supplied by business and charitable trusts, the budget was limited, precluding the use of a photographer or expensive production methods. The graphic and exhibition designers worked closely to ensure the graphic elements would compliment both the display stands and the exhibits. An architectural sheet-plastic material was employed to create the stands themselves, and it was decided to use this theme as a basis for the graphic imagery.

The material is translucent and lightly colour tinted. Cost and practicality ruled out the use of the actual material as an innovative binding concept, instead, the designer used a digital camera to create close-up images of the material, using light and reflection for architectural effect. To add a further level of transparency, the book was covered with a tracing paper wrap simply printed in one colour. The tracing element was also bound into the publication to create section divisions.

It was deemed part of the designer's brief to liaise with the architects wordwide to collect the illustrative content of the book. These included digital photographs of architectural models, drawings and three dimensional renderings. As the time-scale was critical, electronic transmission had to be employed to collate these elements from all points of the globe. The images were supplied in a number of different formats, file types and resolutions. Most were compressed as JPEGs to speed transmission. All the images had to be

re-sampled to TIFF or EPS format to create 300dpi CMYK files suitable for printing. Text was supplied as a digital word-processing file by email and run into the page layouts. The pages were designed entirely on screen and first stage proofs created as PDF files. A set of hard-copy page proofs were also supplied to the client to ensure the 'feel' was balanced and the weights of type sympathetic to the design.

After final corrections were taken in, the digital files were sent on disk to the lithographic printer based in Belgium. The printer ran the files to plate and supplied page proofs so the designer could check there were no file errors or incompatabilities that might cause poor-quality imagery or font conflicts.

Below: **Page layouts in progress in QuarkXPress. Text was imported from emailed word processing documents. Pictures, emailed as compressed JPEGs, were converted to CMYK Tiffs prior to positioning on the page.**

This page: Some of the elements that made up the printed material designed to promote the exhibition: invitation, poster and book, with a spread depicting architectural concepts from one of the winning practices.

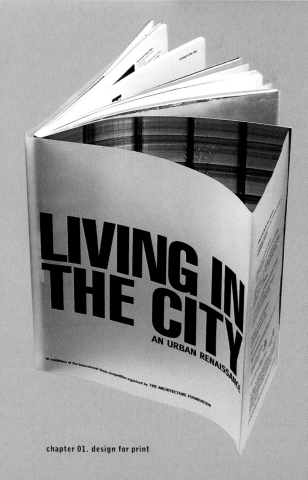

The practices of advertising, corporate identity and branding cut across other sections in this book, yet the profession of advertising has a distinct character that connects it closely with corporate identity and branding but sets it apart from other forms of visual and commercial practice. This section therefore looks at advertising, branding and corporate identity together. Although they used to be billed as separate practices that incorporated graphic expertise, the three aspects became more interconnected, as multimedia agencies, developed in the 1990s, were able to mix graphic and advertising skills and to take on entire promotional projects.

Essentially, advertising aims to produce a campaign – a strategic thought voiced in different ways, to surprise, delight and inform people. Like advertising, corporate identity aims to coordinate the interpretation of a product or service with a distinct visual or verbal 'look', by which it can be recognized. Branding became prominent in the 1990s with the rise of multinational companies that wanted to extend their promotions outside the normal territories of conventional advertising. Before any other quality, all three areas require ideas to be expressed with absolute clarity.

### THE SIGNIFICANCE OF ADVERTISING IN CONSUMER SOCIETY

In each area, graphic design skills are essential. Branding and corporate identity require typographers to craft letterforms and distinguish brand character; and computer-skilled graphic designers to coordinate the connections between all graphic elements, format material for printers (on disk and over the Internet), and define rules that govern the graphics application to different media. In advertising, a graphic designer's sense of organization is essential in order to ensure the flow of information and consistency of treatment. Word-based advertisements depend on skilled and sensitive typography. Most significantly, establishing a brand and developing its corporate identity in an advertising campaign demands graphics expertise,

**PART 02. SURFACE DESIGN**

**CHAPTER TWO**

# DESIGN FOR ADVERTISING

Left: **This ad relies on a tight relationship between the art direction and copy. The organization of props, colour density and picture space has been carefully arranged with the shape and weight of the text. Note the distinct visual style and placement of brand name and logo. These reinforce the brand name and visual identity.**
Duckworth Finn Grubb Waters, UK

Opposite above: **This Coke campaign drew on the brand's famous marque, effectively reminding the viewer of its established familiarity and uniqueness. The art direction drew on the brand's pre-existing archival imagery, which plays to the strengths of digital image manipulation (scanning, re-editing, segmenting, and enhancing).**
McCann Erickson, UK

Opposite below: **In its location a billboard has to be striking, quickly understood and easy to associate with the product or brand. The layout therefore must be clearly organised while the message must be punchy and succinct.**
Rainey Kelly, UK

because it requires the translation of concepts into images and copy, combined with an acute understanding of visual reference points.

The modes of advertising fall into five categories: warning, informing, reminding, launching and promotion. The overriding purpose is to provoke awareness by disrupting viewers' routine by grabbing their attention.

Since the beginning of the twentieth century, the usual means of media advertising was in the press and on billboards, and from 1954 this extended to television commercials. From the 1970s, a more direct form of advertising – sometimes called integrated advertising, advertising design or below-the-line advertising – emerged to counter the over-familiarity of mass advertising. A more recent form – ambient advertising – uses landscape and the placement of brands in situations where their message is most likely to be well received, such as a car manufacturer promoting safety by sponsoring and branding the clothes of a lollypop man.

The expansion of promotional forms has required designers to apply their skills more widely because, in all forms of advertising, the brand and the message have to be applied consistently and understood in the same way.

Life tastes good

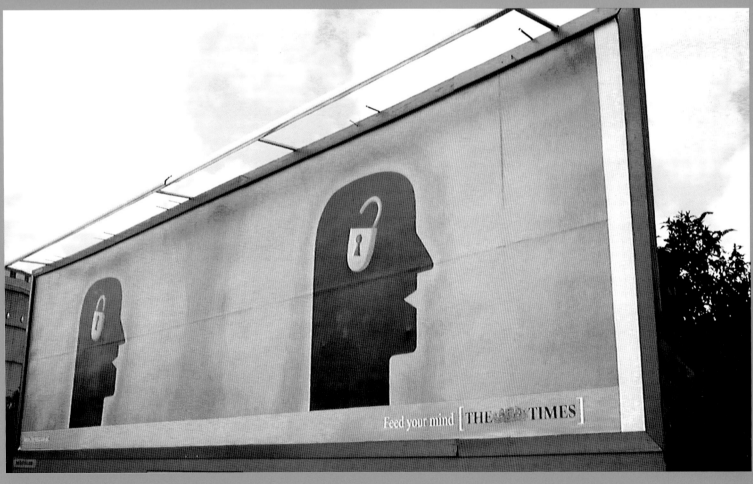

Feed your mind [ THE TIMES ]

**SPECIALIST PEOPLE** Within the set-up of a media advertising agency, there is typically a creative team that shapes the campaign and feeds ideas to graphic designers and typographers. Designers are usually called when ideas need to be presented at pitches, at review stages and for final artwork. The precise nature of campaign development varies between agencies but one would broadly expect to find the following:

## CREATIVES

The creative department is made up of art directors, who construct the artwork, and copywriters, who determine the use and wording of copy. Both are answerable to creative directors, who control the overall direction of campaigns with financial and planning directors. Art directors and copywriters often work as a team, an approach that emerged from New York's Madison Avenue in the 1960s. All three creative jobs require graphic design training, and it is with the creative department – usually called 'the creatives' – that graphic designers, typographers and brand-design specialists work most closely.

The input required from graphic designers centres on turning rough ideas in the form of scamps (see page 95) into finished digital artwork that brings together all elements – type, image and corporate branding. Images can be developed digitally and sent via e-mail. Graphic designers need to ensure that the campaign appears consistent with the other applications of branding and corporate identity.

## FACILITATORS

The media campaign is usually connected to, and co-ordinated with, other areas of brand-building, such as price promotions and more targeted direct advertising. This is usually negotiated with the client's own marketing department and the project management team, which consists of the creative director along with planners, who translate the client's needs into the creatives' brief, and account handlers, who control the finances of a campaign. In all aspects of advertising freelance work, graphic designers are likely to come into contact with facilitators (often called 'suits'), who employ typographers, illustrators, animators, computer-graphic layout specialists and production specialists on a project basis. Graphic designers are also likely to come into contact with project time-planners (called 'traffic'); their job is to ensure that deadlines are met. Media-space buyers negotiate with billboard site owners, press and other media owners to organise the placements of advertisements. In some

cases, specific advertising sites require designers to tailor their artwork at short notice in liaison with the media-space planning team.

Graphic expertise is usually introduced when the creative direction has been agreed, although the brief on which designers work tends to be established early in the process. Increasingly, because brand-marketing directors move jobs frequently, clients tend to employ their own third party, a 'brand guardian', to oversee their product's long-term development: these people are concerned with all aspects of the brands development, from campaign direction and corporate identity through to consistency in the development of product packaging. The lines of responsibility often inter-connect, according to the variety of media used in an advertising campaign.

As in other fields of graphic design, work is nearly always produced on an Apple

Above: **Art-direction led advertisement. The product is clearly central to the artwork, preventing it being confused with another brand, while the negative space emphasises the simple arrangement. In the past the footballer's crafted outline would have required a skilled model maker and photographic trickery. Today it is more cost-effective to simulate from a sketch model in either Photoshop or FreeHand.** Tribal DDB, Spain

Bottom: **This advertisement needed to include detailed product information, so bold art direction makes the text (headline and body copy) readable within a striking, stylized composition. The branding (top left) and product shot (bottom right) are strategically placed to ensure** image and text connect with the make and model. The illustration was specially commissioned, then scanned into the agency's ad format. The image was then produced in Photoshop while the stylized copy was created in Adobe Illustrator.
DDB, Singapore

Right: **Copy-lead advertisement. The justified copy is easy to read because of the liberal spacing between and around the text. The illustration provides the copy with a distinct visual point of reference, leading the eye into the text. Copy is often written straight into FreeHand, therefore careful copy checking beyond electronic spellchecks is essential.**
Brook Street, UK

You are your own business. Me PLC doesn't owe its existence to an employer. As chairman and workforce, you supply your services to whoever needs them. And if you want to close the factory down for a couple of months, well that's your business too. What used to be called temping is now called smart. Using your main asset (a very powerful piece of wrinkly grey software) to the best advantage. Brave? Scary? Maybe at first. But not as scary as staying in the wrong job until you hate it. Why not make an executive decision to diversify? Talk to Brook Street. We'll help you make a career of it.

Macintosh. Work is increasingly moved between individuals and groups via ISDN, FTP sites and the Internet, so computer-skilled graphic designers have in recent years become integral to the advertising process – throughout the transition from the strategies (in the brief) to visualizing and development stages and through to the completed artwork ready for production.

In such a busy digital environment, the graphic designer must have a thorough grasp of file management and be conversant with file formats and compression techniques, in the interests of rapid and accurate communication. Producing prototypes is helped enormously by choosing the right software. Final print-quality presentation can be produced for client approval and 'one-off' or limited-edition giant posters can be produced on inkjet printers for trial marketing. On a smaller scale, photorealistic proposals for hoardings can be easily photo-montaged in Photoshop. Advertising and branding usually require designs in a wide variety of publications and formats. The ability of software to scale and reassemble design elements in different aspect ratios gives the graphic designer great flexibility and makes it easier to create adaptations.

**DESIGN CONSIDERATIONS** Within advertising there are many different types of promotion, and agencies tend to specialize. The two most prominent are media advertising and direct advertising. Media agencies produce mass-exposure, high-publicity work through billboard, press and commercial advertising, while direct advertising – often called one-to-one – is more closely geared to target markets and does not have the same audience reach.

## MEDIA ADVERTISING

Billboards are usually produced for 48 or 96 sheet sites or single-sheet rectangular format (1 sheet = 15 x 30 inches). On a smaller scale, but in larger runs, 6 and single-sheet poster campaigns are used to promote events rather than products. In both cases graphic designers liaise with advertising directors to make imagery and layout plans fit the format.

Press advertising ranges from double- and single-page spreads at one end of the market to column-width advertising at the cheaper end. Most advertisements require graphic judgement from an early stage. Factors such as typesetting, colour and organization of space are determined before photo-shoots and other production material are commissioned. Unlike brochure design, designers have less choice over paper or format, and the brief stresses corporate qualities that need to be clear in the artwork.

Television commercials also require early graphic input. Illustrators are hired to sketch out storyboards from art directors' notes, which help the creative team to communicate precisely what they require from film directors. Because of the expense in hiring film crews, on-location storyboards are checked constantly to ensure that accurate footage is recorded, that the timing of sequences is met and that recorded material fits precisely with the requirements of post-production teams. Digital typographers and graphic designers are usually required to produce animated text sequences – added during post-production editing – to link the film with the end frame. In most commercials the end connection between final product shot, branding and strapline is the most crucial graphic element.

## DIRECT ADVERTISING

The most common form of direct advertising is direct mail (DM), using postal services to reach selected potential or existing customers. Most DM specialists are graphic designers, because the work involves graphically presenting special offers, service schemes, brand magazines and service information through the design of mailshots – flyers, brochures and packaging. Databases and mail merge software simplify and facilitate the personalization of direct mailshots. The format and appearance of DM work are usually the remit of graphic designers, in negotiation with the client's marketing team. For bigger advertising pitches using DM, one-off 'interactive' self-liquidating promotions (SLPs) tend to be commissioned. These are specially designed limited-edition branded goods that connect to publicized special offers, and are usually developed from a media campaign. Point-of-sale promotion requires digitally skilled graphic designers to connect all areas of brand advertising and promotion work. Usually in shops and supermarkets, point-of-sale formats include freestanding boards, dump bins, banners, 'wobblies' (plastic mobiles suspended from shelves) and 'buzz stops' (vertical advertising hoardings between shelves). Digital graphic skills are particularly needed to scan and manipulate environments during concept development.

Right: Self-liquidating promotions (SLPs) are campaign extensions designed to add to a brand's promotional 'hit'. This megaphone slotted into a press, poster and TV campaign for a soft drinks company picked up on the colour and branding of the product while the SLP type, a megaphone, reinforced the company's extravagant personality.
Triangle Communications, UK

WE'VE SQUEEZED
A DESKTOP
INTO A PORTABLE.

## DESIGN CONSIDERATIONS FOR MEDIA AND DIRECT ADVERTISING:

✱ An advertising campaign must have impact, relevance, and 'connect' simply with the intended audience.

✱ Advertising must not lose sight of its subject – the graphic content is essential in this.

✱ Clarity – in print advertising 80 per cent of the space usually conveys the idea, and 20 per cent the additional information.

✱ Analysis of the brief defines precisely what is required – the ideal is to reduce the proposition to a single sentence – and defines the types of skill required of a graphic designer.

✱ The prominence of the logo or product shot must be considered, remembering that the purpose of the graphic input is to emphasize the advertised goods.

✱ The brand characteristics must be systematically adhered to in terms of layout, tone and treatment of the copy.

Top: This ad for the Welsh Tourist Board was designed for 48 and 96 sheet billboards, which enabled the small inset image contained in the top left to contrast with the less constrained image representing the free open expanse of Wales.
Impact FCA!, UK

Above: This press ad uses a visual pun as a lead into the body copy. Note that the text is separated from the image so that it does not distract from the image or text's clarity. The text is further simplified with separate headings to make it appear less bulky.
Duckworth Finn Grubb Waters, UK

**CORPORATE IDENTITY IN ADVERTISING** Corporate identity is the commercial face that represents a company, where branding is its commercial application. They often get confused because the term 'brand' is the name given to a company's identity, while 'branding' describes the marque by which a company, product, or service is recognized. Expressed simply, corporate identity is the creation of the brand, while branding is how it is then applied through all areas of communication.

The corporate identity has to represent the values by which a company should be known, but in recent years major brands have turned their products into sub-brands; and consequently advertising activity has diversified. In modern communications agencies, the roles normally associated with branding and corporate identity tend increasingly to cross over.

The most common outlets for corporate identity include journals and in-store magazines, which are typically quarterly publications that show, through their editorial contents, how the company's products and services connect with the presumed lifestyles of consumers. Graphic design considerations include the creation and implementation of the brand's corporate rules regarding layout, and the organization of leader stories, advertorials and features in a visually stimulating manner.

Clear rules as to how the corporate identity will be used in different media have to be established. These typically range from stationery and advertising to digital applications. Appropriateness and consistency are key considerations. How changes affect the reading of the brand is a significant issue in the development of a corporate identity: does it still retain a connection with earlier brand associations?

Bigger brands have tended to develop and implement corporate identities through their own retail environments – most notably superbrands such as Nike and Disney Stores. Such total branding involves the bringing together of all visual aspects and the development of corporate signature styles to create a brand experience.

Corporate identity, therefore, requires background knowledge of the product's or firm's chief characteristics, the type of market in which the clients want to develop, and the nature of promotions to which they want to commit.

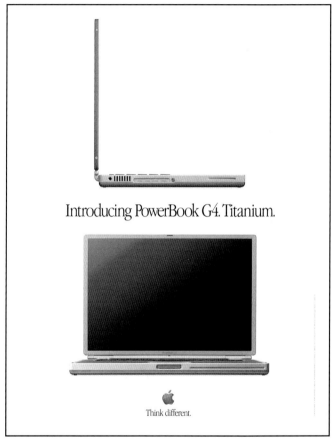

Above left: **The Flash ads for internet search engine Ask Jeeves appeared on websites and search engines attracting a large number of 'hits'. With on-line ads a system of 'hyperlinks' (sub-pages) need to be created, with a consistent thread of corporate identity running through web pages.**

Above: **Most creative industries use Apple computers because their systems are geared to creating and manipulating digital images. From 2000 Apple made a virtue of this in their advertising. The shape of the Titanium powerbook became the advertising 'hook', conveying a sense of stylish innovation and creative freedom as the unique selling proposition.**
TBWA/Chiat/Day, USA

## DESIGN CONSIDERATIONS FOR CORPORATE IDENTITY

Graphic consultants typically are involved in key stages of corporate identity work: primary research and recommendation, visualizing (through sketch work and digitally imaged scamps) image concepts, development and detail, then implementation (digital type specifications and media appropriation). It is important for designers to be able to blend traditional and digital skills in order to get the right results in as little time as possible.

Corporate identities need to convey a sense of belonging, must be representative and must be clear. Designers need to ensure that the placement of, and any appropriations to, a brand marque are consistent with core brand values. They should check to see what rules govern its usage. The visual dynamics of a corporate identity must be well measured in terms of appropriateness to market and consistency. This is absolutely essential to the inherent character of the product or firm it represents.

Having extracted key graphic qualities, the designer will need to consider the need for flexibility and assess how these qualities can be effectively reproduced at different scales and in different contexts.

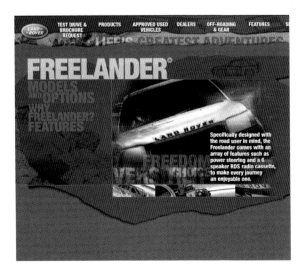

Above: Land Rover's direct mail has been credited with developing their existing customer base. Using data to target established and potential customers, the agency has developed a variety of promotional material that has coordinated user group outings, mailer posters and small publications. Together it forges a bond between customers and the brand ethos. The range of paraphenalia is connected through strong corporate identity, which underpins the entire range of promotional work including the Land Rover website (left).
Craik Jones, UK

**BRANDING** Compared with corporate identity, branding is directly connected with raising awareness. It usually involves the development of a brand's identity within the everyday surroundings of its target market, using graphic techniques to ensure that the brand is associated with a particular space and mood. Branding therefore fits between direct advertising and corporate identity, because it commercializes the brand by applying the graphic identity to appropriate contexts.

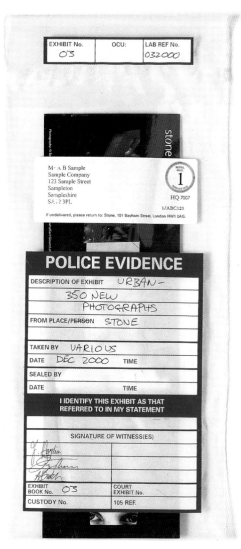

Above: **This limited edition business-to-business mailer treats a Tony Stone picture library image as police evidence. The team that designed this as part of the stock archive's re-branding had to develop the total** package, linking separate elements such as a flyer, poster, cover letter and sealed bag. All elements were rendered in FreeHand and printed onto the different media.
Tequila, UK

The best-known aspect of branding is product placement, instigated by 'marketers' who directly engage with graphic designers. The role of the designer is to apply the corporate graphic style to situations that, in most cases, require re-thinking in terms of how an existing identity can be tailored.

Recently, branding has engaged a wider range of specialist graphic practices so that environments and products – from coasters and clocks to nightclubs and public spaces – have become vehicles for promotion. Photoshop is an ideal tool for producing mock-ups showing products and brands in different situations. However, final artwork will usually be produced to the desired specifications in FreeHand or Illustrator – vector-based files being more versatile for a variety of scales.

The objective of placement branding, called ambient or 360-degree advertising, is to engage customers the moment they are most likely to want the product – for instance, a drinks brand in a bar. Graphic designers are typically employed to re-style and appropriate graphic elements, taking into account how the branding will be understood in its given context. The development of typographical rules for on-line branding is essential, and usually involves collaboration between digital graphic designers, copywriters who shape the wording, and web designers who apply the corporate identity rules and graphic elements to suit the context.

Branding is also called on to extend direct advertising activity. Examples include branded booklets, collector cards and correspondence, usually produced to promote product ranges and sent to existing clients to maintain customer dialogue.

In recent years brands have developed their identity by diversifying into other markets. Brand stretching can simply involve a brand name being applied to another product, but more often it involves developing a brand through a new product range – for instance a drinks brand expanding into leisure clothing, where new product ranges are links to the brand's main area of operation.

In some instances clients have their own brand guardian, who ensures that the advertising strategy and other new ideas fit with the existing brand ethos and the company's other development plans.

Right: Even in the design of the Porsche mug, the placement of the marque and copy are key design elements, as is the sourcing of a mug manufacturer with the appropriate surface finish, proportions and details for Porsche's brand identity. Such qualities may be defined in a corporate identity specification manual.

Right: The Smirnoff Experience – a branded dance event – was a version of 360° advertising, where the landscape was dominated by a single brand. Such sponsorship strategies reinforce the association between a venue and a distinct brand or product. They are co-ordinated with a range of branded design material including posters, environmental graphics and self-liquidating promotions.
KLP Euro RSCG, UK

Right: Initially produced as a brand extension of the fashion label Benetton, Colors magazine espouses many of the values associated with the brand's established global identity. The magazine added depth and kept the spirit of Benetton's brand ethos, which had been developed through earlier ad campaigns.
Design by Benetton Publishing, Italy

## DESIGN CONSIDERATIONS FOR BRANDING

Graphic consultants are typically involved in three stages of branding development: primary research and recommendation, visualizing the brand in context, then working out implementation feasibility.

The role of graphic designers in branding involves consultation and recommendation more than re-design. Branding must graphically reflect, in situ, a company's aspirations in a wide variety of contexts, ensuring that the visual distinction of a brand is clearly evident and that its primary function is to condense key characteristics into a single 'signature' – a visual typographic or graphic element. This will be the marque by which it is recognized.

With promotional work in mind, the branding should incorporate commercial hooks that suggest how the brand typography and graphic styling could be adapted. This may suggest to a brand's marketers or advertising creatives the key qualities that can be picked out as a selling proposition

The context in which the brand is placed has to be clearly relevant and easy to associate. It is important, if it is to work effectively, that the branding cannot be misconstrued and that any brand extensions of the work must connect with the core ethos of the brand's other promotions.

**PLANNING AND PRODUCTION** Careful planning and control of production are key to a successful advertising campaign. With so many creative professionals involved, it is vital that the graphic designer is aware of all the critical stages of the process.

## KEY STAGES IN THE PLANNING, DESIGN AND PRODUCTION OF A PROMOTION CAMPAIGN

**Stage 1** is the brief – defining the campaign objectives. The creative brief is broken down in order to interpret statistical evidence, to define a 'hook' as the most suitable selling proposition, and to define appropriate modes of delivery (and appropriate media) to reach the defined target market. The components are translated into a project plan that defines art direction, and suggests tone of voice and the most appropriate types of graphic designer (and illustrator) for the project.

**Stage 2** concerns the defined key words and proposition – concepts for advertising. This is the task of thinking through ideas on paper using layout pads and markers to produce scamps – ideas in rough, simply communicated. At this stage, the concepts are shown to the rest of the creative team, then to the planning team (occasionally with client representatives) to ensure that all aspects of the brief have been addressed. At this first visualizing stage, art directors work through and negotiate ideas with copywriters, who will consider the ratio of type to image.

Initially a campaign plan is defined – developing the strongest strategies, and detailing the concept – and a plan for art direction and execution is set out. Ideas are presented in-house (using scamps and mock-ups) and adjustments are made, with graphic specialists employed to tidy the presentation. The agency's project team puts a detailed presentation plan together. This is followed by the external (client) presentation for which key ideas are polished (with external graphic design expertise) to presentation level. By this point graphics software such as FreeHand or Illustrator and photomanipulation tools such as Photoshop will play a vital part in the process. Clients are usually presented with a central campaign plan and a series of alternatives, so that a final direction can be agreed and signed off by the client.

Right: The stages shown in this diagram are typical of those commonly found in media advertising agencies. Digital graphic designers are mostly called upon in the run up to the key presentation stages, such as the prentation of strategy, concept, and for the final artwork.

**Stage 3** concerns final concept development – fine tuning for production. Art direction is detailed, and specialist typographers, photographers, film director, illustrators, specialist media experts are commissioned. Any other promotional aspects are also tied into the overall strategy. Commissioning of media is then made, and a timetable is set, with 'traffic planners' controlling the meeting of deadlines. Printers are booked and media space buyers negotiate the appropriate venues, release dates and length of campaign run with account planners and media space sellers.

The agency team meets with all the client representatives for final project clearance. At this stage follow-on promotions may be discussed.

**Stage 4** is when all printing and production takes place and the synchronized campaign is launched.

Above: **A detailed scamp, used as a visual to convey the concept to clients, and the resulting press ad, prepared for a double-page glossy magazine (within the crop marks). The detail of a crying car was one of a sequence of 'moodboards', produced in marker and pencil, to guide a film crew in the shooting of a television commercial.**
BMP, UK

## BASIC REQUIREMENTS FOR GRAPHIC DESIGNERS WORKING IN ADVERTISING

A graphic designer working in contemporary corporate identity, branding and the various forms of advertising promotion will need a 'book' or portfolio of ideas to demonstrate his or her thinking. It should demonstrate skills as a visualizer and the ability to generate highly finished detailed graphic design, layout and typographic work. It should also prove ability to use the appropriate graphic software.

Increasingly advertisers themselves are developing the capacity to use digital design tools, i.e. to produce work digitally on computer equipment. However, it is the graphic designer's creative expertise that is mostly called upon. To work in promotions, you will need the following basic equipment.

✳ **Hardware:** Apple Macintosh, colour printer, scanner, access to email.
✳ **Software:** Adobe Illustrator or Macromedia FreeHand (original artwork creation), Adobe Photoshop (image manipulation)

You should also consider adding some of the many special effects plug-ins available for Photoshop, Illustrator and FreeHand. Make sure your portfolio shows your flexibility and competence both with the software packages and with combining traditional and digital techniques.

# 02.02

## DAEWOO MATIZ ADVERTISING CAMPAIGN 2001

The agency campaign team, led by their creative director, liaised with Daewoo's marketing director and team. The agency re-presented developed project work to the Daewoo team at interim presentations and final presentation stages.

The first stage of the process was to define the requirements of the brief and the type of finished outcome that was being sought. Agency planners and the creative director constructed a brief for the creative teams, based on consumer research and initial client meetings. The key quality picked out from the brief – the Matiz's manoeuvrability in urban conditions – was translated into ideas through roughs and initial scamps.

It was agreed that the agency would develop press, poster, billboard and self-liquidating promotional material. Such work often has to co-ordinate with other direct promotions, such as point-of-sale showroom displays. At this first development stage the campaign direction was reappraised, next stages were agreed and a time scale was put in place. Daewoo's marketing director signed off the plan of progression for the next phase.

The creative team for the job consisted of graphic designers, a creative director, two creatives (sharing art direction and copywriting roles) and a planner. Scamps of the poster were developed from rough sketches, incorporating many of the corporate layout elements and logo. These are often collaged in FreeHand, Freelance graphic designers were briefed at the studio, and then developed the work, corresponding via email and phone. A 'book' of interim solutions was presented to the Daewoo team for approval.

Decisions were made within the agency on the most appropriate solutions to go forward to the final presentation of ideas. Three different versions for each promotion strategy were developed for the presentation, which were presented with detailed scamps. The creative

director planned the presentation as a demonstration of how the work addressed the brief, met existing Daewoo objectives and breaks new ground. Some ideas were rejected at this last stage before the development of final artwork.

The winning concepts were then refined though scamps and mock-ups, with regular creative team development meetings. Having defined the direction of the final execution, graphic specialists worked on the typography and graphic arrangements for the poster and corresponding promotional material. Production technicians were contracted to work out feasibility and costings with account planners, then the agency's 'space buyers' investigated relevant venues for the campaign duration. Final variants in design detail were presented to the rest of the creative team at an 'internal crit', where graphic treatments were selected for detail design. Final mock-ups were produced for client approval using digital packages.

At the final client presentation, campaign work was presented to Daewoo's project team by the agency's creative and planning directors. The work was approved and signed off for production, pending minor graphic amendments. 'Traffic' planners then co-ordinated final location shoots for the art direction, while typesetters were employed to coordinate the final copy arrangements. Space buyers signed up to poster and billboard sites while printers and manufacturers were contracted to produce the final printed artwork. Simultaneously, call centres were organised to deal with enquiries and coordinated promotion offers. Contractors were hired to install the posters.

All that remained to be done was to print and install the posters and launch the campaign.

Left: **The agency brief, developed from client meetings**

Below left: **Initial sketches, first concepts produced as rough visuals, which are used for** in-house discussions and development meetings only.

Below right: **Final presentation scamp, where text and image elements were assembled in Photoshop.**

Bottom: **The completed poster.** The final version was produced as a Photoshop document, and was transferred to Adobe illustrator format for print production.
Duckworth Finn Grubb Waters, UK

**DUCKWORTH FINN GRUBB WATERS**

41 Great Pulteney Street, London W1F 9NZ. Telephone: (020) 7734 5888.
Facsimile: (020) 7734 3716. Email: dfgw@dfgw.com

## BRIEF

What is this brand called?  What is this campaign/ ad called?
Daewoo Brand Relaunch - Matiz

What is this brand's DNA?

Who do we want to buy it?

Anyone's who's looking to buy a new car who is fed up with the pressures of urban driving. Whether they're young or old, a businessman or a creative type, they will all share the same frustrations: congestion, lack of parking spaces and dismal public transport all make urban driving a nightmare.

The Daewoo Matiz is the perfect urban car, in fact its even won the 'Best City Car' Award to prove it. It's nippy enough to move though traffic, and small enough to slip into the smallest of parking spaces.

The Matiz has also won the 'Best Budget Car' and if you have to commute into work, might well work out annually, as not much more than the cost of your travelcard

Why should people buy this brand?

The award winning Matiz, designed to ease the pain of urban driving

The Daewoo Matiz is small and nippy enough to be the ultimate in urban driving, and it comes at an affordable price; that's why its won the Best City Car and the Best Budget Car awards

| Requirement | Appearance Date | Budget Guidelines |
|---|---|---|
| | | |

| Signatures | Date | Internal | Present | Creative Team(s) |
|---|---|---|---|---|
| Plan/ Acc. | | | | |
| Traffic | | | | |
| Job Number: | | | | |

Duckworth, Finn, Grubb, Waters Limited registered in England number 2372731
Registered Office: 41 Great Pulteney Street, London W1F 9NZ.

That'll be the ⊘ DAEWOO Matiz

That'll be the ⬙ **DAEWOO**

Every day, we come into contact with packaging of differing shape, size and purpose, informing us of the merits, dangers, quality or value of the products they contain. Some packs are designed to be discarded immediately after purchase, others are integral to the life of their contents. The graphic designer has to create compelling and attention-grabbing packaging items and take into account the legal requirements, trading rules and environmental concerns that govern the industry. Packaging must function physically as well as being visually attractive and enticing.

The ability to visualize two-dimensional designs in the round – as provided, for example, by QuarkWrapture – is essential to the digital graphic designer who has to imagine the packaging in its made up form to determine how text or images will sit in relation to components such as folds, gluepoints or lid mechanisms.

Preparing digital files of the complete pack design for production is the responsibility of the designer. To facilitate this, much of the software used in package design allows for manufacturing or cutter guides to be imported. These are used as templates for the graphic content of the pack.

Different pack shapes are continually being developed which can be manufactured from an expanding range of materials. Polyethylene, high-grade plastics, acetates and many other new materials, have been added to the already extensive range available to the designer. These materials, each with their different textures and surfaces, provide both opportunities and challenges for surface application and production.

Branding is essential to packaging design and is much more complex than simply the application of a logo. Typography, shape, image, layout, choice of colour and tactile qualities all contribute to developing product identity.

Visuals on screen can be seductive so designers have to be careful not to be beguiled by the ease with which software allows them to create a packaging design. What is seen on screen will ultimately have to be

**PART 02. SURFACE DESIGN**

**CHAPTER THREE**

# DESIGN FOR PACKAGING

Left: **To a consumer, this bag represents style and luxury, but strip away the cosmetic elements of the design and you are left with a simple paper bag. The design is no more practical, despite the extra cost in materials, but is now an effective marketing tool for the brand.**
Design by Kenzo, France

translated into a physical, fully functional three dimensional product. It is important, therefore, to include mock-up construction as part of the design process.

Testing a package design by producing an accurate mock-up, well ahead of the full-scale production, and checking that the design itself and the surface graphics work together is essential. Once constructed, a package can dramatically change in appearance from the original design. Type, for example, may become distorted, cut-out windows may not align adequately enough to display the product or, just simply, the overall design may have less impact off-screen. Keep printing out and test assembling work frequently. This can save you much embarassment when it is time to show ideas to your clients.

Above right: **This award winning cover for the Pet Shop Boys 'Very' CD stood out in the competitive charts crowd by defying the traditional approach to packaging design. Taking advantage of alternative manufacturing techniques resulted in, not only a practical packaging solution, but an effective publicity device. The designer conveyed a message to the consumer of an individual and creative band setting themselves apart from a crowded industry.**
Design by Pentagram, UK

Right: **The plastic carrier bag was once an undesirable but very cheap device for carrying shopping home. With advances in printing technology, the colours, texture and quality in production of this bag means it can now proudly be used to successfully represent a contemporary brand image.**
Design by Paul Smith Ltd

Left: **Adobe Illustrator** is a popular choice among professional designers, due to its compatibility with Adobe Photoshop; in fact, although it is a powerful vector-driven illustration tool, most of the Photoshop default filter effects are available and can be applied to imported bitmaps in a document. Tools and modifiers are located in various Palettes, which can be organised around the work area in customisable groups, or hidden away.

Left: **Corel's** flagship product, CorelDraw, tends to be more popular with office and home users. While the three most popular drawing applications do not differ much in price, the Draw package includes not only the vector-based drawing application, but a full version of Corel's bitmap editing application (Photo-Paint) and a handful of other useful tools for screen captures, texturing, tracing, and more.

**DESIGN TOOLS** Graphic designers normally have a good understanding of all the major graphic arts software including three dimensional modelling applications but, at minimum, should be fluent in at least one drawing program, when working with packaging.

Computer-generated artwork can be extremely accurate, allowing the designer to work to precise tolerances. This has knock-on benefits for the manufacturing processes.

Designers often tend to favour one program over another for reasons of familiarity, but DTP programs – more suited to multi-page work, are less frequently used for packaging design. However, artwork for manufacturer's cutting guides and templates can be imported and locked into these programs and graphic elements used as necessary. Dedicated drawing programs such as Illustrator, FreeHand or sometimes CorelDraw are widely used as they have many functions that assist the design development process. Almost infinite scaleability and distortion controls together with lockable layers and guides, give designers greater flexibility for experimentation and for previewing their creations at different stages.

The advantage of working with layers, which can be locked and/or hidden, allows numerous permutations and variations of a design to be made on screen without accidental deletion or movement of key elements.

Repetitive transformations, 'click and drag' duplication and knife tools are just some of the highly productive features of drawing programs. In common with DTP programs, other graphic elements including photographic images, text and manufacturer's guides can all be imported. Bitmap editing programs are used extensively for modifying and preparing images for packaging design.

An interesting feature of 'object oriented' drawing programs is the facility that allows the user to assign different output halftone resolutions to individual elements, thus allowing a high degree of control over differing graphic components when printed onto different surfaces.

Files exchanged between different computer platforms can throw up incompatabilities so it advisable to check on this before committing files to the final production stage.

Generating digital artwork and transmitting it to clients and manufacturers, by high-speed telephone lines, has greatly reduced the time span between concept and production, but this advantage can only be maintained by accurate file preparation and platform compatibility.

Above: **Macromedia FreeHand** is the main competitor to Illustrator and is very similar, with the exception of some minor differences in the way tools are sorted and implemented. Panels and Inspectors are used to display tools and options. Support for documents with multiple pages, the Perspective Grid, and powerful type handling tools including support for hanging punctuation are some outstanding features.

**MATERIALS** Products of most shapes, sizes and weight generally need some form of packaging. This must be suited to the individual product to ensure adequate protection as well as ease of opening and good customer appeal.

One aspect of packaging design that cannot be dealt with by computer software is the choice of the right material. The substrate's behaviour when folded, bent, stamped, moulded or blown is crucial to how the final product will look. This is simply something you have to learn from experience and by making or commissioning mock-ups.

Paper and cardboard are widely used in the packaging industry. They are relatively inexpensive and have a versatility that makes for simple and quick processing. Additionally, they are materials that designers can also use easily for constructing presentation mock-ups. Embossing, creasing, cutting, folding, slitting, gluing and the printing of inks, varnishes and other finishes are all straightforward processes suitable for use with paper and cardboard.

Recycled cardboard is used for many forms of packaging. This lowers unit costs and also carries the added bonus of being 'environ-mentally friendly', a quality that is exploited by manufacturers of 'wholesome' or 'green' products. Inexpensive card can be treated with a range of coatings to enhance its performance. Water - and oil-resistant laminates, for instance, can be applied for effective food packaging or other moisture-producing goods. Card is often coated purely to resist marking that can occur from frequent handling.

Other materials are regularly used in conjunction with card packaging to provide strength or to give extra visibility of the product. Acetate windows, for example, can be be glued into position over an area that has been die-cut from the card sheet.

Intricate or fluid shapes cannot be easily constructed from card so many of these designs are produced by using plastics and films. Injection moulding, in which melted plastic is forced into a mould, is widely used, though set-up costs can be high and only large production runs bring the unit cost down to acceptable levels. A popular type of plastic for packaging is PET (polyethylene terephtalate), which is easy to shape and good looking.

Plastics use numerous chemicals in their manufacture and do not degrade quickly, making them difficult to use for products that in themselves are considered environmentally friendly. Designers need to be aware that materials can 'speak' to the audience as clearly as graphic imagery does.

Glass, once a popular packaging material, has seen a decline in use. It is more temperamental than plastics, such as PET, shatters easily and cannot withstand extreme temperatures. However, its transparency, moulding capabilities and self colouring, together with its suitability for frosting and engraving, give it a tactile and aesthetic appeal, appropriate for giving products an unusually luxurious feel.

Metal, as a packaging material, accommodates extremes in packaging price points. At the lower end of the market it is used in great volume for tinned foods, aerosols and oil containers, as well as being used for luxury goods, such as gift-set tins printed with interesting graphics – making them collectable once the contents have been used. Metal is also suitable for recycling as it is easy to melt down and re-form. However, there are fewer shape options from which to chose as most tin production is based on two or more pieces being welded together.

This page: Different food types demand various packing solutions depending on the nature of their contents. The breakfast cereal (below) needs to be sealed in airtight container to avoid spoiling. Heat sealing, plastic zip sealers and foil packing help the longevity of the product. Eggs (far right, below) have always been awkward to package. This effective solution is created from one sheet of card, making it easier to manufacture compared to more common moulded designs used today.

A simple cardboard tube used to be the only pack to buy Smarties in. But market forces demand interesting and novel approaches to retailing and so this toy-like pack was created for Mini Smarties – Exactly the same product but an exercise in alternative formats.

The glass bottle for Coca Cola, however, has remained a favourite, indeed a classic design. Essentially unchanged since 1915, the shape is a registered trademark and proves that innovation in packaging is not always the best approach. The filter coffee pack (top right) makes use of foil wrapping and vacuum packing to retain freshness.

All materials have their own unique qualities and behavioural properties. A lot of packaging incorporates several materials which have to combine successfully. It is a good idea for designers to take the time to familiarize themselves with the manufacturing capabilities and performance of each of the materials they intend using.

Understanding the purpose and function of a package design is of prime importance to the graphic designer. The major consideration for large, bulky items such as, for example, computers, microwave ovens and washing machines, is ensuring the packaging provides adequate protection and has prominent instructions for lifting and storage. In a retail environment large items are usually displayed unpacked suggesting that compelling, marketing graphics play a subordinate role in these instances. Despite this, there are manufacturers who use every opportunity to advertise their products and recognize that even large cardboard boxes offer a chance to promote the qualities of the product within.

**KEY KNOWLEDGE** So diverse are the methods of packaging and materials used, that designers are constantly having to up-date their technical knowledge both in terms of production, digital software upgrades and new applications designed to facilitate and expand conceptual work and the creation of digital artwork.

Above: **Packaging for large domestic appliances** usually make use of basic corrugated cardboard with a single colour application of type and virtually no coated finishes. Here the experience of buying a innovatively designed product such as this is enhanced by the pack design. The four-colour image on coated stock, the intricate and environmentally friendly card inserts all point to attention to detail and encourages consumer confidence in the product.
Design by SCA Packaging, UK

Right: 'Squeezable' bottles formed from flexible plastics are cheaper than metal or glass alternatives and are more convenient for the consumer. This innovative tube incorporates a small silicone valve which self-closes immediately after use. The graphics are printed on a soft, flexible, transparent sleeve which is then shrink-wrapped around the tube.
Design by Fuji Seal Europe

Cutter guides are used frequently in the manufacture of card packaging. Printing card packaging is usually done by offset lithography and the steps taken by the graphic designer to create graphic files for reproduction are similar to those for any general design for a print job (see Print section). However, once the sheet is printed, it will then be cut, creased and perforated in order to form a three-dimensional pack. The printed graphic work has to fit accurately within the physical shape to be cut in order to display as intended. For this reason, cutter guides are supplied to designers (usually as EPS files) from which to work. These guides accurately show where the cuts, folds and creases will be made, thus providing an accurate template to show the designer where to place the surface graphics.

Cutting and creasing equipment runs at high speeds so can have plus and minus tolerances and specific 'bleed' allowances that have to be taken into account when graphic artwork files are prepared.

Different materials and packaging shapes may require a number of alternative methods of printing and/or have properties that might affect the overall design. For example, corrugated card has a coarse surface which, if uncoated, soaks up ink and the fluting on the reverse side acts as a cushion making printing flat areas or delicate halftone work difficult.

Flexographic printing (see page 78) is used to print onto rounded or curved surfaces, as on washing-up liquid bottles, although precise registration of colours is difficult to achieve. Fine text and hairlines also tend to suffer, breaking up and distorting as a matter of course. Transparent stickers are

Above: **Packaging of crisps never took any interesting forms until the Phileas Fogg Tortilla crisps pack was created. To create this eye-catching design required the commitment of the client and the technical know-how of the designer and manufacturer.**
Design by Lawson Mardon Packaging, UK

Above right: **Square cartons of juice used to be a challenge to open without spillage. Plastic screw top pourers have now been incorporated into the pack, improving the customers experience with the product.**

increasingly being used as a more accurate alternative with assured, high-quality, printed results – but at an increased cost.

Most metal packaging design is printed as flat sheets which are subsequently pressed, or stamped into the required shape or component.

Unit cost is critical in the packaging industry. Print runs are usually very high compared to general publishing work. The number of colours, glue points and separate processes in a pack design affect the production costs, so the designer's ingenuity and creative skills will often be exercised to the full when working with low-level budgets. Safety in packaging demands care and consideration and can impose significant restrictions on design. Packaging must protect toxic or sharp objects from being accessible to children or piercing the pack and all food products must have tamper-proof devices such as protective films, ring pulls and pressure buttons on jar lids, incorporated into the pack design. Additionally, adequate warning or directional texts (also in braille) have to be prominently displayed on packaging that contains any form of hazardous product.

**DESIGN CONSIDERATIONS** The average pack on the store shelf has a tough job to do. It has to attract the customer by promoting its contents in competition with many other similar products around it and without making false promises. It must also be highly functional so that it can be safely and efficiently stacked, and be easy to use for the consumer.

In creating or re-designing a package, the graphic designer has to weigh up the advantages of following trends in typography, colour, imagery and layout against the fact that these can date quickly. Although we constantly see new packs appearing on the supermarket shelves, it is surprising how long branded items keep their identity and in many cases, packaging designs have to be created to be both durable and outlive transitory fashions.

Designers need to develop a strong visual language and understand the effect of colour and be sensitive to the way in which the consumer is influenced by different styles of design. Illustration and photography can play an important role in packaging design, evoking aspirational lifestyles and ambience. Specialist image makers should be commissioned for this purpose.

Making one product more desirable or chosen in preference to another brand, is a challenging task. A considerable amount of packaging design is direct and focuses fully on the virtues of the product, although other designs are deliberately created to appeal, obliquely, to lifestyle values so that the virtues of the packaging content are relegated to second place. This is seen clearly in the worldwide use of popular 'designer' labels and logos, subliminally suggesting that, by purchasing these products, the consumer will automatically adopt an enhanced lifestyle. Some packaging shapes have adopted their own branding characteristics in their own right, as in the triangular pack for Toblerone chocolate and the Coca Cola bottle shape, now registered as a trademark.

Above right: **Kodak** have successfully used colour to brand their products. The particular shade of yellow has become synonymous with Kodak film. It is not the name but the colour the consumer looks out for on the store shelf.

## BRANDING AND COLOUR

Recognition plays an important role in branding, particularly in supermarkets and other self-serve environments where shopping time can be limited. It is so much easier to reach out and pick up a familiar item or scan the shelves for products identified by colour association (see Designing with Colour). There are, however, occasions when powerful branding transcends traditional colour association. The turquoise colour used on the Heinz Baked Bean labels is so well embedded in the minds of most consumers, that the more usual association of blue/green in food with mould is not automatically made. Selecting colours appropriate to a product that also forms part of a design that will stand out from other competitive brands, many of which display similar colourways, is an interesting challenge for the graphic designer.

In packaging, typography acts as the voice of the product. Appropriate choice of typeface can help to evoke the right mood, suggest authority and generate confidence. When working three dimensionally, it is important to ensure that information is displayed on the correct surface and presented in a logical order. Contents, weight, size, colour, style or model number must be clear and easy to read.

Below: This is where the designer's work will compete with the rest. The object of the task becomes apparent when faced with this wall of colour, type and image. Surface graphics are relied on totally in a display of this kind as all pack formats are the same. The most successful design will have communicated a great deal of information such as the merits of the contents and the brand value, in the notoriously short attention span of the passing customer.

**Left:** Visualising a pack's design, before committing to paper or card mock-ups, is made easier with computer software. Virtually all the tools in QuarkWrapture are identical to those in XPress making the surface design simple and straightforward. When exported as a Quicktime movie the finished pack may be viewed folding itself up from flat to the assembled piece and then viewed from any angle.

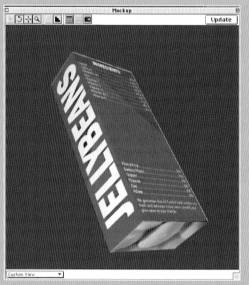

## INFORMATION REQUIREMENTS

Pack designs need to communicate information about their contents as well as persuade the consumer to make a purchase. There are a considerable number of elements that have to be incorporated into a pack design – some seemingly excessive but usually necessary for safety reasons or legal requirements. Barcodes, ingredients (vital to those with allergies and important to those counting calories), instructions for preparation, use or assembly, warnings, sell-by dates (overprinted separately), technical data and promotional advice, all have to to taken into consideration and accommodated within the design. Additionally some of these elements, such as barcodes, are fixed in terms of size, position and colour, and these cannot be ignored or visually relegated simply because they might degrade the look of the pack design.

The graphic designer should also consider that most packaging is normally first seen as a collection – row upon row of the same product identically packaged. A stylish design with powerful impact viewed in isolation, either on screen or as a physical mock-up pack, may look less successful in a general display context and viewed from a variety of heights, distances and angles. Using a three-dimensional modelling program or dedicated packaging software, such as QuarkWrapture, in order to see realistic three dimensional renderings of multiple packs from a variety of view points is useful for this purpose. Wrapture also allows the pack to be seen in the round as a QuickTime movie. Image manipulation programs such as Photoshop, enable the designer to montage pack designs into in-store photographs and view them in context alongside competitors' products.

**PLANNING AND PRODUCTION** Packaging briefs are usually more comprehensive than those for other areas of graphic design. In large retail organizations, the brief is usually drawn up by senior buyers after consultation with the manufacturer's marketing department. Marketing departments and manufacturers themselves may also commission designers directly. The product is often already in existence and the target consumer, retail outlets and a unit price for the packaging (as a proportion of the selling price) are already known.

Designers need to obtain as much of this information as possible and also consider potential modification and application of the design to future range extensions or different consumer markets.

Unit costs will determine the number of colours and construction methods that can be used, but inventively simplifying one aspect of a design allows elaboration of another.

If the product in question can be accommodated in a standard pack design, the creative process can begin straightaway using the relevant templates from the manufacturer. If the pack has to be purpose made, it is likely that the designer will need to confer with specialists. These may be in-house cardboard engineers or specialist mould makers, die-stampers and packaging manufacturers. Glues, inks, materials and assembly techniques are so varied that collaboration and research is strongly recommended.

Below: **Cardboard engineering plays an important role in the design of protective cartons for fragile products such as this Wedgwood china. Dye cut corrugated board inserts fit both the box and lid to hold individually shaped items securely. Inserts can be stamped and creased from a single sheet, or cut and slotted together for extra strength.**

Designs can be created on screen using a drawing program with images imported from bitmap imaging software although, ideally, a dedicated packaging program with constructional and three dimensional viewing facilities, should be used. This can be followed by a physical mock-up for client approval although the quality of three dimensional packaging programs may sometimes obviate this need. PDF files (see PDF files – Print section) can be sent directly to client marketing managers who can return them to the designer annotated with comments and any necessary amendments.

Final digital files should be prepared with great attention being paid to dimensional accuracy and colour specification before being sent to the production contractor. This may be a printing company with access to specialist cutting and finishing processes or a specialist packaging manufacturer with printing capabilities. The designer's files are used to make printing plates or stereos for final printing.

Colour proofs should always be obtained and checked for colour fidelity and hand-cut samples made up to check for constructional weaknesses or inaccuracies.

There should be close contact between designer and the production team throughout the production period. The final stage is for the proofs and made up packs to be signed off by the client.

# CASE HISTORY       MISCHIEF – PULL ALONG TOY

The brief to design packaging for a range of 'own brand' wooden, pre-school toys, to compete against well-established brands was given to the designer. The client wished to avoid brash and garish designs associated with cheaper, plastic toy packaging. The packaging was to accurately represent a higher-quality product with a potentially long life-span.

The products were aimed at children aged between twelve months and three years. However, as the purchase would be made by an adult, the packaging had to appeal to their perception of quality and value for money. It was considered important to allow access through the packaging, to the toys inside, so that potential customers could feel the texture and quality of the wood used. This need for accessibility involved cutting a panel from the main pack, which could weaken the overall package structure, so minimum guidelines were drawn up to ensure optimum strength and durability.

A packaging engineer was commissioned to develop the structure of the packs for this range, taking into account the client's requests for accessibility. To ensure the mock-ups created were accurate, a drawing program (Macromedia FreeHand) was used to produce scaled line drawings of each toy. This provided accurate information to help the engineer create precise dimensions for each of the proposed packs.

After evaluating the full range of toys to be marketed, the engineer designed a range of ten boxes to accommodate a total of twenty products. The number of boxes could have been further rationalized by constructing a range of more evenly-sized boxes, however, this ran the risk of criticism of 'over packaging' as the customer could be left feeling cheated after finding a small toy in an oversized box.

The packaging engineer then tailored each pack to individual requirements for securing each toy within the outer pack. Simple but effective strengthening techniques, including double-folded handles, were designed to ensure the product could be safely carried. Problems, such as ripping at stress points could occur during handling if such details were overlooked. The intention was to have as few tie or glue

Above: **The packaging engineer supplied these scaled drawings of the product to establish how much space is required by each item. An outline of a possible box shape is placed around each item to determine the minimum number of boxes capable of packaging the entire range.**

Above right: **The mock-up helped to illustrate the validity of a box shape to the client's manufacturer. This starting point answers initial questions such as cost or shelf area required. Once approved the progression to further mock-ups and the final design can continue.**

points as possible to help reduce costs. This was achieved by creating supports and grooves within the cardboard to enable the pack to be created efficiently from one piece. Minor adjustments were easily made, redrawn and quickly re-presented using the drawing program. Finished, physical mock-ups were then constructed.

The design of the packaging structure was subsequently passed to the graphic designer, who created surface graphics in the same drawing program, developing three options for a client presentation.

The selected design used a rich, earthy terracotta colour to both represent the toys' natural origins and quality. The colour had a traditional quality which contrasted well with the strong, lowercase Gill Sans typeface that was used. Cutter guides were supplied via email to the graphic designer and were transferred to layers in FreeHand. Other layers were placed underneath for text, colour panels and logos to manage the origination of digital artwork efficiently.

Once the final artwork was approved, the files were sent via email to suppliers in Korea, Thailand and Taiwan for manufacture. Printer's proofs were received and colour corrections to match those of the client-approved mock-ups were requested before the job was finally approved for production.

Below: The final printed product with an insert structure holding the product in place during transit and on the shelf. Sales of this range have been very successful with a 54% sales increase within two months of being launched.

Above: The final artwork is ready to email to the various Far Eastern countries who will produce the packaging. Finishing details such as age warnings, bar code spaces and colour specifications are checked and signed off by the client. Die cutting details such as the circular window were incorporated not only to add interest to the pack, but to enable the customer to see and feel the product more readily. This was a request made at the briefing stage.

Even hanging a small sign outside the local shop will need some thought. Will it be seen from the end of the street? What will it look like at night? How can it be cleaned? Will it need planning permission? Larger sign projects are even more involved. An ordered mind is needed to pull the complex threads of a signage system together.

Anyone who has ever taken a wrong turn, got lost and asked for directions from a passer-by will know how confusing verbal directions can be. As the Chinese proverb goes, 'one hundred tellings are not as good as one seeing.'

This is the reason we have signs; to help us travel independently. Signs distil information to the absolute minimum, they speak to you just at the right moment, they keep us moving. Seeing one good sign is better than a whole crowd of helpful locals.

Signs are often considered as merely two-dimensional directional aids – as arrows on posts or lists fixed to walls. A lot of this type of signing surrounds us: construction sites use basic, temporary signs, hospitals need rigorously functional signs, and department stores rely on floor-by-floor directories to list each sales area. These are all good, conventional signs, with each serving different, but important roles.

But there are many opportunities to branch out into three dimensions, where signs can become an integral part of a company's identity and embody the spirit of their brand. On a larger scale, signs can also be landmarks or even advertisements. If the purpose of a sign is to help you identify your destination, then sculptures or even an icon such as the Statue of Liberty can also act as a sign – after all, the statue unmistakably proclaims 'America' even without carrying the name. So signing can take many different forms. While conventional signs quietly go about their business directing you from point A, there are many other ways of announcing your arrival at point B.

**PART 02. SURFACE DESIGN**

**CHAPTER FOUR**

# DESIGN FOR SIGNAGE

Left: These directional arrows are large scale sculptures, each weighing two tons and reaching nearly eighteen feet high. With landmarks this size the designers believe that it would take a dog to get lost.
Design by Pentagram, UK

Right: How large can you get? This sign just can't be missed – it not only signs Warner Bros flagship New York store but it also keeps you up to date with the latest company successes. Cleverly, the sign is presented by one of the company's most important assets, Bugs Bunny. A perfect mix of information and brand experience.
Design by The Partners, USA

**GRAPHIC DESIGN AND SIGN DESIGN** The graphic designer draws together creative expression and analytical problem solving. Sign design demands that the analytical problem solving must come first, in order to inform creative expression appropriately.

Left: **Tall, thin monoliths made of frosted polycarbonate sleeves allow ambient light through and make the dark type stand out in a crowded retail environment. Vinyl cut lettering is applied to the hollow inner surface. This can be peeled off and updated when the store layout is changed.**
Design by North Design, UK

Below: **This museum orientation map uses silk screen printing and vinyl frosting on the reverse side of a large sheet of glass. When secured with heavy duty stainless steel fixings it seems to float away from the wall.**
Design by Atelier, UK

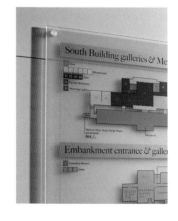

Designers have to consider that many who momentarily glance at their signs will be on their way to somewhere else, wrapped up in their own worlds, engrossed in the exhibition they've come to see, finding their way to the train, or simply on the way to the toilet. In this sense, sign design can be a straightforward occupation – merely guiding a fellow human being from one place to another, without fuss or bother. That is when signs really work in the real world. However, to be able to achieve this functionality together with style, panache and wit is the designer's creative challenge.

Sign design is a distinct area of graphic design in that signs take longer to plan, develop, make and install than many other graphic design projects, with, perhaps the exception of permanent exhibition projects (see Exhibition and Display). They are also around for a lot longer – making mistakes painfully lasting for the client (and the designer) involved. Signage is a design area that can be very rewarding for the graphic designer in that it can make a significant contribution to a visitor's experience of a building or space.

### DIGITAL TOOLS FOR SIGN DESIGN

Although sign design demands a different approach from many other areas of design, the tools a signage designer needs can be found in virtually any properly equipped design studio. Signage design requires strong type and graphics, so the key digital tools of this trade are either FreeHand or Illustrator – used for design, graphics production and typesetting – and a good range of typefaces. QuarkXPress is sometimes used, but it isn't really useful as a true drawing tool. Photoshop can be invaluable for creating mock-ups of signs montaged into photographs, but is generally not so useful for actual artwork production. Similarly, three dimensional modelling and CAD tools can be an asset for creating more effective presentations of work and might be used extensively by architects involved in the project, but aren't used for core design and production tasks.

Many signs are produced using cut-vinyl lettering and shapes. These are produced on vinyl-cutter machines, most of which can work happily with vector-based EPS graphic files exported from any professional drawing program. However, some less-common production tools, such as computer-controlled milling machinery for cutting and routing metal or wood items, may require other file formats. DXF is likely to be the format required in these cases. This format is more commonly used by CAD software, but FreeHand and Illustrator can export 2D DXF graphics when required. Note that type may need to be converted to

Right: This sign system for the
Bristol Legible City Project was
built of component parts that could
also be used for street furniture
and bus shelters. Made from
stainless steel supports and
vitreous enamel panels, in the
street scene these kindred
elements provide a coherence and
sense of identity for the city.
Design by MetaDesign, UK

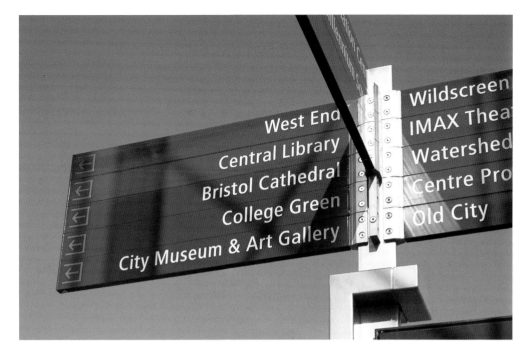

editable shapes first to preserve the desired look and feel, and plan with the machinery operators to make some test runs before committing to a production schedule.

Silkscreen printing is a very common print process, and lends itself to the reproduction of strong line artwork with flat colours. It is ideal for signs that have to withstand temperature and weather extremes, and exposure to public abuse. For more temporary uses large-format digital printing is becoming increasingly popular. Digital printers can handle complex imagery with graduated tones and vignetting. These graphic techniques are very difficult to achieve using more traditional sign production processes. It is very cost-effective for short run and one-off signs and posters, but the drawback is the fragility of the medium. Results are easily damaged, and in particular are prone to fading even when protected by lamination or encapsulation. More lightfast inks are being developed to address this problem, but be careful when considering this production method for anything but temporary signs.

Below left: British Airports
Authority, London VIP lounge,
internal signs. In keeping with the
calm atmosphere of a VIP lounge,
these signs were treated like
pieces of art – made from
embossed leather, simply framed
and hung like works of art. They
present a contemporary British
feel to business travellers on a
stop-over between flights.
Design by Pentagram, UK

## SPECIALIST PROCESSES NEEDED FOR SIGNS

The environment in which signs are placed and the roles they must take on will influence their physical construction and form. Only then does the designer have a surface upon which to consider graphic elements.

The signs shown on these and following pages have all been influenced by their environment. They differ in a range of ways: visually, in the use of materials, and in manufacturing processes. Specialist processes for sign-making are almost limitless as the lifespan of signs lends itself to a wide range of durable materials including metal, glass, plastic, wood, stone, slate, woven fabric and even leather. (see Exhibition and Display). Lettering and images can be screen printed, inkjet printed, etched, cut out, routed, carved or moulded. Methods of fixing can be as varied as any other architectural construction and it is this rich variety of materials, formats and fixtures that makes sign design such an interesting area in which to be involved. Virtually all the image-making processes whether for creating film for silkscreen printing or for driving a router to carve into wood, can be driven by designer-generated digital files, either directly or indirectly.

Left: These signs for a listed 1950s
theatre are simple elliptical
'blades' with a period typeface
screen-printed onto powder-
coated trays. They are finished
with stained hardwood trim.
Design by CDT, UK

**DESIGN CONSIDERATIONS** The start of the sign creation process is to take an in-depth look at both the signage problem in hand and the client's brief. Once the designer is fully informed about the project, there are a few guiding principles that can help the design development.

It is good design practice to make signs simple, understandable and to the point, as well as inventive where appropriate. The site is all-important and signs should be designed to integrate into, and function in, this environment. What might look eye-catching on screen in the studio might be lost in the vastness of a building space or when erected outdoors and placed on the horizon. It is imperative to be consistent throughout a scheme, remembering that one sign always follows another. Signs need to engender trust in the user by being both clear and consistent.

Signs must work for as many groups of people as possible, not just the average, but the tall, the short, the less sprightly and able, as well as those confined to wheelchairs. A surprising number of people have trouble with their eyesight. In some contexts multiple-language signs might be required. Signs obviously have to cater for everyone.

There are few rules covering colours, type sizes and pictograms. However the experienced graphic designer will know that colour can be used effectively as a coding device and also that colour choice and combinations are affected by different lighting conditions and any dominant colours within the sign system environment. Pictograms need to be unambiguous; they may entertain, but primarily they must inform, and the type size must be legible at the correct reading distances. Special-access groups often provide guidelines for designers and their guidelines may be incorporated into signage contracts. Common sense should always prevail, and the designer who focusses on selecting a robust typeface, an appropriate colour palette, and using it in a creative but consistent way, will usually meet with success.

## CHOOSING A TYPEFACE

It is important to note that most of the typefaces available to designers today originate from letterforms developed for printing. Certain letterforms were drawn for use with particular printing processes, paper or for a specific purpose such as for books or newspapers. Few letterforms have been specifically drawn for display and signing purposes, so designers should rigorously test their selected typeface at different sizes.

Any letter enlarged above 72pt will take on a new persona. Choosing a typeface for a sign system can therefore be rather difficult. When selecting a typeface for signage purposes you should take into account the following:

| | | |
|---|---|---|
| 1. Cap height | Should be high in proportion to width of letter | |
| 2. X-height | Should be large (see designing with type p.38) | |
| 3. Ascenders | Should ideally be same as cap height | |
| 4. Descender | Should be as short as possible | |
| 5. Counter shapes | Should be as open as possible | |
| 6. Type design | Should be as strong as possible, with a selection of weights for emphasis | |
| 7. Serifs (if used) | Should be strong – bracketed or slab | |

Sometimes the available range of typefaces, although vast, simply doesn't offer what a job needs. It is perfectly permissible to turn some type into editable drawn shapes in FreeHand or Illustrator, and then to tweak and modify shapes to get the letterforms you want. But remember that these won't be real editable typefaces, just letter shapes you can arrange by hand.

Letter spacing and individual letter pair kerning need particular attention in sign work. As signs carry relatively few words the structure of each word needs to be visually correct to ensure clarity and legibility (see Design Basics).

Left: **The National Maritime Museum, London, internal signs. A simple sail and mast concept is a clever and appropriate design solution for a maritime museum. Note how the sign is held away from the brick work – a conventional flat wall mounted sign would look 'stuck on' as an afterthought. The brightly coloured sails are easily spotted and the large type is very readable despite being on a curve.**
Design by Pentagram, UK

Below: **Striking modern colours are used to help travellers to find their correct queuing areas at this bus station. The large-scale graphics contrast well with the background colours and are placed at a level above the crowds where they can still be read from quite a distance.**
Design by Allford Hall Monaghan Morris and Atelier, UK

Above: **Signs for the visually impaired use colour for maximum contrast so that a sign can firstly be located. Then once drawn to it, the sign can be read using the raised tactile pictogram and braille.**
Design by RNIB, UK

## CHOOSING COLOURS

Being able to read large text on a contrasting background is normally sufficient, but locating the sign in the first place can be a challenge. When considering a colour scheme, the colour of the sign itself should contrast with its environment. If colours are pre-determined – such as those of a corporate identity – it may be difficult to achieve a good contrast. In such instances, adding a distinctive but simple border round the sign, or using rules to break up text or inserting a special design feature for the visitor to look for may be a solution (see Rules, Design Basics). Working with most graphic arts software will enable the designer to sample numerous colourways quickly and simply. A coordinated colour palette can be achieved using the HSB (Hue, Saturation, Brightness) features. Select colours to emphasise information or to colour code areas.

Before picking a suitable set of colours however, consult those involved with the final signage production. If, for instance, you're planning to use cut vinyl, your choices of colour will be limited to those available in the material. This is also a production process which doesn't lend itself to the use of many overlapping colours. Learn as much about your intended sign-production process as possible, preferably from those who will be responsible for creating the actual signs, before committing to a particular set of designs.

Right: A freestanding museum sign that can be removed when the space is needed for functions. The clear information is presented at eye level downwards, allowing for wheelchair users to read the information in comfort.
Design by Atelier, UK

## POSITIONING

The designer's family of sign types (see page 120, The Design Process) will need to develop from the environment in which they are to be placed. So a typical sign family may comprise a free-standing structure, a wall-mounted or hanging sign, a statutory sign, and perhaps one or two individual variations for particularly tricky areas. Working with this family of sign types, a walk through the site (physically, electronically or mentally) is needed to establish the earliest points at which a visitor needs to see each aspect of information.

Motorway signs are a good illustration of this principle. Users are usually travelling at great speeds so these signs are provided well before a turn off – allowing time to get into the correct lane, slow down and prepare for exiting. Placing signs ahead of the exit means that drivers remain calm, make no sudden movements and are able to get to where they want to go with relative ease. The same principles apply to all signs even at the comparatively gentle pace of walking through the foyer of an exhibition hall or strolling through a park. Repetition of information is not a problem – remember that visitors often enter environments from many different directions and the repetition of information will help nurture trust in the sign system.

Naturally signs need to be positioned where they can be seen. The ideal is to locate signs so that information is presented just above normal eye level for general ease of reading, which will also accommodate wheelchair users – with tactile signs appropriately located for the partially sighted (which may be additional to the general sign system). However, the concentration of visitors in that particular area should always be considered. If signs are to be located in crowded areas there may be no other option but to place the signs higher so they can be read by everyone at all times – even though this may be at a distance.

Right: Whether above a motorway or in a hallway the principles of signage positioning remain the same. In the 1970s French designer Jean Widmer worked with a team of specialists to examine the legibility and positioning of motorway signs. One of his recommendations was to position exit signs at 2km and 1.5km ahead of the slip road as well as on it.

Lighting is a factor to consider when positioning a sign. What looks good on a screen presentation, doesn't always work in situ with the harsh glare from sunlight hitting a reflective sign surface. This glare may become a dark shadow later in the day – with the sign disappearing altogether at night if not illuminated. Avoid reflective materials, keep to matt finishes and ensure that signs are properly illuminated.

## IMPLEMENTATION

Digital artwork can be prepared using a standard drawing application. Sign manufacturers may use their own specialist software for certain processes, so the designer's digital files will need to provide accurate information regarding type, spacing and typeface. In some instances it may only be necessary to produce 'master' artwork for a typical sign from each member of the sign family to serve as a control model. From these control models prototypes can be made and in turn used as the final controls for the complete system. A visit to the factory to check manufacture and fine detail is worthwhile as errors can be difficult to rectify at a later stage.

Sign manufacturers will usually be contracted to install the signs and during this crucial stage it is worth daily visits to the site. On completion there will be a walk-around tour with the client to pick up on outstanding issues. Identifying these issues is known as 'snagging'.

Once the project is complete it is important that the client receives 'as built' records for future maintenance. Meticulous filing, data back up and recording of the design drawings during the development of the project can be transformed into a handover manual comprising instructions on maintenance, repair and updating. This should also include all the final sign schedules; their positions set against floorplan journey routes, technical drawings and fixing instructions.

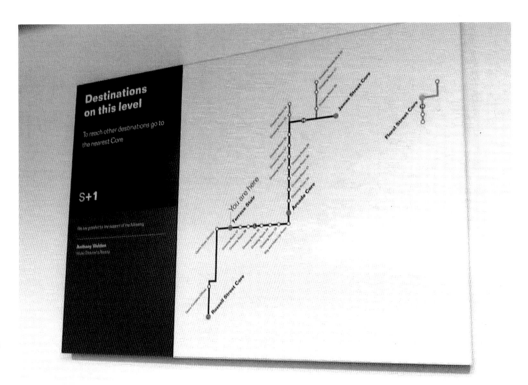

The Royal Opera House, London, backstage sign. This sign has and integrated tray into which slots a digitally printed route map of the back-of-house area. With constantly changing accommodation in this part of the building it was essential that the signs could be updated by the client themselves. Digital maps held on system provide a cheap and simple self-maintenance solution.
Design by CDT, UK

## MAINTENANCE

Good sign systems should last for many years since they are generally serious capital investments. Designers have to rely heavily on the professional expertise of sign manufacturers for advice on the practicalities of appropriate materials, paint finishes, fixing solutions, and other production processes.

It is important to convince the client that materials and build quality should never be cost driven – skimping on a second protective paint coating, initially to save on production costs, may result in rapid fading from the sun's ultra violet rays after a few years. It is more expensive to replace a whole sign system earlier than normal, than it is to prepare more robust signs to begin with.

Vandal proofing is an important factor in sign design. Signs should be strong enough to support physical abuse and their surfaces may have to withstand 'tagging' with spray paint, marker pens and relentless flyposting. Signs are a magnet for vandals so surfaces must be easy to clean and signs should be designed to enable quick replacement of component parts.

Such components need to be simple enough to order and to fit – ideally by the client's own maintenance teams. This is where the 'as built' handover documentation becomes essential to the client. All final design solutions should detail each component part and provide ordering and fitting instructions. Self management is important to many clients, as their site activities may change in line with their business. Signs therefore, may need to be frequently amended, taken down or added to by the clients themselves.

**PLANNING AND PRODUCTION** On large signing projects it is essential to become involved as early as possible. This involvement helps the designer understand an architect's vision for a building or space and this should influence the final signage solutions. It also provides the opportunity to integrate signs into the fabric of a site; thereby reducing the number of signs needed to be applied to wall surfaces.

## DESIGN TEAM

If the project is a large one, there will be a number of parties involved. First, the client, who should outline the extent of the project and provide any corporate guidelines that may be applicable. Second, the architect, who should provide the brief on the thinking behind their design, the purpose of each space, and the materials to be used. The architect will be closely shadowed by a construction manager and a quantity surveyor who will supply delivery schedules, budgets and liaise with other contractors on the designer's behalf. Additionally, there will be a selection of interested parties including local planning authorities, fire and safety officers, access groups and possibly heritage organizations. And don't forget the users – they will need to be consulted, for instance through focus groups.

## RESEARCH

The designer should start by studying the site plans thoroughly – not forgetting all the external approaches. Signs should be seen by the users before they arrive on site. The design team members should then be consulted individually and sounded out for their concerns for the project.

A site visit by the designer is important particularly for observing how people move through the space. If the environment is not yet built, designers should visualize themselves as visitors and walk their way through the plans. Journey routes and all possible destinations should be mapped. This process will indicate the points with the greatest number of intersections and decision-making points for visitors. These points are key sign positions. Lists of all the information a visitor may need to know at these points should be made. In preparing these lists it will be found that some are quite short, others long. The amount of information a sign has to carry and its position should dictate its physical form. For example, an extensive list of information might result in a large freestanding sign, whereas small amounts of information may necessitate a small, wall-fixed or perhaps suspended sign. By examining the site, a family of signs will emerge. It is best to keep the family numbers to a minimum, as numerous sign variations will be not only more costly in manufacturing and future maintenance but also potentially confusing for the user.

## THE DESIGN PROCESS

When the site has been fully researched, the designer should begin by designing a representative example of each member of the sign family. This can be achieved using most page layout or drawing programes. These initial concepts should then be presented to the project team. It is best to make paper prints at full scale and stick them onto walls in situ if possible. Only then will the project team understand the full impact of the concepts.

After client approval, the graphic designer will prepare a design specification for each sign type. Talking directly with the sign manufacturer is vital at this point. It will help with any necessary design refinement for production and costing, and the manufacturers should be willing to prepare early prototypes.

Below: **Typical floorplan with journey routes and sign points identified. Each sign point will be numbered and a sign schedule prepared (see opposite).**

Below: An extract from a sign schedule showing sign identification number, sign type, what it has to carry, how it is to be fixed, and how many needed.

Right: An extract from a sign specification tender package showing the level of detail needed for a prototype.

Left: A finished sign from the same project.
Design by Atelier, UK

Directional sign

6mm exterior grade MDF panel mounted to foamex spacer with 3M VHB tape

2mm aluminium plate mounted to MDF panel with 3M VHB tape

10mm high density foamex spacer screwed to wall counter sunk heads). fixings will be invisible.

Signs will be produced in 2 different scales and will vary in height.
Small scale signs
width: 360mm  height: 100 – 450mm
Large scale signs
width: 600mm  height: 170 – 700mm

Room number colour to be one of six special PMS matches

100mm–450mm or 170mm–700mm

600mm or 360mm

**Mid basement**

| number | area | code | legend | Fixing/Construction | quantity |
|---|---|---|---|---|---|
| 1 | **B** | Direct | Silver + Gilt/Gold Boxes<br>Micro Mosaics | screened or vinyls on glass wall/wall mounted | 1 |
| 2 | **4** | Room | Room 4 | wall mounted | 4 |
| 3 | **4** | Info | lift access details/In event of fire do not use lift | wall mounted | 1 |
| 4 | **4** | Direct | Room 4 – Silver<br>Gold Boxes/Miniatures/Porcelain Boxes/Jewellery + Plaquettes<br>Indian Silver/Treasury/Shop/Toilets/Exit | wall mounted | 1 |
| 5 | **C** | Direct | Micro Mosaics/Jewellery + Plaquettes<br>Indian Silver/Treasury/Toilets/Shop/Exit | screened or vinyls on glass wall/wall mounted | 1 |
| 6 | **5** | Room | Room 5 | wall mounted | 1 |
| 7 | **5** | Info | Research room<br>about Research room appointments | wall mounted/door mounted | 1 |

It is important for the graphic designer to be fully involved in the preparation of prototypes, the tender documents and in reviewing the tender submissions. In cost-driven projects, designers often find themselves being the sole champion for quality. Accepting the lowest tender for a sign system can be a false economy as quality may suffer, resulting in a higher incidence of damage, repair or replacement. A close working relationship between the designer and the sign manufacturer is essential if the preparation of artwork is to be trouble-free.

## DEVELOPING A HIERARCHY OF INFORMATION

Who will be the main users of the signs and what information should they carry at what point? This information should be ordered according to its level of importance. For example, in a public building such as a performance venue the main user will be a member of the audience. First they will want to know where the box office is in order to pick up their tickets, then where the auditorium is, which side of the auditorium to enter to get to their seat and how much time they have before they have to take their seat. If they have time to spare they may want refreshments and to sit down while they wait or they may want to locate the cloakroom.

Understanding the user's requirements, helps the designer organise the placing of elements on a sign and determines the level of emphasis. By taking on the role of a member of the audience, the designer will probably arrive at the following hierarchy: box office, auditorium, seat numbers, clock, cafe and cloakroom. Obviously the box office is a key source of information and will be in large type along with directions to the auditorium. The clock needs to be nearby and easily readable from the sign point. Seat numbers are another level of detail and can be smaller. Facilities such as the cafe and cloakrooms can be indicated using pictograms. Thus, an information hierarchy emerges directly from identifying the needs of the user.

# 02.04
## CASE HISTORY | THE ROYAL NATIONAL THEATRE

The extensive refurbishment of the Royal National Theatre, London, introduced more facilities and new entrances to the building. It had been a common complaint that visitors found it difficult to find their way around and so the new sign scheme was an important part the refurbishment. CDT Design was commisioned to develop a new signage system.

## STAGE 1

A number of problems were faced. The structure itself is a protected building, is multi-levelled and has many entrances on many floors. To make things even more confusing, where traditionally there is just one main auditorium at a theatre, the Royal National Theatre has three.

To win planning consent for a new sign system in a listed building there has to be an improvement upon the existing signs, in sympathy with the architectural features of the building. The whole site was carefully studied, noting the raw shuttered finish to the concrete, the chamfered corners, and the recessed holes in the walls left when the tie bars holding the shuttering together were removed after the concrete had hardened. These details affected the form and detailing of the final sign solution. This was composed of modular slats with chamfered edges, which when stacked together echoed the wall shuttering. The signs wrapped themselves around columns which also had chamfered corners. As an interesting finishing detail some signs had subtle recessed holes that matched the tie bar holes in the walls. The building was built on a 45- and 90-degree grid, with all the walls, supporting columns and even the floor tiles conforming to the grid. This determined the choice of Ehrhardt as a suitable typeface – with bracketed serifs set at 45- and 90-degree angles it echoed the spirit of the building.

Above: **The three theatres at the RNT are clearly identified and the colour associations are established well before a visitor enters the building. Here, the signs act as both a draw to the main box office from the outside and serve as a sun blind for the box office staff on the inside.**

## STAGE 2

Making sense of the building required more analytical thinking. While each theatre had its own catering facilities there had previously been instances where visitors took pre-performance refreshments in the wrong bars and then found themselves trying to enter the wrong theatre for the wrong performance! After studying the floor plan, the whole theatre was divided into zones to ensure that every sign within each theatre area was prefixed with the theatre name, and then colour coded to each zone. This colour coding was adopted by the architects during the interior refit. Wall coverings and furniture were selected to match the zoning system.

The multi-level nature of the building meant every entrance had to have a complete directory of facilities available at each theatre and (particularly important for latecomers), directions for getting directly to each theatre quickly. With its imposing concrete, steel detailing and dark tiled floors the RNT is quite a monotone building, so the signs introduced 'spots' of colour acting as a trail to each theatre.

## STAGE 3

With the introduction of new entrances and new facilities, the way in which visitors used the building was going to change. Schedules of information were compiled that listed every possible visitor requirement for key points around the whole of the building. The information listed dictated the type, size, position and fixing for every individual sign. In the early stages many of the signs were designed then printed out full size and pasted on the walls in situ. Three-dimensional prototypes were also tested in the same way, this time in conjunction with the lighting designers who tested the readability during day and evening light conditions. Some fixing tests were also carried out to accommodate the irregularities of the wall surface. These early prototypes acted as control samples against which the complete sign package was checked for quality during production and installation.

Left: The main internal signs wrap around supporting walls to avoid being hidden from other angles.

Below: Visitors are greeted by large directory panels detailing all facilities available at each theatre, each of which has a colour zone.

Above: To avoid any confusion, all facilities relating to a particular theatre were prefixed with its name.

Top: Large external banners were designed to be seen from the other side of the River Thames and from the flyover bridge nearby.

Early design work was produced in QuarkXPress and the final artwork was prepared using Adobe Illustrator so the manufacturers had outline paths for printing purposes. The signs themselves were manufactured from extruded aluminium, sprayed with several protective paint layers, and the type and pictograms were screen printed on top. All fixing screws holding the signs together and onto the wall were concealed for security reasons.

This entire signing project took a little over two years to complete from early concepts to the final installation. All of the work – schedules, flow routes, tender package, engineering drawings, final typographic proofs and fixing details – was then compiled into one 'as built' hand over document for RNT's maintenance department.

Graphic designers working on exhibitions face the challenge of creating a thematic design for viewing in large spaces at a human scale and in a variety of different dimensions. They must be able to think three-dimensionally, often having to visualize the exhibition space from architectural drawings and consider the general themes, atmosphere, tone and messages that need to be communicated to the audience.

The overall visual identity, the display panels, and the accompanying publicity material – the two-dimensional aspects of an exhibition – are the main responsibility of the graphic designer. Digital technology makes for imaginative and flexible design and production, and also allows for easy sharing and exchanging of files by email or ISDN – a great advantage in exhibition design, which can involve designers from many different disciplines working together towards a common goal.

The three dimensional aspect of exhibition design is produced by specialized exhibition designers, who may have had architectural or interior-design training but can equally come from a variety of backgrounds. Spatial awareness, developing themes with a narrative, interpreting subject matter effectively, working closely with the graphic designer, communicating to the target audience and producing detailed working drawings (on AutoCAD) for contractors are all paramount to the exhibition designer.

It is generally not necessary for the graphic designer to be familiar with either AutoCAD drafting packages or Form Z (software that creates walk-through vistas), although both are integral components of the exhibition design process. It is also useful for members of the design team to exchange and understand each other's digital files. Graphic designers working on exhibitions normally produce flat artwork for panels using vector-based software, such as Adobe Illustrator, FreeHand, PageMaker and QuarkXPress, which allow for radical change in scale without loss of quality. Images scanned or created in Photoshop can be imported into all these programs together with text from word-processing software.

**PART 02. SURFACE DESIGN**

**CHAPTER FIVE**

# DESIGN FOR EXHIBITIONS

Above: **Pearling and fishing in the Arabian Gulf, from the National Museum of Dubai's Underwater Gallery. The underwater effect is achieved using reflections and floating glass panels. Clear and full-strength images are mounted onto glass, and projected gobos and water images complete the picture.**
Design by Event Communications, UK

Left: **The entrance to the Fondation Folon exhibition in Brussels, a permanent exhibition on the work of the artist Jean Michel Folon. Euroculture, the designers have perfectly captured the poetic, dreamlike qualities of the artist's work in the design of the exhibition space, which starts by allowing the visitor to enter through a giant book which slowly opens as the visitor moves past the admission desk.**
Design by Euroculture, Belgium

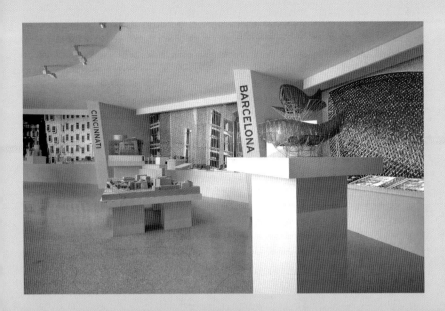

**Far left:** Guggenheim Museum exhibtion on the work of the architect Frank Gehry. Gehry's drawings, enlarged and printed onto the walls, show his fascination with capturing a sense of motion. To produce this effect, the artwork was printed onto the maximum width of paper available (though any length is possible, widths are dependent upon the size of the roll the printer takes), mounted onto MDF and heat sealed or wrapped for installation. Alternatively, laser cut vinyl can be applied to painted walls, and again heat sealed if it is in danger of being damaged.
Design by Guggenheim Museum, USA

**Below: Legacy** – Testament to those who survived, In Flanders Fields exhibition, Leper, Belgium. This memorial exhibition makes use of war-damaged sculpture rescued from Ypres cathedral, set against an etched glass panel depicting the names of survivors. Specially commissioned images of other memorials are placed behind in the form of large photoprints mounted onto Foamex. The low lighting helps to convey the sombre atmosphere.
Design by Event Communications, UK

# THE NATURE OF EXHIBITION DESIGN Exhibitions vary widely in their nature and complexity, and so can assume a variety of shapes, sizes and forms. However, conveying the message appropriately is key to every situation, whether the context is a simple panel system or a full-blown major exhibition.

## EXHIBITION OPTIONS

The simplest cost-effective way to communicate a message to an exhibition audience is to use portable panel systems. These can take the form of multiple, flat-panel and fascia configurations, pop-up, telescopic wire-framed structures or pull-up, single canvas panels. These modular exhibition systems allow simple, digital graphic panels to be economically produced on a wide range of materials including paper, PVC, gauze, cotton and canvas. Graphics designed for these systems need to be durable and light. This type of exhibition or display is used wherever portability is an important consideration.

Shell schemes are a cost-effective solution to exhibiting at trade shows. Supplied by the venue organisers, they consist of standardized basic units that feature power and lighting, and onto which individual company fascia and wall panels can be attached. They often form an integral part of the overall trade show personality.

Above: **Visuals of large graphic panels used for The Eaton Group's Five Year Business Plan – 4th Year, Management Briefing. The final digital prints were mounted onto 10mm Foamex and heat-wrapped for durability. JPEGs and EPS files of design work produced for the company's advertising campaigns, brochures and signing are brought together in a series of three two-metre high graphic panels.**
Design by Perks Willis Design, UK

Alternatives to shell schemes consist of three dimensional designs built by specialist contractors and are consequently much more expensive.

Purpose-built exhibitions are usually complex, high-budget design concepts built for a specified time span ranging from a two- to four-week-long trade show to a temporary year-long exhibition or permanent museum gallery. These exhibitions are built to a design created by a specialist exhibition designer and, whether long or short term, are built to last for only a designated period. The graphic designer's role involves designing and overseeing the production of the exhibition identity and related design publicity material, often in the form of oversized, digitally printed banners and introductory vinyl cutout lettering. It is the responsibility of the designer to specify the correct materials for mounting, sealing and finishing graphic panels. The durability of materials used is dictated by the size of the budget and is directly proportionate to the lifespan of the exhibition.

Permanent exhibitions may have a lifespan of ten years, sometimes more, and tend to be located in museums or galleries. The planning stage of such exhibitions can spread over several years. Large budgets and maintenance programmes are necessary to keep them in pristine condition, and to support areas within the exhibition that have to be reworked due to changes in science or popular thinking. The designer's role, however, normally ends when the completed design is 'handed over' to the client.

Educational exhibitions, which may be long or short term, are concerned with

Below: Screen grab showing the use of Form Z software, as used in the Arte Povera exhibition in Tate Modern, London. Once the process of feeding in dimensions, thicknesses, and other data has been completed, it is possible to produce vistas of gallery spaces from many different angles and get a very accurate impression of the intended design scheme.
Design by Philip Miles Graphic Design, UK

communicating complex concepts in an effective and inspirational way. Subject specialists liaise with educationalists and designers to ensure that teaching points can be clearly interpreted by the audience. Interactive devices, although expensive, can significantly enhance these key teaching points, encouraging audience participation and adding greatly to the educational experience.

In situations where a purpose-built exhibition needs to travel, a whole new set of criteria has to be taken into account in the design approach. Durability, packing, weight, and possible language issues need to be addressed, particularly if the exhibition is touring abroad, and a successful travelling exhibition will, wherever possible, make inventive use of panel stands as packing cases. The graphic designer, normally designs accompanying touring manuals, giving clear instructions on installation and dismantling.

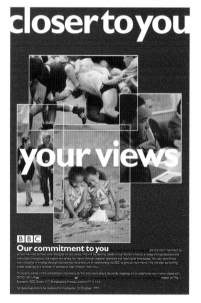

Left: Visuals showing a set of panels designed to fit into a travelling modular system for use in the BBC's public consultation on proposed changes to regional services in London and the South East. A simple, eye-catching design, this had to be instantly accessible using stock photography, striking colours and simplified maps.
Design by Perks Willis Design, UK

Below: Oversized display banner, Times Square, New York. Banners can now be printed onto an extensive variety of materials, in huge sizes, sometimes covering whole sides of buildings. In Times Square, waterproof banners such as these provide an alternative to neon, LCD and lenticular displays.

Left: Detail of multimedia wall in the Finney Gallery, National Museum of Football, Preston. The wall is formed through a complex layering of information, which has produced a 'reportage' style integration of film, sound, lighting, objects, photography and text. Many different materials have been used to create this exhibit – wood fibreboard, glass, galvanized steel, and plywood, together with 3D lettering, floor lightboxes and object cases wrapped in supergraphics, all interspersed with monitors and speakers. These are all mounted on a steel support frame.
Design by Land Design Studios and The Chase, UK

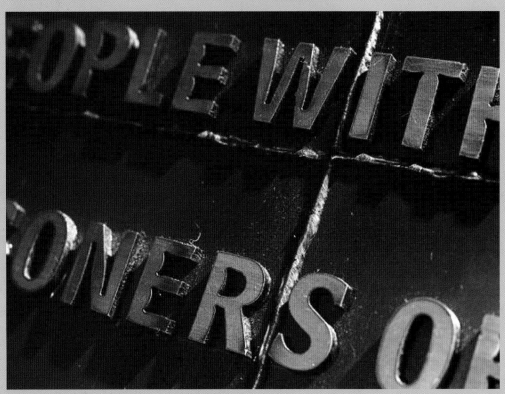

Above left: Multi-layered map showing the social order of Europe after WWI, screenprinted in three colours and fired onto ceramic tiles.
Above right: Detail of metal lettering, Holocaust Exhibition, Imperial War Museum. The font used is Bell Centennial, produced in 5mm thick fret-cut mild steel. It is constrained by welds of steel. The steel wall outlines the aims of the exhibition, and also functions as a projection screen for war film footage.
Design by DEGW, UK

**EXHIBITION GRAPHICS PROCESSES** Digital technology has radically changed the labour-intensive and limited production of exhibition graphics. This once depended on photo enlargements and photo techniques as the core origination media. Designers can now be much more ambitious. As technology develops, the creation of digital artwork and digital production becomes a more comprehensive and integrated procedure.

The extensive capabilities of giant ink-jet (or bubble-jet) printers allow for artwork files to be run out at virtually any size and on a variety of substrates. Transparencies are scanned to produce high-resolution digital files, and the designer combines these with text and other images. Retouching and manipulating images in Photoshop allows total freedom. Areas of interest or special significance can be highlighted or played down by modifying colour and contrast.

Laser-cut type output from digitized artwork allows for great flexibility – virtually any design can be converted into a path for the laser-cutting program. Matt and gloss vinyls are available in a wide choice of colours, and self-adhesive, frosted films can be used to give the illusion of sandblasting onto clear surfaces. Raised type can also be laser-cut using polystyrene or metallic finishes – almost anything is possible. Spacers mounted between wall and lettering can create the illusion of depth and shadow. Different surfaces can be built up to provide a three dimensional finish.

Silkscreen printing (see page 115) panels and graphic surfaces is a far more labour-intensive, high-budget process than producing prints digitally. It does, however, produce a sharp image in beautifully flat, hard and durable inks that can be matched to the PANTONE system, unlike digital output, which can only simulate PANTONE colours with varying results. Silkscreening also makes it possible to print directly onto glossy, curved surfaces. The use of 'tough inks' eliminates the need for protective sealing, and allows matt and gloss finishes to be mixed.

Below: **Designs for metal gobos, From The Beginning, Natural History Museum, London. Lasers are used to cut intricate designs from metal discs. When installed into a projector system, coloured lights can be shone through, and the resulting image made to move through gallery spaces giving another dimension to the exhibition design.**
Design by Exhibition Plus and Perks Willis Design, UK

## MULTIMEDIA EXHIBITIONS

The use of multimedia adds an exciting dimension to exhibition design and provides almost limitless opportunities to feed the designer's imagination. Multimedia productions can be projected onto panels or played either on freestanding monitors or on screens set into part of the exhibition structure.

Lenticular panels, created from a high-tech photographic process, provide a low-tech form of animation by a simple flip from vertical to horizontal.

Touch screens can be incorporated into the design to show animated or interactive programs, or both, giving viewers more in-depth information about a specific subject and increasing the direct involvement of the audience in the process. Specialized interactive designers can transform a concept into a fully functioning, moving machine that works electronically, mechanically or manually, but the graphic design element of each of these exhibition components is still the responsibility of the graphic designer.

Lighting and lighting techniques are another important part of exhibition design. Gobos – small metal or glass discs with either cut or printed designs – are a versatile way of making lights move either slowly, or in dramatic shooting movements. Specialized companies produce these items, however, the designer should bear in mind that a projector is needed to use them. Coloured gels can be added to produce different colourways. Gobos are a very good way of reinforcing areas or themes (or even exits) in exhibitions and can be projected onto floors, ceilings, and walls or thrown along galleries.

**DESIGN CONSIDERATIONS** The graphic designer is responsible for providing visuals and digital artwork for all the graphic panels, labels and interactive exhibit components throughout the exhibition. These are produced at a convenient scale that is compatible with the size of the panels.

Viewing ergonomics are particularly important, and it is essential to produce a full-size mock-up of a typical panel before spending time developing a design too far. This enables you to check the effectiveness of size and height of titles, text and captions. Lighting conditions also need to be taken into account, as they can radically affect legibility. As a general guide, unless you are designing for very young children, the average eye-level should be set at 1.5m with the majority of the text not falling much below hip-height.

The spacing and arrangement of panels should facilitate overall understanding of the subject matter. Visitor flow and avoidance of bottlenecks is usually the responsibility of the specialized three dimensional designer, but the graphic designer also needs to be aware of these aspects in considering the arrangement of information.

The design of the exhibition identity, including a versatile logo and a related family of associated elements, is of prime importance since it has to carry the visitor through the entire exhibition. Where the brief is to design an exhibition for an organization that has its own distinct and well-structured corporate identity, the implementation of the scheme needs to be faithful and accurate in every rendition—a detailed manual may be available from the company for guidance on this.

1. Partitioning the space creates an orderly flow of visitors around centrally placed exhibits.
2. Dividing the space into smaller manageable areas aids comprehension and allows the subject matter to be broken down into logical units.

3. Regimented positioning of exhibits, allowing random circulation .
4. Regimented positioning of exhibits with regimented circulation.
5. Random positioning of exhibits allowing random circulation.
The solution you choose should be dictated by the subject matter.

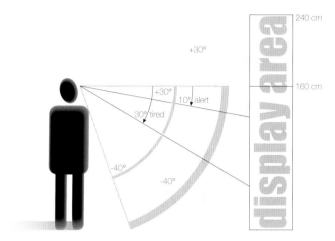

Above: Ergonomic data showing natural viewing heights and angles, and areas of optimum visibility. The upper segment of the display should be viewed from about 2 metres away to successfully scan the information.

Above: From The Beginning, The Natural History Museum, London – an exhibition about the last 600 million years of Earth's history. This visual is from 'Early Earth', a huge exhibit with a large laminate arrow, and doors that vistors can open. The laminate arrow was silkscreened, and the outside of the doors made from digitally produced artwork illustrating the cooling earth. The doors had a heavy duty coating for maximum durability to withstand extensive handling. Inside the doors were a few simple exhibits behind glass with backlit Duratrans.
Design by Exhibition Plus and Perks Willis Design, UK

## PLANNING AND PRODUCTION

Planning an exhibition can be a lengthy process. Agreeing budgets, research, finding locations and checking cost effectiveness must be completed before the design team is appointed. In practice this means that the graphic designer has to be flexible enough to work with restricted budgets and accommodate (or tactfully challenge) preconceived ideas.

The graphic designer's initial role is to formulate the overall design concepts and produce preliminary designs for key panels and related elements for client approval. The style of typography, illustration and photography, and the processes needed to realize them, must be clearly identified. Illustrators, photographers and picture researchers have to be commissioned as well as any other experts including lighting designers or multimedia specialists.

Once a writer has supplied a cohesive script for the exhibition, the specialized three dimensional designer produces detailed plans and elevations. The graphic designer, in turn, has to produce a comprehensive panel specification document to enable contractors to see and understand the full extent of the job. Estimates are then sought to ensure that the intended scheme is feasible within the allocated budget, and the project goes out to tender. When budgetary requirements are met and contractors appointed, design production can begin. The graphic designer then produces digital printouts of single flat-panel designs and views of key sections of the exhibition, using a combination of graphic arts software to realistically simulate the three dimensional environment. As colours vary dramatically from screen to printer, and from the desktop to the press, constant monitoring is essential to ensure consistency. In order to minimize expensive mistakes, individual components of each exhibit are turned into artwork that needs to be approved and signed off by the client before it is sent away for production.

A graphics issue sheet should be designed to tie in with the specification document, to detail and track each component of the artwork. This sheet should accompany every piece of artwork, together with annotated colour visuals, TIFF and EPS files, fonts, etc. Unlike other areas of graphic

Above: **From The Beginning, The Natural History Museum, London.** This photograph shows a view down the gallery featuring a giant mural with a timed sequence of different florescent light effects. An etched stainless steel timeline runs the length of the gallery, introducing the arrival of different creatures to the planet, and a second layer of smaller exhibits and models runs above this tracing the development of life on earth in more detailed form. Larger exhibits stand behind, and vinyl wall graphics complete the picture. Design by Exhibition Plus and Perks Willis Design, UK

design, the exhibition graphic designer may well be providing artwork to a number of different contractors (in different digital formats) for a range of different specialized components, including multimedia, animation or video editing.

Before panel artwork is mounted and sealed to its substrate, a visit with the client to the photographic contractor for the final approval should be planned. Delivery to the site can take place when the finished design is mounted and sealed, but panels will need to be checked again for possible damage, on site, prior to installation.

## CASE HISTORY          RHYTHMS OF LIFE

The exhibition involved a large team of three dimensional designers, graphic designers, illustrators, model-makers, video producers, interactive exhibit designers, lighting designers, building contractors, photographic contractors, picture researchers and a composer, all working with the Natural History Museum's in-house writer and project manager.

Initially, the specialized 3D design company, Exhibition Plus, worked with the in-house team, developing ideas and extending the brief. Only then did Perks Willis Design (PWD) start work on the overall graphic scheme and identity. Because 'Rhythms of Life' was to be a travelling exhibition, Exhibition Plus designed flexible structures in bamboo and timber (to illustrate slow and fast growth) and kite-like graphics encapsulated with a matt finish that could be replaced cheaply when the exhibition was translated for touring. It could also be easily dismantled and packed into large oil-cans, which served as some of the bases for the graphic panels and exhibits.

The exhibition was aimed at families with young children. It had to be clear, bright, fun and animated, and flexible enough to be reproduced in several European languages. PWD's first job was to try to capture the essence of what the Natural History Museum was trying to achieve – to communicate how humans and animals are affected by rhythms around them, primarily day and night, and the seasons – and then produce some key exhibits. Early influences were Keith Haring, The Beano comic and Hergé's Tin Tin – cartoon-like images with lots of natural movement. The colour scheme consisted of seasonal leaf colours, sunshine yellow, midnight blue and rich red. Starting with a set of rhythmic symbols of falling leaves, suns, moons and beating hearts, these naturally led on to the exhibition identity.

After producing an initial graphic panel, a full-sized mock-up was made to ascertain legibility, contrast (in varying lighting conditions), reading heights and distances. Illustrators were then commissioned to work on the kite-shaped graphic panels, with a brief to produce amusing and whimsical images for children aged six to twelve with added 'street cred'. The final panels were to have a mix of photography and illustration.

As an opening piece, large-scale cut-out themed figures of a 'clock boy', tree and dog were designed, to reinforce the concept of time. These were produced as digital prints, mounted onto MDF and then finished with a heavy-duty seal. Type panels were applied as overmounts. Interactive devices were designed, and specifications given to PWD to design graphics for the component parts.

After extensive tendering processes had taken place, PWD started to produce artwork for the exhibition. Transparencies and line illustrations were scanned to produce 'paths' that could be coloured up in Adobe Illustrator. Most of the exhibition was designed in Adobe Illustrator, with Photoshop used for re-touching and superimposition.

Above: Banner showing the exhibition identity and use of related corporate elements. The image needed to be vibrant, appealing to children, and above all seen as having 'street cred'. This banner shows the use of the composite elements of the logo that were used as a background image.

Left: Designs for glass gobos, used to send images shooting up and down the gallery. Glass gobos, although not as durable as the metal variety, allow for more flexible use of colours. These gobo images formed moving markers for various sections of the exhibition.

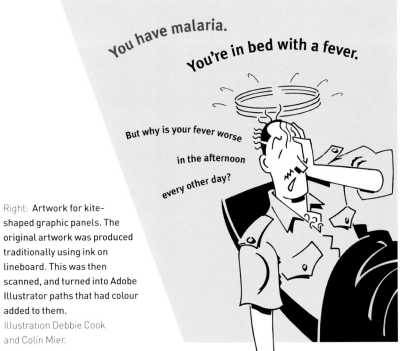

You have malaria.

You're in bed with a fever.

But why is your fever worse in the afternoon every other day?

Sleep – why bother?

We sleep every day because it's very useful.

Dreaming probably helps sort out the day's memories.

While the body's resting, muscle, bone and the brain are repaired and replenished with energy.

We make the most of our food if we save energy by sleeping.

Right: Artwork for kite-shaped graphic panels. The original artwork was produced traditionally using ink on lineboard. This was then scanned, and turned into Adobe Illustrator paths that had colour added to them.
Illustration Debbie Cook and Colin Mier.

Above and right: The matt-laminated kite-shaped graphics and side banners were fixed to the bamboo poles using coloured ties. Interactive exhibits were attached to thick horizontal poles arranged around oil cans or trestle units. Coloured vinyl symbols were applied to the lower surfaces to further enhance the themes.

Artwork was then sent to the exhibition contractor, who produced high-resolution digital prints onto paper, encapsulated them with a matt finish, and finished them with eyelets so that they could be attached to the bamboo frames. The interactive devices also used digital prints and, where necessary, were finished with a heavy-duty seal. Artwork was also produced for converting into Gobos. Elements from the logo, leaves, suns, moons and hearts were all used to highlight different areas of the exhibition. Baggage labels, and clipboards with additional information and facts were applied to the bamboo and other surfaces to provide low-cost interactive devices.

Below right: Detail of small half life-size lenticular panel, which flips between open and closed eyes using a stock photographic image with illustrated overlay. (This small panel was mounted onto a metronome arm). Lenticular panels provide simple low-tech animation, and can either flip from left to right, or top to bottom, depending on the effect required. More complicated lenticular panels can have several images incorporated within them.

# DESIGN
# FOR SCREEN

## 03.01

The impact of the Internet revolution upon our lives is undisputed. The growth of websites is increasing at an unprecedented rate, and the challenge for the graphic designer to apply traditional design practices in this digital environment is an exciting and sometimes daunting one.

In the early days of the Internet, Web page construction was a relatively simple process. There was only one browser for viewing pages, and the constraints of the medium meant that the placement of small images in relation to text was the only consideration. Today, the role of the Web designer has expanded considerably. New technology and improved functionality on the Web has meant that designers can now employ animation, sound, and movies and ever more complex graphic image formats to enhance the user's experience. With software such as Macromedia Flash or Adobe Live Motion, for example, dynamic, highly interactive Web content becomes a design reality. The Web designer has to take stock of emerging technologies and strike a balance between applying proven design principles and technology-driven possibilities. The gap between the early programmers of the Internet revolution and the pure designer has narrowed

to the point where the two are now inextricably linked.

In the early 1990s it would have been hard to imagine that we could access so much information through a personal computer, but today we are presented with billions of pages of information through the Web. It is in this arena that designers can make their mark, using the powerful tools at their disposal to create successful designs and solutions that communicate to a universal audience.

The range of websites, on which designers might be called to work, is as varied as the Web itself, ranging from educational, cultural and non-profit making organisations to commercial and financial ventures. Re-branding of existing corporate identities forms a major proportion of Web design work and many companies who entered the 'cyber marketplace' early are conscious that their initial Web presence is out-dated and in need of a fresh look. New technologies are being introduced which add greater functionality and scope for e-commerce, all of which need an effective visual interface. The graphic designer can find challenging and varied prospects within the world of Internet design.

**PART 03. DESIGN FOR SCREEN**

**CHAPTER ONE**

# DESIGN FOR THE INTERNET

Above: www.egomedia.com
**Ego Media is an interactive design group based in New York. First impressions are everything in the In the interactive design and their website makes extensive use of Macromedia's Flash to enhance the prospective customer's experience.**
Design by Ego Media, USA

## DIGITAL TOOLS FOR INTERNET DESIGN

Internet design is done with a mixture of general-purpose design tools and software made specifically for Web work. Key website layout programs include Macromedia Dreamweaver, Adobe GoLive, Microsoft FrontPage, NetObject Fusion and SoftPress Freeway. Dreamweaver and GoLive are both powerful code editor tools, with Dreamweaver in particular favoured by site editors and programmers, while Freeway (Macintosh only) is more suited to serious design tasks.

Graphic content is best produced using Photoshop, as well as Macromedia Fireworks, a Web-specific graphics production tool. Flash media content is best produced using Macromedia Flash or Adobe LiveMotion, while QuickTime content is made with anything from Apple iMovie through to Adobe Premier. FreeHand and Illustrator are also used for producing graphics for Web use.

Producing page and site mock-ups is an important part of Web design. Photoshop has been quite popular for this task, but it must be said that while this makes exporting graphics convenient, it isn't a good layout tool compared with the Web-oriented Freeway or even QuarkXPress.

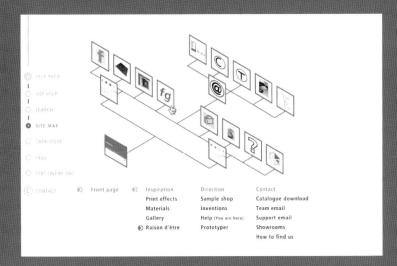

Left: www.foldersgalore.com
Coming up with a site map will help designers develop a logical website structure. Sitemaps are often included as a navigational tool for users. This site map uses multiple rollovers to mark the text labels as users point at the appropriate page icons.
Design by Biggles, UK

Above: www.yugop.com
Yugo Nakamura applies a rich design aesthetic to all aspects of his site. The level of Flash programming required to create such complex interactive tableaux is very advanced – a successful blend of technical know-how and visual craft.
Design by Yugo Nakamura, Japan

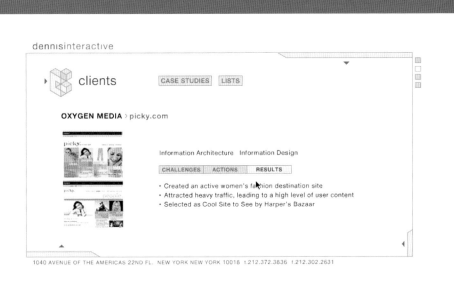

Left: www.dennisinteractive.com
Dennis Interactive has long been an innovative company in the field of interactive design. Their Internet portfolio reveals a varied and challenging client base – testament to their flexibility and versatility in producing on-line work without becoming narrowed to a specific 'look and feel', which can be the fate of many a design conscious enterprise.
Design by Dennis Interactive, USA

**'WHAT IS THE INTERNET ?'** The Internet is a global telephone network connecting computers all over the world, transporting information in digital form. The idea of a network that could share information over great distances with ease was conceived in the USA in the 1960s as a military communications application. By the early 1990s the first computer code of the World Wide Web was devised – an 'illustrated' version of the Internet allowing the transportation of pages, images and video using a relatively simple, editable code.

## THE GRAPHIC DESIGNER'S ROLE ON THE WEB

As with designing for print publications, the graphic designer's role is to produce an appropriate visual structure for Web pages. The fundamentals of design – the use of layout, colour, type and imagery – remain the same, but clearly there is a lot more to Web design than this.

Understanding the possibilities and limitations of Web design is vital. Interactivity, where the page contents can respond to the user's actions in some way, is highly important, as is non-linear navigation, where multiple links between pages allow users to pick what they see.

A grasp of the core graphic design software packages is as useful here as in any area of digital design. It is also very helpful to have some knowledge of the many ancilliary packages on offer for Web design work, and to be comfortable with managing the myriad file formats involved in this field. You'll also need to learn at least one of the key website design tools to some extent. How far you take this depends on whether you plan to deliver mock-ups and guidelines to teams of code writers, make the complete site yourself, or strike some balance between the two. But you do need to understand the principles of the Web in order to design effectively. Being a successful Web designer means being a bit of a jack of all trades – but you'll also need to remain a master of design skills at the same time or you'll become just another visual Web technician.

## BYTES & BITS – HOW THE INTERNET WORKS

Essentially all digital information can be reduced to basic binary code – ones and zeros, or the 'on' and 'off' state of an electrical signal. Any content, text or images, delivered via the Internet must be digitized or encoded into 'bits' at high speeds. In reality, the speed at which individuals can receive information is governed by the quality of their Internet connections via a modem linked to a telephone line or fibre optic cable. The Internet Service Provider (ISP) provides the link between the individual computer and the World Wide Web, supplying a dial-up telephone number that enables two-way

Above: **www.atlantic-records.com** All websites, no matter how diverse their content and appearance are underpinned by HTML. Browsers will allow the viewer to inspect the code, thus rendering the designer's layout and structure transparent to the code-savvy reader. Although HTML provides the basic layer upon which content is built, other proprietary codes such as Macromedia's Flash are used for applications which are not revealed in the source window (shown inset).

transmission of email and access to the Internet. Other services are often offered such as website hosting, e-commerce and technical support.

Fibre optics and satellites, which work at the speed of light, can support the rapid transfer of data but 'old' telephone network technology, often utilized at the first and last stages of transmission, is the cause of the characteristic delay in receiving Web pages over land-lines.

Web pages are drawn on the screen from information encoded using HTML (Hyper Text Mark-up Language). Web page browsers provide the software interface for decoding HTML and rendering the intended visual content on the screen.

The term 'Internet' should not be confused with 'Intranet', which is a closed and exclusive network for individual organizations for the use of their employees only, to send and receive data either locally or globally.

Left: When you first set up your computer you will be prompted to sign up for an Internet Service Provider (ISP) to provide access to the Internet. On the Apple platform the 'Internet Setup Assistant' will guide you through the process; you can choose an ISP based in the country you reside in, or alternatively you can manually enter settings, such as dial-up number and password, from your existing account.

Below: www.google.com
The World Wide Web is a vast and rapidly growing storehouse of information, news and data. Search engines such as Google go some way to cataloguing this information and are an essential on-line tool to master.

Right: www.apple.com
Websites that are too reliant on HTML text for their content may load quickly but are susceptible to browser preference changes by the user that can cause the text to enlarge by up to 300%! This would cause the page view to wildly distort. Apple have constructed their corporate site using predominantly graphic content, which is immune to such preferences shifts.

# BROWSERS – THE WINDOW ON THE WEB

Internet browsers are exactly what they say they are – a means to 'browse' the World Wide Web, not unlike browsing the pages of a magazine or book. The phrase 'surfing the Web' is often applied to this activity and 'browser' is a generic term for the many software applications available for Web surfing.

Although most people think of a Web browser as the means by which they connect to the Internet, it is in fact just a tool used for reading and displaying files found on computers that are themselves connected to the Web. Connecting to the Internet is like connecting to the world's largest computer network. Once 'on-line' the browser is free to search for a sepecific Web page. This will be either the browser's default 'home' page or a specific address that the browser has received in some other way.

When a browser is given a particular address (URL), it sends a request to the machine identified in the address, and obtains a Web page by way of reply. It then displays the page according to the HTML formatting instructions found in the document. When the browser finds references to graphics or other 'rich media' content it returns to the remote computer and requests those items. The results of all this are shown, to the best of the program's ability, within a browser window.

## THE HIDDEN CODE

Web pages can contain a variety of different items, but it is text that forms the majority of the information. HTML-formatted text is certainly not the most flexible or exciting form of typesetting a designer could wish for; the choices of style, fonts, leading and kerning control for example, are limited at best, and all but non-existent for most of the time. There are other options a digital designer could choose, such as bitmap graphic images of text, but these are best suited to headline work rather than setting paragraphs of body text.

While browsers can convert formatted text and graphics without help, they require additional software in order to cope with other media such as QuickTime video or Flash animations. This extra help is provided via Web browser 'plug-ins' – add-on software that extends the browser's capabilities. Plug-ins are either provided as part of the standard browser package, or can be found on magazine cover CDs or downloaded from software manufacturers' websites. Most are free because manufacturers want their plug-in software to become as widely used as possible, in turn encouraging Web designers to use their commercial software. Popular plug-ins include Flash (for interactive animated content), RealPlayer (for video and audio), and QuickTime (for a variety of video and audio content).

Above: **The two main players in the Internet browser war. Each successive update that is released leapfrogs the rival's capabilities, which is an aid to the consumer who benefits from greater usability and performance but often at the expense of stability and reliability. Many popular plug-ins are not pre-installed on these browsers because their manufacturers do not want to offer a competitor's range of products and services. This monopolistic stance inhibits the market growth of new products in many people's view.**

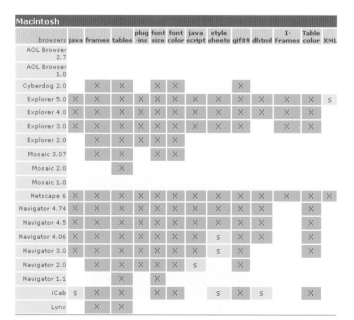

| Macintosh browsers | java | frames | tables | plug-ins | font size | font color | java script | style sheets | gif89 | dhtml | I-Frames | Table color | XML |
|---|---|---|---|---|---|---|---|---|---|---|---|---|---|
| AOL Browser 2.7 | | | | | | | | | | | | | |
| AOL Browser 1.0 | | | | | | | | | | | | | |
| Cyberdog 2.0 | | X | X | | X | X | | X | | | | | |
| Explorer 5.0 | X | X | X | X | X | X | X | X | X | X | X | X | S |
| Explorer 4.0 | X | X | X | X | X | X | X | X | X | X | | X | |
| Explorer 3.0 | X | X | X | X | X | X | X | X | X | | X | X | |
| Explorer 2.0 | | X | X | X | X | | | | | | | | |
| Mosaic 3.07 | | X | X | | X | X | | | | | | | |
| Mosaic 2.0 | | | X | | | | | | | | | | |
| Mosaic 1.0 | | | | | | | | | | | | | |
| Netscape 6 | X | X | X | X | X | X | X | X | X | X | X | X | X |
| Navigator 4.74 | X | X | X | X | X | X | X | X | X | | | X | |
| Navigator 4.5 | X | X | X | X | X | X | X | X | X | | | X | |
| Navigator 4.06 | X | X | X | X | X | X | X | S | X | X | | X | |
| Navigator 3.0 | X | X | X | X | X | X | X | S | X | | | X | |
| Navigator 2.0 | | X | X | X | X | X | S | | X | | | | |
| Navigator 1.1 | | | X | | X | | | | | | | | |
| iCab | S | X | X | | X | X | | S | X | S | | X | |
| Lynx | | X | X | | | | | | | | | | |

Left: **www.webmonkey.com** Web Monkey provides a vital resource for Web developers and designers. Industry enthusiasts who are keen to promote an open-access approach to Web design maintain this free service. The site offers useful statistics on common Web design problems, such as available versions of browsers and plug-ins.

This page: All browsers employ an identical method of locating websites by prompting the user to manually input a website address. Then, hitting the Return key will prompt the browser to locate the address on the World Wide Web. Netscape has the minor share of the market and has to work hard to produce revisions of its interface to retain customer loyalty. New browser revisions may offer different interface styles, yet the real test on their improved performance is their ability to accommodate the latest advances in code types and plug-in types.

Microsoft Internet Explorer is bundled free with virtually every new PC sold. IE and Netscape's Navigator are bundled with every new Apple Mac. Other browsers, such as Opera, are not free but they can provide a more refined performance.

URL (Universal Resource Locator)

## MODERN BROWSERS

The first Web browsers were very basic tools indeed, handling basic text-formatting options and simple graphics. Today's browsers are much more capable. The market is currently dominated by two main players, Microsoft's Internet Explorer and Netscape's Navigator, although there are a few other browsers vying for attention, Opera and iCab in particular. Each browser has its own interface characteristics, and although their functionality is fundamentally the same, Web pages will need testing on target platforms before the site goes public.

Browsers are constantly being upgraded to accommodate improvements and changes in technology and coding. This can be problematic for the Web designer, as different tricks may need to be developed in order to keep control over the way pages behave across different browser versions. Although this is an onerous task, it is vitally important to ensure that the maximum intended audience of a website is reached and that the site's design integrity is upheld.

This page: There are many contrasting views about what the Web should be used for and how content should be conveyed. Jakob Nielsen (www.useit.com) is a staunch believer in keeping the Web firmly rooted in functionality, while those at www.typographic.com want the Web to be as visually rich and engaging as possible.
What matters most for any site is that it adheres to certain elementary design principles and is suited to the content and the needs of the audience. In this respect, both these sites are well designed.

**THE CHALLENGE FOR THE PRINT DESIGNER** There are some fundamental differences between design for print and design for the Web. All Web publishing is intended to be viewed on screen. This means the 'end-user' will determine the precise output of the design by the particular set-up or preferences they may choose for their computer. The challenge for the Web designer is to adapt and learn to make the best of this environment.

Unlike print design, the Web designer has to come to terms with their work being seen in different viewing tools and on different screens, and even with different sizes of text. The most common factors that affect the way a page is seen are monitor resolution and browser window size, Web browser preference settings, and display differences between Macintoshes and PCs. (Remember that although most designers work on Macs, over 90% of Web surfers use a PC.)

In Web design, unless steps are taken to lock things down, everything in a layout can move. Some Web designers do their best to take control over this, locking elements down as much as possible in order to preserve the design's intended appearance. Others try to produce pages that take this issue into account, retaining a measure of the intended appearance ('degrading gracefully') as items shift in the browser's window. This form of design, sometimes called fluid or liquid design, can ensure layouts fit browser windows regardless of window size, but it does impose aesthetic constraints on the designer.

The most common orientation of print design, whether a book, a magazine or an annual report, is portrait. However, computer monitors are landscape-oriented devices, so many existing print designs don't directly translate into good Web page designs. Pages that are too tall to be seen in one go can be scrolled, but this is a poor answer to the design problem. Good design, careful planning and a structured page-navigation system are all an asset. Fluid page design techniques can also be a strong asset, where it suits the desired design structure.

To work effectively, a Web designer should understand the needs and limitations of their work's intended audience, not just the possibilities.

## DESIGN DECISIONS

Some designers prefer to adhere to basic standards that make their work accessible to as many users as possible no matter which browser version or platform is used. This precludes use of the latest technologies and plug-ins, as earlier versions of browsers, for instance, are unable to take advantage of their enhanced features.

Another school of thought is that designers should produce only for the current versions of browsers, thereby taking advantage of the latest developments such as Cascading Style Sheets (see page 149) and XML code. The rationale here is that browsers are free and easy to upgrade and to deny advances in technology is to hamper innovation in design even if using new features risks losing a small percentage of the intended audience.

A solution to the issues of older browser performance, and one that has already been alluded to, is to offer the end-user a choice when they first log onto a site: either a version with cutting edge technology or a 'non-Flash' or 'no frames' standard HTML alternative. This requires more work and planning but will be accessible to a wider audience.

**MONITOR RESOLUTIONS** The variable nature of Web page display on an end-user's computer can be particularly vexing for a designer. One of the most hotly debated aspects of this is the problem of monitor resolutions. A page that holds together well on the designer's screen may completely break on another.

## HOW TO DESIGN FOR VARIABLES

Part of the problem of variable display lies with the technical aspects of type handling between Macintosh and Windows-based computers. Windows uses a different relative point size for text scaling, 96 pixels per inch (ppi) rather than the Macintosh standard of 72ppi, with the result that text formatted in certain ways will look 30% larger compared with surrounding graphic items when viewed in Windows-based browsers. Monitor resolution is the total number of pixels displayed on the screen – this is why Web page measurements are calculated in pixels not centimetres or inches. The greater number of pixels held on a screen the higher the detail as more visual information can be displayed. This factor alone is crucial in deciding upon the optimum size for images and text for a Web page.

Early monitors could only display 640 x 480 pixels on a 15-inch screen. Today monitors are capable of displaying varying resolutions depending on the video card installed on the system. This is why it is vital to design pages that either fit into a minimum size or flex to accommodate varying sizes. The majority of computer users today have 17-inch screens set to 800 x 600 pixels, or laptops with 1024 x 768 pixel displays. Identifying the intended audience and their predicted computer set-up is essential to ensure successful scaling of Web pages. The most common mistake made by designers is to produce pages that are too large for the majority of computer screens – often a designer will work on a 21-inch or larger monitor giving a false impression of scale and resolution quality.

Deciding on the predicted monitor size and resolution is the first step followed by calculating the actual screen space where the

Below: The Apple Macintosh operating system allows the interested user to acquaint themselves with the inner workings of the computer. Changing monitor resolution and colour depth is just one example. Programs like Macromedia Dreamweaver assist the Web designer is foreseeing these operating system parameter shifts, which will affect a design layout.

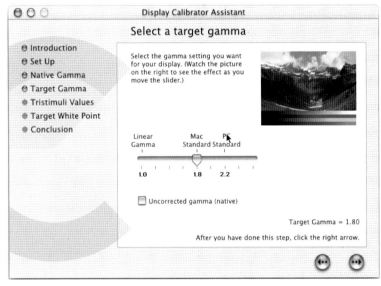

Opposite right and above: Both Macintosh and Windows operating systems allow the altering of monitor resolutions. This is particularly useful for designers who need to be aware of variable end-user monitor settings that can throw a Web page layout completely out of sync with the designer's original intentions.

Web page will be displayed. Browsers occupy a proportion of the monitor window with their varied menu options of tabs and side bars – as do operating systems with their on-screen menus. The area where the Web page will actually be displayed is often referred to as the 'live space', which (unsurprisingly) is another flexible element in the design environment. For example, the latest version of Internet Explorer for Mac has no less than five collapsible panels, each increasing or decreasing the viewable live space area. One normally assumes that the majority of end-users will be content to leave the default panel settings untouched.

There are published charts that specify live space dimensions for browser versions, operating systems and screen resolutions.

These are invaluable to the designer for ascertaining the best all-round page dimensions to use.

It is also possible to create pages that scale according to the width of the browser window. This is particularly useful in situations where the viewer is using a smaller (not maximised) browser window, regardless of the screen resolution. This method involves a careful page layout in an invisible HTML table set to a width of 100%; all the graphic and text elements are contained within the table and strategically positioned to the right, center, or left of the screen. As the browser window is scaled – or as the page is viewed at various monitor sizes and resolutions – the layout elements 're-flow' to fit the width of the page, usually to a minimum of 640 pixels wide.

**FILE SIZES** No matter how stunning a website design may be, if it takes too long to download (and anything much over ten seconds is too long) then it cannot be counted a success. Until broadband cable Internet connections become universal, the Web designer must design for the user with a 56k modem and a copper phone line designed for the comparatively low demands of voice transmission. In practice this means getting the most out of small files.

## IS YOUR WEB PAGE SLIM ENOUGH?

Usability and efficiency are the currency of popular websites, therefore page download time is critical. The speed at which a page is displayed in a browser window is directly related to its file size. The drive to minimize the total file size of a given page is fanatically pursued by Web designers.

A fast loading page will greatly enhance the first impression of a visited site and hopefully attract the viewer back for repeated visits. Other factors such as the speed of the modem connection, available bandwidth, and the efficiency of the connected server will also influence the download time. The way in which a page is rendered by a browser follows Western style text formatting by reading the page from left to right, top to bottom. As content is revealed in this progressive manner it is important to understand how different media affect the overall display sequence. Images, for example, will be displayed at a slower pace than HTML text.

To gain an understanding of page file sizes it is useful to outline how data is measured.

File size is calculated in bytes, a byte is eight bits, 1024 bytes is a kilobyte, or 1K. Bandwidth is measured in bits per second, 1000 bits is a kilobit, and the capability of modems is expressed in kilobytes per second. The fastest a modem can manage in reality is approximately 4 kilobytes a second (a 56K modem refers to kilobits, not kilobytes). The published data rate of a modem is always the maximum so in practice a 56K modem will connect at somewhere between 38K and 44K depending on the quality of the

telephone line connection. A more realistic guide is an A4 sized page with average text coverage the file of which will measure approximately 6K and take 2 seconds to download on a 56K modem.

So what size should your Web page ideally be? Some maintain that an entire page should not exceed 20K in total. This is, of course, often highly impractical, as unavoidable graphics such as corporate logos or the need to use high-quality images will easily push the total size over that threshold. A more realistic guide is 50K, which should take approximately 15–20 seconds to download on an average connection. However, this does require some deft planning and tight compression ratios for any included graphics. The real test is assessing the amount of time the intended audience might be prepared to wait.

Text file sizes are the smallest, followed by graphics, with video, sound, Flash and Shockwave in the rear. Flash and Shockwave do have their own in-built, pre-loading capability which can hold the viewers attention whilst the remainder of the content is downloading. Likewise, progressive JPEG and interlaced GIF images will load almost instantly and achieve full clarity in stages.

Below: **On Macintosh and Windows operating systems it is possible to get an exact indication of file size directly from the desktop (for Apple, click the file icon once → Apple Key + I, for Windows, click the icon once → right click on the mouse → Properties). This is invaluable when preparing content for a website. Macromedia Dreamweaver will perform a similar function when content is first imported into the application to use in a Web page layout.**

Above: **inpaku.j-phone.com**
**This site uses a clever combination of optimised GIF and JPEG image files to give the appearance of a 'full' page. Slabs of Web safe background colour underpinning carefully positioned superimposed images can produce a graphically impressive site that does not betray the necessity of fast loading files.**

**An approximate guide to various Internet connection devices and their data processing:**

| Connection | is rated at | typical throughput | to be safe |
|---|---|---|---|
| 14.4 modem | 14.4 Kbits/sec | 1.2 Kbytes/sec | 1 Kbytes/sec |
| 28.8 modem | 28.8 Kbits/sec | 2.4 Kbytes/sec | 1.8 Kbytes/sec |
| 33.6 modem | 33.6 Kbits/sec | 3 Kbytes/sec | 2 Kbytes/sec |
| 56K modem | 53 Kbits/sec | 4 Kbytes/sec | 3 Kbytes/sec |
| Single ISDN | 64 Kbits/sec | 6 Kbytes/sec | 5 Kbytes/sec |
| Dual ISDN | 128 Kbits/sec | 12 Kbytes/sec | 10 Kbytes/sec |
| Cable modem/ADSL | 512 Kbits/sec | 40 Kbytes/sec | 20 Kbytes/sec |

**COLOUR AND TYPOGRAPHY** Print-based designers making the switch to Web design must be aware of various differences and limitations involved in file output. One major difference is the expanded, yet unpredictable, RGB colour space; another is the typographical limitations of HTML and Web browsers.

## WEB COLOUR

For those familiar with designing for print, the Web environment offers some new concepts and practices in using colour. In general, the Web designer has to think of colour in a very technical manner. Traditional rules involving CMYK and PANTONE colours do not apply.

Most computer monitors today display millions of colours by mixing red, green and blue light, as a television does. The light viewed is 'transmissive' (projected from the screen) and not reflected, as in CMYK colours printed on a physical page (see Colour). Browsers have their own in-built colour rendering systems, which can sometimes alter a colour unexpectedly on monitors set to 256 colours. Colours on a Web page that are not part of any graphic (pictures or backgrounds, for example) are specifically identified in the HTML code, which raises

Right: It is vital for the designer to use colour effectively on the Web and respect its limitations and characteristics. Adobe Photoshop 6 has included the option to select Web-only colours from the Colour Picker to make this task easier. This will ensure compatibility with browsers and consistency of colour rendering when a page is published.

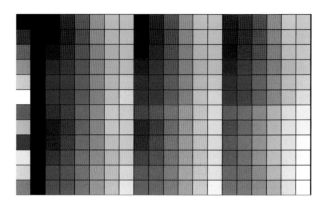

Below: Mundi Design's Web Colour Theory, one of the many resources available to help Web designers comprehend the sometimes confusing nature of screen-only colour. The on-line resource provides an interactive 'hands-on' approach with which the designer can experiment with various colour schemes.

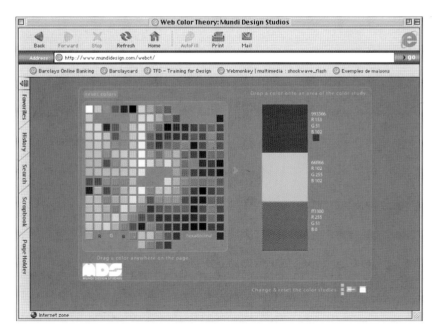

some restrictions on colour use. The final consideration is that the default Windows and Macintosh 8-bit system palettes (a uniform sampling of 256 RGB colours used to display system-level operations) display a slightly different set of colours. The Macintosh system palette is actually the closest to how browsers render colour which is useful for Macintosh Web designers.

The redeeming factor in the confusion of RGB colour presentations is the use of a Web-safe palette. The Web-safe palette consists of 216 colours made up from the Macintosh and Windows system palettes, which all browsers are able to render accurately. If the designer uses the Web palette, consistency is assured across both platforms.

When saving images in the GIF or PNG-8 formats the Indexed colour mode is used; it is limited to any combination of 256 colours or less, and as such it can support any of these smaller colour palettes. It is also worth noting, however, that many (if not most) current computer systems in use are capable of 16-bit colour or higher, which enables browsers to display a much larger range of colour and virtually eliminates Web-safe colour limitations.

## WEB TYPE

HTML is a proficient tool for coding and sending basic formatting instructions to different computers. Its original purpose was to place the ultimate control of presentation of information in the hands of the end-user. This simplicity and lack of precise control means good typographic detailing is difficult to achieve. Designers do not like the lack of typographic control available using HTML, but it is the fundamental standard of Web page design. In the most basic form of HTML there are only three types of fonts available: proportional serif (Times New Roman on Windows, or Times on MacOS), generally used for body copy; proportional sans-serif (Arial on Windows, or Helvetica on MacOS), often used for headings and large type; and fixed-width (Courier), best for columns and tables. These are considered the default Web fonts because they are the only ones that are guaranteed to be installed on virtually all systems; the use of typefaces not installed on a given system will cause that text to be displayed using one the default fonts.

New font development coupled with widespread free font downloads has enabled

Above: **The array of available fonts for print publishing is vast; the choice in Web publishing is not. The elements of compromise and forethought need to be deftly applied to a project to attain a good level of typographic style. Web designers can access a number of on-line resources, such as Microsoft's True Type Font Utility, to aid better type use in a constrictive area of Web publishing.**

Below: **General font attributes can be altered in all WYSIWYG editors, although testing or previewing the page in a browser is crucial to ascertain its published appearance. To make certain of a fonts behavior the only failsafe method is to upload the page to a server and view it on a number of operating systems and browser types.**

designers to use a greater variety of type styles; for example, Microsoft's Verdana – developed specifically for use on the Web – is enjoying widespread popularity as one of the best sans-serif fonts for Web use on both platforms. In addition, CSS (Cascading Style Sheets), and certain browser plug-ins enable designers to refine the way type is displayed in specific browsers.

The formatting options used to set the text sizes can be crucial to the way things appear on different browsers and computers. The basic formatting controls work on some of the oldest browsers, not to mention screen readers for blind users. However, these don't solve the issue of the way Windows scales fonts, with 12 point text displaying closer to 16 points. To solve this, and to provide greater formatting control, more sophisticated formatting instructions can be used. CSS, for example, embeds a set of instructions in the page, including rudimentary letter spacing and leading control. Writing CSS coding yourself is not easy, but fortunately most serious Web design tools make CSS style creation pretty simple. Dreamweaver is tuned for this kind of work, and some software makes it as simple as ordinary text formatting.

The final option is to create graphic images of text. This technique, while usually not suitable for large blocks of text, is ideal for preserving exact typographic detail for headlines and similar elements. Do this with tools such as Photoshop, FreeHand, Illustrator, and Fireworks.

**WEB GRAPHICS** Designers face a new set of constraints when working with graphic images on the Web. Images sent over a network and viewed on screen have to be low-resolution – monitor resolution 72ppi. They must also be small files if they are to be viable Web page elements. Currently there are two dominant graphic file formats on the Web, JPEG and GIF, with a third contender, PNG attempting to find popularity with Web developers.

Web graphics are compressed versions of original picture files. The production methods employed to create graphics are similar to print in so far as images are created or sourced, drawn, or scanned, manipulated, and then saved for publishing. It is the RGB image mode, resolution, and output stage that are uniquely different. If a Web designer remembers that everything happens on the screen it is easier to develop a more proficient working practice.

To create effective Web graphics a certain amount of image information must be sacrificed in order to create file sizes small enough for Internet delivery. A loss of sharpness or subtle detail compared to high resolution print scans is natural. The relatively crude 72 pixel per inch resolution of Web-ready graphics combined with the lossy compression methods impose limiting factors that Web designers just have to accept.

Production of Web-ready images is generally done in Photoshop ImageReady, Fireworks or PaintShop Pro, and all provide some form of image preview to find the right trade-off between high compression with lowered quality and low compression with large file size.

Below: **The importance of experimenting with file format compression settings cannot be overstated for Web graphics. Even the basic rules can be misleading depending on the specific nature of the graphic being used. A good practice for the Web designer is to always keep the original prepared graphic. Then, export a range of compressed files to view comparatively within the most popular browsers, ideally also over a number of monitor types.**

## GRAPHIC FILE FORMATS

**GIF** (Graphic Interchange Format) is the veteran of the Web, being the first file format to be supported by Web browsers. It remains as the most popular graphic format on the Web today. GIF files index colour information within a maximum 8-bit palette (akin to older monitors), which gives them 256 colours to choose from. Compression is achieved by rationalizing rows of pixels with similar colours, making it most suitable for graphics with flat areas of colour, such as text and logos.

**JPEG** (Joint Photographic Experts Group) files contain 24-bit colour information (6.7 million colours). They use a different, lossy, compression method, where some image information is discarded rather than rationalized as with GIFs. A sliding scale is used to choose the level of image compression. With medium or high settings

Original image

jpeg

gif

Left: Adobe Photoshop 6 provides the opportunity to view a number of progressive compression states of a single graphic image before the decision to export is taken. File size is given as well as an estimated download time on a typical modem connection speed.

there can be little noticeable loss in quality. JPEG files are ideal for photographic images with complex pixel gradations, but are not suitable for flat colour areas as unwanted mottling can occur.

**PNG** (Portable Network Graphics) is an adaptable format allowing 'lossless' compression with 8-bit indexed and 24-bit true colour, but it is finding it hard to dislodge the dominance of the other two.

A golden rule in Web design is never to scale or otherwise edit images once they've been converted to Web-ready format. It is always best to keep your original source files, and go back to those if scaling or other significant changes have to be made. JPEG files in particular should never be edited and resaved; each time this is done the JPEG compression process destroys a bit more image information.

Left: As JPEG images work best with smooth tonal changes, better compression and cleaner final results can be achieved by blurring anything in the image that isn't part of the central focus. Here a JPEG image has been reduced in size to minimize download time. The resulting pixelation can be disguised by applying a gaussian blur from the filter→blur menu. This gives an overall smoother, though softer appearance.

## HTML – 'THE HIDDEN CODE'

HTML code is the framework of the Internet upon which the visual interface hangs. It lies behind every Web page giving instructions to the browser on where to place images, render text and manage assorted media. It is the foundational building block upon which all Web development has been built. Its principal function of 'hyper linking' (the ability to link between pages and addresses on the Internet) remains one of the most potent tools on the Web today.

HTML is composed of sets of nested instructions, called 'tags', that hold formatting and layout information pertinent to the page, such as font styles and background colour. These special instructions are not themselves displayed in the browser window, but affect things which are. For designers not used to looking at a page of HTML code it can appear rather daunting. On closer inspection, however, the code, while sometimes rather convoluted in structure, is actually quite logical.

### HTML TAGS

The master tag is the HTML tag, the opening <HTML> tag and the closing </HTML> tag. These encapsulate everything on the page, like the front and back covers of a book. The contents of the page sit within this tag in various nested groups. At the top of the page is the <HEAD> and </HEAD> tag pair, which hold items describing the page. This includes the page title, copyright information, and keywords intended for some of the Internet's search engine indexing tools. (Keywords for search engines can help get sites into the listings of search engines, so when people search for related items the sites you design are among those offered. But with many millions of pages available and the fact that some search engines actually ignore keyword lists, this does not always work miracles.)

### HTML KNOWLEDGE

Designers need to understand HTML to a reasonable degree in order to work with specialists such as database programmers, even if they will never actually hand-craft a page themselves. The HTML files that browsers read are simply ordinary text files, so you can edit them and create new pages from scratch using nothing more than SimpleText or TextEdit. Building Web pages by hand using text editors used to be the only option available, and many experienced Web programmers still use this approach. Fortunately, today's professional visual Web design tools are easily good enough to produce work to the level of the best hand coders without the designer having to key a tag at all. So while it is important to understand the structure and principles of HTML, don't believe the myth that you are not a Web designer until you can type everything in by hand.

HTML is a language which is continually growing, with new tags added from time to time. Browser revisions accommodate (and sometimes drive) these changes, for example, supporting JavaScript (an embedded control language for making Web browsers perform complex functions) and CSS, which engenders structured control over layout and type.

Above: **It is a very handy skill to be able to look at a page of HTML code and 'decode' it – although not essential for the designer using a WYSIWYG program. Often unused tags are left in the code when using applications like Dreamweaver, this can sometimes produce unwanted disruptions to a given page. To know and edit the basic tags in HTML is both time saving and professional.**

**WHAT YOU SEE IS WHAT YOU GET – AUTHORING TOOLS** There is a huge number of Web design or authoring tools to choose from. At the professional level 'WYSIWYG' ('What You See Is What You Get') software, such as Macromedia's Dreamweaver or Adobe's GoLive, offer a desktop publishing-style work environment favoured by designers. With precision tools for layout, image placement and text editing, these packages are ideal for print designers wishing to enter Web publishing.

The consumer market for Web design is catered for by low-end software that provides basic formatting options but lacks the flexibility and control offered by the professional tools. They can provide a useful introduction for the general user, but designers will imediately feel frustrated by their limited abilities.

## PROFESSIONAL AUTHORING TOOLS

Professional website design tools, often called WYSIWYG (What You See Is What You Get) tools, are the best for designers, as they offer methods of working that approximate DTP-software behaviour with reasonable success. With these tools the designer arranges the elements on the page and the software writes the code required to recreate the layout in a Web browser. Dreamweaver and GoLive prefer everything apart from text to be prepared for the Web beforehand, and can provide 'smart links' with Fireworks or Photoshop ImageReady for image optimizing. Freeway can work with DTP formats such as TIFF and EPS graphics as well as JPEGs and GIFs, creating and optimizing Web graphics along with the page code.

Above: Freeway's approach to layout is based on traditional DTP behaviour, scaling graphics and styling text on the page. Guides can be dragged onto pages manually or set up as regular design grid structures.

Left: Adobe GoLive's basic layout structure is based on placing grid objects on the page, and design elements within the grids. It has extensive options for handling QuickTime movie contents, and a timeline editor for managing page-level animations.

Graphics are usually prepared for use in an image editor such as Photoshop. Site mock-ups can be done in a number of different applications, but designer, developer and programmer specialization – as well as the increasing complexity of Web design applications and Web programming – has led to teams with split designer/programmer workflows using Photoshop as a layout tool. Most Web design applications such as Dreamweaver and GoLive are still very designer- and programmer-friendly, enabling designers to maintain control over more of the production process, or vice-versa. Still, many designers prefer creating layouts with layout or graphics tools, such as QuarkXPress or FreeHand, or using a Web DTP tool such as Freeway, so as to avoid having to work with programming code entirely.

## WYSIWYG

Entire sites can be constructed and edited with WYSIWYG tools; hyperlinks can be made and tested, interactive forms, buttons and rollovers created and pages uploaded to the hosting Internet Service Provider. Flash and Shockwave files can be included as elements on a page, but often they are used to create stand-alone pages or sets of pages. They both use a traditional, time-line format for creating animation with the capability to script links to other pages, movies, Internet addresses or for sending mail. The advantage of using Flash and Shockwave for Web design is that they can be treated as 'embedded' files, or objects, within HTML. This means that they cannot be altered when displayed in a browser, assuring design fidelity. Flash, in particular, is favoured by Web designers for this fact alone.

## SHOCKWAVE

Shockwave is the Internet export format of Director, Macromedia's CD-ROM authoring software. It is used extensively for on-line gaming because of its powerful Lingo scripting language, which facilitates versatile interactivity. Shockwave can contain sound, animation, graphics and latterly 3D components. However, it is far more complex to work with than Flash, which offers many of the same features.

## FLASH

Flash is Macromedia's Web animation tool; it is used for simple animated logos as well as creating entire sites with navigation structures. Flash uses vector technology, similar to Illustrator and FreeHand, which is ideal for the Web because of the small file sizes and scalable qualities characteristic of vector files. It compresses sound using the Web's standard MP3 format, contributing to efficient download times. The Flash plug-in is found already installed in millions of the world's modern Web browsers. However, this doesn't mean that all these browsers will have the latest version of the plug-in or haven't had it disabled for some reason. It is good practice not to design sites that require Flash unless you're confident that enough of your target market will have a recent version installed.

Left: www.fray.com/hope/thecity/ Web pages can be displayed as multiple frames within a single window. Many Web designers try to avoid this technique, but this site shows how this can be put to excellent creative use. Black and white photography and graphic typography helps to make this site a particularly powerful interactive experience.
Design by Powazek Productions, USA

Left: www.fray.com/hope/2000/ Sometimes the best Web designs are the simplest, at least as far as the final result is concerned. This Web page uses sliced graphics and overlaid text to produce a strong, creative impact.
Design by Powazek Productions, USA

Above left: www.trafficthemovie.com This Flash dominated site to promote the movie 'Traffic', presents the visitor with a sequence of visual puzzles to solve before the next stage of the site can be accessed. 'Traffic' entertains while drawing on the viewer's intuitive abilities.

Left: www.brightlingphoto.com This site uses carefully prepared photographs, subtle rollovers and a simplified iconic representation of the user's place in the site. The result is understated elegance and a site which is extremely easy to navigate.
Design by Biggles, UK

**Left:** Specific attributes of Flash can be manipulated within Dreamweaver, not on an authoring level, but on the control of playback properties.

**Above:** www.swatch.com This site for the Swiss watch makes full use of Flash animation to involve and entertain the visitor.

**Above right:** The Flash interface is difficult to find your way around at first, although Flash 5 is much closer to the standard of DTP application interfaces. It has the advantage of integrating well with Dreamweaver, giving the designer the chance to play the Flash movie directly within the editing area.

**Right:** Freeway is a viable alternative to Dreamweaver, particularly for the Macintosh platform. It has great versatility and flexibility compared to many of its rivals.

**chapter 01. design for the internet**

155

**INTERACTIVITY** To interact with a computer is the fundamental principle of communication in the digital world. Almost without exception every type of content on the screen requires some level of user interaction. Websites are designed exclusively for this purpose – to encourage the visitor to explore and access areas of the site that offer up information. Web designers have to fully understand the concepts of interaction in order to use them appropriately.

## CREATING HYPERLINKS

Interactivity is a key element of any website, making the design dynamic and encouraging the user to stay and look around. The simplest form of interaction is clickable hypertext links. These provide links to other pages via clickable text items. Visually, graphic buttons and image maps are a more sophisticated form of link, but the technical aspect of the link is produced in exactly the same way.

The process of producing links varies slightly from one website layout tool to another, but the principle is the same. The examples shown above demonstrate creating hyperlinked text using Dreamweaver, and creating a graphic link using Freeway. In Dreamweaver the process begins by selecting a word or piece of text on the page. Click in the 'Link' field in the 'Properties' palette, and type a complete URL or pick one of your other pages from the pop-up menu. When the page is tested in a Web browser the linked text will take the user to the specified page when clicked. The process in Freeway is very similar. It begins by selecting, in this case, a graphic on the page. Then press on the globe icon at the bottom of the window and pick one of the pages in your site, or select 'Other' and type the URL into the URL field in the 'Hyperlink' window. Preview the result in a Web browser and the graphic will take the user to the linked page when clicked.

Above left: **The principle of text hyperlinking can be applied to any graphic element on a page as well. It is always important to check for broken links when publishing a site. Trying to navigate your way around a site with over a thousand links can be a very arduous task! Most WYSIWYG applications offer a fast and efficient method to check the integrity of all links with a page as well as an entire site.**

Above: **Mapping the links from a page can be a tedious business, but with complex sites it can be vital to keep track of your overall site navigation structure. Look for site and link mapping features in your Web design tool in order to keep on top of this when handling large projects.**

## ROLLOVER BUTTONS AND IMAGE MAPS

Rollover buttons are used to make graphic link items more interesting visually and to provide feedback to the user so they know an item is definitely a clickable link. Rollovers use a second graphic, which is shown in place of the first when the user points the cursor at the item, and are most commonly used to simulate a button that either lights up, appears to depress, or display some other form of detail change. They are produced using JavaScript instructions, which are placed in the HTML along with the image references in order to create the image-swapping behaviour.

part 03. design for screen

Below: **Four possible states of a clickable hypertext link.**
**Plain Text:** This is plain black HTML text, set in Verdana.
**Linked Text:** This text is hyperlinked and bold; hyperlinks are set to dark red on this page.
**Visited Link:** This text is hyperlinked and bold, but has already been visited; visited links are set to brown on this page.

**Hover (CSS):** Using Cascading Style Sheets, this link has been given a Hover state. When the mouse pointer hovers over it, it turns bright red to indicate that it can be clicked.
**Active Link (CSS):** Using Cascading Style Sheets, this link is made to turn orange when clicked; however, this can also be done in plain HTML.

Image maps work by plotting separate areas of a larger image and linking each area to a separate URL. This creates 'hot spots' within the graphic that take the user to different destinations when clicked. The graphic itself is an ordinary image file, and the map coordinates, which plot out the hot spot areas, listed within the HTML code. Image maps allow a very visual design method and don't demand that the designer slice their image up into multiple parts to create each graphic link. There are two forms of image map; client-side and the more unusual server-side. Client-side image maps hold everything to do with the map, including all the URLs, within the HTML page code. Server-side image maps send custom messages to a remote Web server that passes back the final destination URLs.

Above: **Macromedia Dreamweaver 4 incorporates the 'hot-spot' tools into the Properties window. This makes for very easy hyperlink editing when working with images on a page. Hotspots can be linked to invisible elements on an HTML page ('Anchors') and separate pages contained within a Frameset. This can be advantageous for producing quick side menus – when clicked, these change the content in the rest of the Web page.**

Below: **Graphic buttons and image maps work in exactly the same way as hypertext links but they do offer the designer infinite scope for creativity.**

**JAVA AND JAVASCRIPT EXPLAINED** Java and JavaScript are two distinct coding languages used to add interactivity to Web pages. Java is an object-orientated 'full' programming language that can be used to create complete applications. The Web manifestation of Java is in the form of Java Applets – independent, mini-executable programs placed on a page, like an image. JavaScript is a client-sided scripting language that allows the creation of rollover effects, the opening of pop-up windows and many other interactive page functions.

JavaScript is a text-based scripting language that is used to make specific instructions for browsers. These are placed into regular Web pages alongside the HTML code and are read and acted upon as required. Web designers frequently use JavaScripts without even realizing it as part of rollover effects and similar Web tricks.

Java on the other hand is a complete programming language; intended for use as a platform-independent language to develop Web-accessed software, it is frequently used to make self-contained miniature applications, or Applets, which can be embedded into Web pages. All the major browsers can be configured to support Java Applets but unfortunately they can be unreliable in handling them. Also, as the result of a court battle with Java developers Sun Microsystems, Microsoft was restricted to using an older version of Java in their products. They responded to this by dropping Java altogether from the Windows XP operating

Above: **Just like regular TV, Apple's QuickTime TV offers the viewer the choice to switch between channels and view different programs or content on-line. In reality, bandwidth difficulties make this a somewhat less than smooth affair. A good ISDN line will permit this to operate more effectively.**

system and the Internet Explorer browser. While Sun has since offered a new, freely downloadable Java Virtual Machine for XP, it is difficult to predict whether users will bother with the download, as Java applets have dwindled in popularity due to their reputation for slow loading and buggy operation. Applets provide an array of functions from games to numerical computations. For designers they are useful for text effects, scrolling marquees and flashing text to name just a few. They are practical for sites that require fast response from user input because they compute on-the-fly using the host computer's processing power. Designers who are not programming conversant can download pre-prepared Java Applets from sites such as http://javaboutique. internet.com and place them directly on the page.

JavaScript is written directly into the HTML code. It is generally very stable, as long as it is well written. It can perform rollovers, randomly display content on a page and load content into new browser windows as well as a host of other functions. Designers do not have to learn programming to use the basic JavaScript functions as the main website design packages will generate the code.

### SOUNDS AND MOVIES

Sound and movies (video) on the Web are commonplace, but handling these weighty files can be a testing experience for the designer. Both formats require specialist applications to prepare them for publishing, and a good bandwidth connection to allow uninterrupted playback or fast download to the client computer.

Below left: Undoubtedly the most widely used multimedia player application, Window's Media Player started out as a very basic utility, finding its legs on the Windows 95 platform. It has evolved into a powerful, automatically upgradable suite of tools, and its latest version, designed for Windows XP, allows for extensive visual customization.

Below: The Apple QuickTime interface is a strong competitor to the Window's Media Player. It is regarded as being very stable on both platforms and will handle a broad range of media. The familiar controls of treble, balance, bass and volume are built into the interface control panel for manual adjustment.

## SOUND FORMATS AND CHARACTERISTICS

The most commonly used formats for audio and video Web publishing are MP3, QuickTime and RealAudio. These formats all use forms of 'streaming' technologies which allow playback to begin without having a complete file downloaded, thus presenting a continuous stream and avoiding a lengthy download. Sound quality is determined by file size so CD-quality sound is not best suited to the Web. Sound files are often compressed to reduce download time, thus sacrificing the full tonal range of the original file. Speech is acceptable at 11kHz sampling rate, whereas music is better at 22kHz, both in mono. Flash uses sound very efficiently.

## VIDEO FORMATS AND CHARACTERISTICS

The QuickTime format ('.mov' file extension), the Video for Windows format ('.avi' file extension), and the Moving Picture Experts Group ('.mpg' or '.mpeg' file extension) operate on both Macs and PCs. Windows Media Player files ('.wma' or '.wmp' file extension) only work with the Windows operating system. Characteristics are similar to sound in that large file sizes give better quality. RealVideo is a common cross-platform format on the Web, although a plug-in is required on the end-user's side and a dedicated RealMedia server is needed to host the video. Some form of streaming, plus a relatively low frame rate (such as 12fps) and small window size (perhaps 160 x 120 pixels) is the only solution to delivering video smoothly.

Left: Banner ad design is a key part of design for the Internet. Creating an eye-catching banner that entices the viewer to click, yet fits into the typical banner graphic dimensions and can be compressed to a high degree is quite an art.

Left: Designing templates for database-driven publishing is a key part of commercial Web design. The trick is to make a layout which works both technically – fitting the contents from the database without breaking – and creatively.

## DEVELOPING A WEB DESIGN STRATEGY
Web design has become an industry in its own right with its own unique workflow, structures and ethics. Digital designers have had to develop strategies that work and operate in this field. Websites are not just marketing tools for the corporate world, they are focal points that enable businesses to stay at the cutting edge in highly competitive markets.

Traditional designers will be pleased to note that it is a good practice to start website designs with paper. After all, we read screens more slowly than paper, and even today's software isn't as quick and flexible as pencil-and-paper sketches. It is often best to visualize ideas, work out navigational structures and site maps on paper before going to the computer. To design the navigation of a site is a creative process in its own right involving considerable planning, and, with complex sites, teamwork.

Set yourself a clear brief with well defined objectives that can be articulated to the client (quite often clients are not familiar with the nature of Web media). Build in a time scale as this will help to deter clients from adding more content as the job progresses, which is often very tempting with the 'openness' of this particular medium.

When moving onto the computer, don't be diverted from your original plans. Keeping an eye on the overall project is vital, although inspiration for a job often comes from stopping and moving off the screen for a moment to regain objectivity. Web pages contain many ingredients that can quickly evolve from the original conception. To help design the layout, create a grid based on a maximum character count taking into consideration the intended platform (remember text can become oversized in some browsers unless formatted in specific ways). Consider the number of graphics you are using and assess their file size and download times. If you are using other applications such as Flash, set your parameters to be compatible with placement on a page. Remember that a Flash movie will take considerably longer to design and create than the page on which it will eventually reside.

An overriding factor in your design strategy is an understanding of the audience's computer capabilities. Designers usually work on powerful, well-equipped computers. It is easy to overlook this and produce a design that is too unwieldy for the average user. Also take into account browser versions and the age of the computers that the user may have. This will always affect the design approach. Don't include sound if the intended audience is unlikely to have a sound card in its computer.

The more attractive and popular a site becomes the more likely it is that download times will increase the frustration of the users. Successful Web designs are those that strike a balance between form and function.

Above: Freeway's approach to layout is based on traditional DTP behaviour, scaling graphics and styling text on the page. Guides can be dragged onto pages manually or set up as a regular design grid structure.

**PLANNING AND PRODUCTION** The planning and production of Web design are different from those for traditional desktop publishing. The technical and developing aspects of the medium should always be capitalized on but never allowed to override the design concept.

A diverse range of roles are needed to design and produce a successful, large-scale website. These could include graphic designer, market researcher, project manager, programmer, production manager, picture editor, sound production manager or video editor. This covers such a broad set of skills that no individual is likely to have them all, so in practice, freelance designers will sub-contract work to other specialists for specific tasks. Sub-contracting can be expensive so it is important to be aware of the scope of the project and adjust the overall design fees accordingly. For example, when a site requires a lot of expensive CGI scripting for e-commerce or on-line booking, this could form the major financial part of the job, with the design costs being relatively modest.

A fundamental planning consideration is deciding whether a site is linear or non-linear in its navigation structure. More than likely it will be the latter, in which case a legible '3D' site map should be created, clearly indicating all the possible linking routes for the user to explore. Refer to this often during the production process to avoid becoming confused when tying pages and sections together.

It is advisable to mock up key pages in graphics tools, such as Photoshop or Fireworks, and get them approved by the

Below: www.tate.org.uk
The value of a clear and simple layout can never be overestimated. Keeping an eye on the actual problem and giving the audience something accessible is a prime objective in Web design. Information should be easily retrievable without too many layers of navigation to wade through. The alphabet is one of the oldest ways of organising information and is still one of the best as seen in this page from the Tate Gallery website.
Design by Nykris Digital Design, UK

client before moving over to your website design package. Or, if your package is sufficiently DTP-like you can move straight to it from paper sketches.
Dreamweaver and GoLive do not allow for magnification of page elements or enlarged views of graphics, so you'll need to inspect and test the quality of all the graphic content in an image editor prior to importing.

Testing is absolutely critical and should not be compromised in any way. A designer is advised to use both a Macintosh and a PC for this purpose, although using Virtual PC on a Mac is a perfectly acceptable solution. Remember that graphics on a PC will appear a little darker than on a Mac, and HTML text can appear larger in Windows. It can be useful to set up a private testing folder on a remote Web server so the client can monitor progress and view 'live' pages. Testing work without first uploading to a remote server gives a false impression of download times. Remember to build in enough time for exhaustive testing and keep the client updated as things progress.

TA͞TE

Tate Home

home | supporters | contact us | shop online

From adolescence I had visited the Tate, read the Art books and generally pulled a forelock in the direction of the cult of genius, on cue relegating my own creativity to the Victorian image of the rabid dog. We know well enough that this was how it was supposed to be. The historical literature on 'rational recreations' states that, in reforming opinion, museums were envisaged as a means of exposing the working classes to the improving mental influence of middle class culture. I was being innoculated for the cultural health of the nation.

I have tried in this collection to play with the broken links within the Tate's collection, grafting on the skins of people who are close to me, dragging parts of the collection through the mud of the Thames, and infecting some of it with a relevant disease. This is a personal response to the cultural attitudes that I found within the aura of the collection.

J. M. W. Turner

William Hogarth

Gawen Hamilton

Thomas Gainsborough

John Singleton Copely

John Constable

---

Above: **www.tate.org.uk/webart/mongrel/collections/**
The right balance of image and text can provide the best platform to invite prospective viewers into a site – and then keep them there with consistency of layout throughout! Navigation bars and menus come in all sorts of shapes and sizes. Whatever your choice, beta-test it on those unfamiliar with your way of working.
Design by Nykris Digital Design, UK

Right: **www.core-design.com**
Flash is not reliant on HTML to reveal its content. As long as the right plug-in is installed on the browser Flash will play 'within itself'. This is why many designers favour Flash as text size and layout proportions are not adversely affected by browser preferences. This games development company makes great use of Flash to give the visitor an impressive dynamic experience.
Design by Core Design, UK

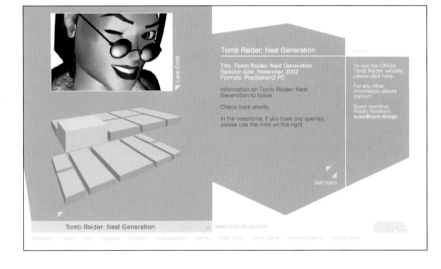

| 1. Pages | max 25k file size (inc graphics), max 795 x 500 pixel area |
|---|---|
| 2. Text | minimum size 3 (12 pixel cap) |
| 3. Graphics | convert all graphics to RGB. Titles as transparent GIFs, all other graphics as JPEGs max size 16k |
| 4. Background | common to all pages |
| 5. Hyperlinks | to email - check  to URLs - check and update |
| 6. Browsers | compatible with V.4.x and up/ P.C. and Mac/(alternative text only?) |
| 7. Test | test all links on both platforms |

Left: A simple checklist is always useful before a project gets under way. Web projects can quickly mushroom out of their intended scope if careful planning is not adhered to. Paper plans are invaluable to refer back to when the screen becomes too cluttered or over-familiar. A disproportionate amount of time can be wasted at this stage of production if all the thinking is done on screen.

# 03.01

**CASE HISTORY**

## WENDY CAULES CERAMICS

Wendy Caules is a ceramicist who lives and works in the UK. Headprecious Design was commissioned to produce a website that would provide a showcase for her work as well as a contact point for customers. The emphasis was on simplicity of layout in order to allow the work itself to breathe and stand out. The client specifically requested that the navigation should be 'straightforward' yet 'intuitive'.

The website would comprise a homepage with links to pages with samples of work, a live email contact and a curriculum vitae page. Within the sample pages it was suggested that a QTVR (QuickTime Virtual Reality) movie could be used to show a 360-degree view of an individual piece.

### THE FIRST STAGES

After the brief was agreed and the launch date set (to coincide with an exhibition of the artist's work) the next stage was to capture images of the work. Most examples of the work tended to be in 35mm transparency format, which is not ideal for high-quality reproduction. It was, therefore, decided that Headprecious Design would photograph the work using a digital camera to obtain a suitable format for Web publishing. An extra day was added to the schedule for photographing the work in a studio. The resulting images were used as a starting point for the initial design ideas and mock-ups. Samples of four

This page: **QuickTime Virtual Reality** was used to offer a 360 degree view of a ceramics piece, accessed via a pop-up window from the main portfolio page. Relying upon the intended audience's recognition of visual symbols as navigational devices (buttons) relieved the need for a large amount of HTML text to be included in the site.

different design concepts were presented, each incorporating the photographic images with varied options for type, layout and navigation structures. The artist chose a design that had a bold, clear 'look and feel' with a dominant photographic element, large-scale type heading and three visual (non-text) navigation buttons. The background graphic on the homepage was chosen to run throughout the site to help maintain consistency. It was agreed that the only section that would use HTML text would be the curriculum vitae page.

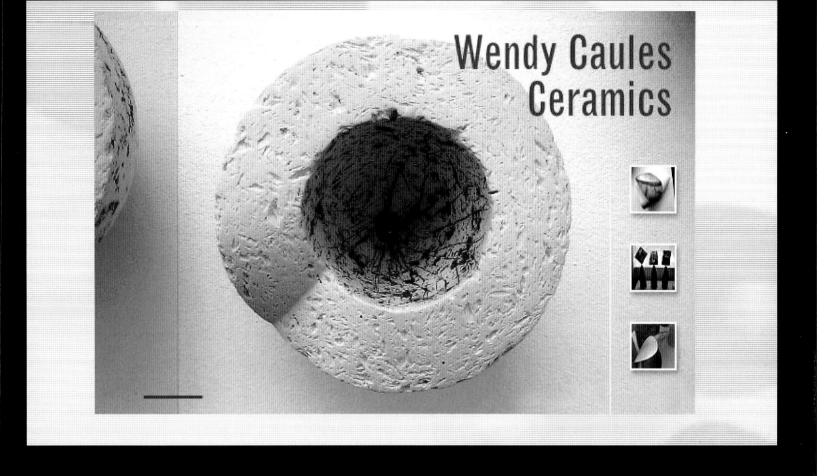

# Wendy Caules Ceramics

The background image was constructed in Photoshop using a technique that maintained the image quality but allowed for a small file size, allowing a shorter download time. The technique employed a screen of alternating 50 per cent transparent horizontal white lines, two pixels apart placed over a subdued montage of photographed ceramics pieces scaled to a 'live space' area measuring 800 x 466 pixels.

## OPTIMIZING THE SITE

To achieve a smooth screen rendering, the homepage graphic was spliced into three vertical sections, measuring 22, 35 and 10K respectively. Although this still constituted a large file, each image would download progressively and simultaneously, presenting a fluid screen draw. To ensure visual content would be present on the screen immediately, low-resolution, grey-scale versions of the three large graphics were created to render quickly followed by the full-colour versions overlaying them as they downloaded. The same technique was applied to all the images on the work sample pages.

Buttons were made as rollovers, incorporating simple graphic symbols to indicate their function in the rollover state, with small-scale images of ceramic pieces indicating the

Above: **By slicing the main graphic on the homepage, a relatively large-scale image could be employed to create visual presence. As well as the design considerations, an equally important aspect of the project was to ensure successful indexing for search engines. The timescale involved for this should not underestimated, and correct meta-tagging on the homepage itself is the first step. Pointing search engines at the site can be a lengthy process.**

static state. The buttons were subsequently placed in layers on top of the main graphic and scaled to match precisely.

## THE FINAL RESULT

The entire homepage measured 97K, resulting in an approximate download time of 25–30 seconds. This was within the acceptable timeframe for the intended specialist audience group. The brief, to create a highly visual site with detailed graphics while at the same time maintaining a fluid rendering of pages, was achieved.

Multimedia, also known as hypermedia, is the broad term that encompasses any communication medium that combines the use of sound, graphics, moving image, video and animation. It generally involves some form of interactivity, which distinguishes it from simple video productions. It is fast becoming integral to our daily lives, with the advent of new iTV, WAP mobile phones, touch-screen information kiosks, Internet enabled pay-phones, DVD, CD-ROM and sophisticated TV graphics. Designers are increasingly involved with the continuing growth of interactive technology.

The CD-ROM, once hailed as the replacement for the printed book, was one of the first vehicles for interactive, 'multimedia' products for the mass market. Traditional publishing houses ventured into this medium with re-workings of existing texts with little success. It became

obvious that reading on screen was not about to replace the convenience of the book. DVD (Digital Versatile Disk) has secured more of a market identity largely due to its focus on entertainment and music industry. DVD is a rich medium that provides high-quality playback of video and music with many other features such as user interaction and editing as standard.

The most noticeable form of multimedia is television graphics (advertising, trailers, title sequences and weather charts) produced using digital technology but mainly delivered by analog transmission. (This will be totally superseded by digital transmission.) Since television covers many areas of information and entertainment, it gives the digital graphic designer a wide range of creative opportunities and by its transitory nature also encourages experimentation and innovation. Design has flourished in the area of information screens and kiosks found in banks, airports, museums, in-store points, stations and public spaces. Unlike their hard-copy counterparts, information kiosks can be updated easily, and hold large amounts of information. Moving images and animation add to their interest and entertain the veiwer.

Artists have adopted multimedia as a viable medium for self-expression, from on-site exhibition installations to Internet delivery. The internationally acclaimed video artist, Bill Viola, has a long respected 'tradition'

**PART 03. DESIGN FOR SCREEN**

**CHAPTER TWO**

# DESIGN FOR MULTIMEDIA

Right: Touch-screen information kiosks, such as this example from the National Portrait Gallery in London, can offer a wide choice of media to the viewer. Illustrations, graphics and video can be rendered quickly and efficiently with dedicated hardware. The constraints for the multimedia designer are far fewer than they are for Web publishing.
Design by Cognitive Applications, UK

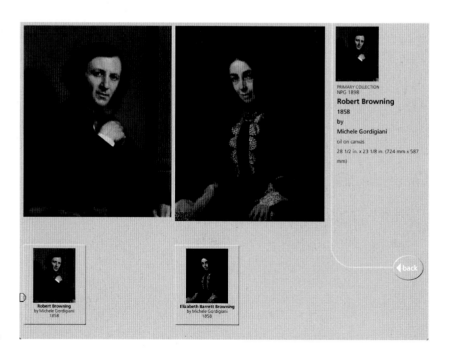

of embracing new media and technology in his work. The Web artist, Barminski, exploits the full power of sound and animation to present his idiosyncratic view of popular culture using Macromedia's Shockwave.

We exist in an environment where our senses are constantly bombarded with sounds, words and images. Designers, artists and developers are responsible for the many forms of information and entertainment that we experience. Designers have to reset their working parameters constantly to keep abreast of new developments, techniques and applications. Multimedia designers may well be musicians, fine artists, film- and video-makers, writers or editors. However, digital graphic designers find that their visual language together with their experience in managing words and images provides them with an excellent basis for multimedia work.

Below: **Multimedia allows the designer to create a high-quality sensory experience using dynamic video and audio. Large high-resolution moving images such as this are impossible to transmit over the Internet, yet will not tax the huge data carrying capabilities of a DVD disk.**
Design by Tomato Interactive, UK

## MULTIMEDIA AND WEB DESIGN – THE DIFFERENCES Much of the technology used to create multimedia projects is similar to that used to create Web pages, but there is one major difference. Multimedia work is not constrained by the limitations of the Internet.

Unlike the Internet, in which the all-important download time is reliant on the unpredictable speed of the modem, multimedia, whether it is a CD-ROM or touch-screen museum installation, is powered by the computer's own internal processor. The advantages of this are clear. First, the viewer sees 'real time' playing on screen, and second, far larger file sizes are permissible and therefore a greater range and quality of content and media is available. The obvious benefit involves the use of video and sound, both of which are memory and disk-space hungry. A DVD can deliver full stereo, surround sound, and uncompressed-quality audio and video, which would be impossible to deliver over the Web. The use of full-screen animation, a wider choice of fonts and complex graphics, are all additional choices for the multimedia designer.

### WHAT IS 'REAL TIME PLAYING'?

Real time playing should be qualified: the speed at which data can be read from a CD-ROM or straight from the computer's hard drive depends on the processing power and internal architecture of the machine and the speed of the CD/DVD reader. Top end machines utilize very fast hard drives and large amounts of RAM (on-the-fly processing) to render multimedia on-screen smoothly. Lower end 'pro-sumer' machines offer a reduced capability. There is always a delay in the transfer of the information held on a compact disc. Video playback from a

CD is usually set at 12 frames per second as opposed to a much higher rate for dedicated video players. This is because the CD-ROM drive cannot read the frames fast enough to present a fluid picture, hence the characteristic jerky motion. This does present a dilemma for the multimedia designer, although the speed of CD-ROM drives is improving. Content optimized for the latest CD-ROM drives will not work properly on those machines with older, slower drives. This is not dissimilar to the issues for Web designers of browser age and compatibility. However, the constant renewal and advance of computer processing power offers greater choice for multimedia developers, both professional and amateur. Editing full-screen, broadcast-quality video on a 'home' computer is now possible with the advent of Apple's Final Cut Pro software and digital, video-ready G4 computers.

### THE END-USER

Where the multimedia work is to be delivered will determine the quality and size of the product. A dedicated custom set-up, such as a museum installation, will provide opportunities for maximum quality, whereas a consumer CD-ROM may be produced to suit the most popular home computers. Multimedia is often delivered over a closed network using a powerful central computer to send the work to smaller, satellite machines. This is much more efficient than using the Internet and is most often used in Intranet systems for company data, training workshops, in-store information points, and similar restricted environments.

Multimedia products offer a broader, richer and more expanded range of outcomes than Web products, which by their very nature are anchored to the current constraints of the Internet. Interactive television, although in its infancy and burdened by low screen resolution, provides a particularly exciting prospect for multimedia designers.

Above: **A DVD disc looks identical to a CD-ROM disc, but its capacity to hold data is many times greater. The latest computers available to the consumer market come equipped with DVD-ROM. This allows vast amounts of hard-drive hungry data, such as raw video footage, to be archived effectively for later retrieval.**

This video was created within a corporate identity campaign for a technology infrastructure company. The video incorporated digital video, still photography sequences, 3D modelled elements, and graphics animated and edited in Adobe AfterEffects. The video conveyed the seamless transparency of technology between the everyday user and behind-the-scenes networking systems.
Design by InterStitch, USA

This page: **Tomato Interactive** has produced some visually stunning and exciting multimedia work over the past five years. By combining live concert footage, as seen here with Underworld's 'Everything Everything' DVD, with graphic imagery and inset video the audience is presented with a multi-layered aural and visual experience.

Design by Tomato Interactive, UK

**THE DESIGN PROCESS** The multimedia design process is by definition diverse and the designer has to adopt many roles. Working through ideas and concepts on paper is useful, and defining the project parameters is essential. Many multimedia prototypes are very complex with the integration of sound, moving image, video and graphics presenting the designer with a formidable challenge.

Almost without exception, multimedia models are non-linear, that is, they present an interface to the user that is composed of multiple choice options and paths to select. A well-designed navigation structure will significantly improve the enjoyment and accessibility of a piece of work. Good navigation design is an artform in itself and certainly should not be undervalued. The problems associated with user boredom, characteristic of Web publishing, are not so prevalent in multimedia work. It is assumed that a potential audience will be more focussed and, as the medium delivers a quicker response to user interaction, not need to wait so long for screen content. This distinctive quality of CD-ROM multimedia products should be balanced against the fact that they are less easy to update than Web pages.

## HIGH EXPECTATIONS

Client expectation can present problems for the designer. The nature of multimedia allows for a rich and varied content, but the time and cost in preparing this content can be significant. So how does a designer positively engage the client whilst at the same time highlighting the potential pitfalls and limitations of the medium? Clients who are not fully conversant with the scope of the medium often anticipate an 'all singing, all dancing' product. One solution is to present a scaled range of product levels, offering the necessary graphics, navigation structure and production methods necessary to complete the work to a satisfactory standard for a lower budget. A menu of additional options, such as more video, larger-format video, and more animation and sound can then be offered. The onus is then on clients to balance their expectations with project budgets. Providing a demonstration of a range of options will be very helpful in this process.

If a designer is part of a large organization with access to many technical resources, many of these issues are more-easily solved. The 'internal' client may well be aware of the possibilities and options available from the start. For the freelance designer there is a more challenging task, as all the resources will have to be independently sourced. This is why many multimedia designers build up contact lists of programmers, video editors and sound designers to call upon. This aspect alone encourages an interdependent approach to multimedia design processes. Designers can increase their skills and expertise by working in a 'design community', sharing their knowledge and learning from others. This makes for a very exciting and challenging career shift for many designers switching from traditional print and publishing backgrounds.

## AUTHORING APPLICATIONS AND THEIR ROLES
In the professional market, Macromedia Director, a multimedia authoring software package, is the dominant player. It allows the designer to manipulate sound, graphics, moving image and video directly in the editing environment without the need for further plug-ins. Director uses Lingo, its own powerful scripting language, for complex 'behind-the-scenes' programming actions that provide a rich resource for user interaction.

### DIRECTOR

Director uses a metaphor of a theatre production for its authoring environment, comprising a 'stage', 'cast members' and a 'score'. For designers this is an excellent format as it demystifies what could potentially be a rather complex workspace. The screen functions as a stage upon which the designer can directly place cast members from a database of elements (graphics, sound, video, etc.). The cast are then orchestrated within the score (a multi-layered traditional animation timeline) to animate frame by frame. Cast members become 'sprites' when they are placed on the stage, leaving their original files untouched in the cast database. Sprites are clones of their parent cast members and can be modified on the stage without increasing the file size of the finished movie. They can be animated, resized, made transparent and scripted to perform and respond to user interaction using Lingo. Finished productions can be made into stand-alone cross-platform applications using a 'projector' which does not need the Director software to run. Projectors launch the authored Director movies, which can be set to fill the entire monitor screen, obscuring the desktop, to deliver a professional presentation.

If used effectively Director can provide a complete digital production solution for multimedia CD-ROM, DVD and touch-screen installations. In terms of Web publishing, Director has found favour with many on-line games developers who exploit its option to export projects as Shockwave movies. Macromedia has actively encouraged a growing Web community of third-party developers who test, share and expand the capability of Director. They, in turn, have helped it to become extremely versatile for integration with other formats such as Adobe's PDF, Apple's QuickTime and HTML. For example, a CD-ROM production could include a 'live link' to a website or have the option to open and view PDF files whilst the Director movie is running on the user's computer in the background.

### AFTER EFFECTS

Adobe's After Effects has become the industry standard package for producing broadcast-quality composite digital video productions. It is an amalgamation of Premier and Photoshop. Graphics, sound, music and video can be imported and then edited to create a layered composition which can be exported in any number of popular file formats (QuickTime, Windows Media Player) or exported directly to a professional video post-production system such as Avid's Media 100. After Effects can utilize a range of PhotoShop filters to apply effects and transitions over a time period. This software is frequently used to create title sequences for TV and multimedia presentations. Although mainly non-interactive it can be exported for Web publishing and include some user interaction elements.

In the multimedia market there is a range of proprietary animation and 3D software, such as Cambridge Animation System's 'Animo' and Avid's 'Softimage', used in the entertainment, video and film industry. They are exclusively designed for high-end animation, editing and production. Companies like Industrial Light & Magic have set new standards in 3D character animation and digital special effects.

Left: Adobe After Effects gives the multimedia designer scope to combine sound, video, type and static imagery into a single time-based movie. The published movie can be used for professional broadcast applications, video or as an element in CD-ROM and DVD productions. After Effects, simply put, is Photoshop with a time-line and sound added.

Above: Macromedia Fireworks is a Web-specific image editor with some animation features included. It makes a pretty good job of animated GIF production, but it isn't in the same league as Flash or Director when it comes to interactivity and serious animations.

Left: This is the Macromedia Director authoring environment showing the main windows used to create and edit a movie. Ideally, two monitors or one large one are needed to display the multiple windows Director uses. The interface is fairly intuitive and can be used to produce successful productions without the need to write Lingo scripts .

Above: Director gives the author many pre-prepared Lingo scripts to use in a movie, making life easier for the hesitant scripting author. The Behavior window offers drop-down menus to select the most commonly applied scripts in well organised sub-categories. Scripts can be used to control playback characteristics, memory use, sound, visual effects and user interaction.

**chapter 02. design for multimedia**

Above and left: **Adobe's After Effects** is essentially an animated version of Photoshop. It allows layers to be imported from Photoshop and retains familiar palette features and tool properties. Sound, imported video footage and graphic stills can be composited together into a smooth, exported QuickTime movie, which can then be integrated into a multimedia production on CD-ROM or DVD.

**PLANNING AND PRODUCTION** In many respects multimedia planning and production is closer to desk-top publishing than it is to Web publishing. There are fewer constraints than in Web design; the outcome can be produced, manufactured and published to exacting, high standards without the loss of control associated with Internet delivery.

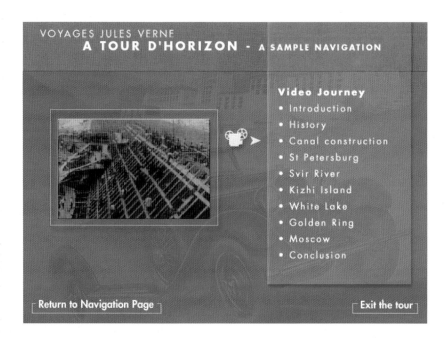

Above: a screen from a promotional CD-ROM for Voyages Jules Verne Travel. The re-purposing of existing promotional or advertising material, supplied by a company, can be effectively implemented into a multimedia production. Posters, photographs and video can be re-edited with Adobe Photoshop and Premier to sit within a new production.
Design by Phil Taylor and Phil Jackson, UK

Despite this extra control over design, development and production costs can be great, with the problems of rising costs to cover additional sound, video and animation. Invariably, multimedia projects are large undertakings with many unseen issues unfolding during the production and authoring stages. It is essential to establish a fixed price for the initial design and concept stage and then build in a tiered fee structure to cover production costs dictated by any revised expectations or supplementary requirements of the client. Sub-contracting is common with multimedia projects and should be thoroughly researched and planned. For example, using advanced Lingo scripting in Director will often require out-sourced programming expertise, even for the experienced Director user.

Some CD-ROM productions can be too big to fit on a single disk. If a client expects a large amount of high-quality stereo sound and full-screen video for their product, this may push the project over the maximum 700Mb capacity of a compact disc. Somewhere content has to be trimmed down for the whole project to fit on the disc. Graphics and text do not usually present a problem for the designer owing to their (relatively) small file size so most 'compression of content' must be made to sound and video.

Fortunately DVD products have a much larger capacity and can accommodate rich media content, making them ideal for a broader design scope.

### 'TEST TEST TEST !'

Testing is absolutely vital for multimedia productions. Web publishing has its challenges, with varying ages of browser versions and monitor resolutions, but multimedia has all these and more! A typical CD-ROM will have to function on computers with different specifications of hardware on varying revisions of operating system software and be compatible with application software and third-party applications. When a client wants to include video, a choice between QuickTime or AVI format has to be made.

QuickTime will play seamlessly on a Macintosh (and in some respects is a more stable format than AVI files), but will not play by default on Windows. Although the QuickTime software is readily available and easy to install on a Windows machine, clients are often sceptical about the ability of the intended audience to install such software. Testing strategies have to be assembled and implemented for every aspect of a project to ensure maximum compatibility and usability. Compromises may have to be made, a situation all too familiar to Web designers.

Cross-platform compatibility is one of the most sought after goals in multimedia. Although the Apple Macintosh market is small in comparison to that of PCs, clients may wish to reach as wide an audience as possible by including a Mac version in their planning. Professional developers often have a testing room set aside with a range of older machines of varying specifications to test a product for flaws and conflicts.

**CASE HISTORY**

# WOODWARD PORTRAIT EXPLORER
# NATIONAL PORTRAIT GALLERY, LONDON

The Woodward Portrait Explorer is a permanent touch-screen installation designed by Cognitive Applications, based in the UK and the US. The Portrait Explorer system extends the approach of the acclaimed Micro Gallery guide in the National Gallery, in London.

The installation functions primarily as an informative guide for visitors to the gallery, with insights into thousands of works of art in the collection, video interviews with artists and many other interactive features.

Designing a multimedia system for public use, such as in a gallery, requires careful planning and execution. Typically an interface design will employ visual metaphors as navigational icons. Presenting a 'human' interface is critical to the useability of the multimedia system. With Web design the interface has to exist within the constraints of browser configurations and limitations, and can be altered by the end-user. Touch-screen installations, which run directly from a hard drive or CD and so permit greater control for the developer. This requires the application of considered and tested design concepts. For example, if the design calls for finger/touch interaction to activate a cursor instead of a mouse, larger buttons will be needed on the screen. The familiar metaphor of 'push-buttons' with drop shadows may seem out-moded in today's computer-driven design, but in an established, traditional gallery setting they may be critical in ensuring that the system is accessible and user-friendly to a wider public.

Rory Mathews, Design Director at Cognitive Applications, UK, considered three important questions before designing the museum installation:

* What is the subject matter?
* What environment will the system be seen in?
* What are the aims of the system?

The most fundamental question concerning the Portrait Explorer system was, 'What, in essence, is an art gallery about?' The answer to this was, 'To provide an environment in which to present works of art, and to allow the opportunity for the visitor to expand their knowledge through exposure and education'. The system would need to accommodate a wide range of people and not exclude anyone within the 'typical visitor' profile, which does not really exist in a large, open-access public space. An interactive multimedia system would need to be in tune with this environment and aligned to these aims. The Portrait Explorer system was designed to offer a refined interface that achieved these aims after an exhaustive reappraisal of the objectives during the design process.

## THE MAIN SUCCESFUL CHARACTERISTICS OF THE SYSTEM
* The system has its own visual identity, but complements the character of the museum and its collection.
* The system's graphic design, interface design and technology – like good book typography – are designed to be virtually transparent to the ordinary user.
* The design does not compromise the integrity of the works of art by gratuitous use of animation or image manipulation.
* The design will always be complementary and subordinate to the works of art discussed in the system.
* Because the system is designed without modish design or technological gimmicks it will not become dated quickly.

A visitor to the National Portrait Gallery can enrich their experience greatly through interacting with the Portrait Explorer system. Through the considered use of animation, video and image manipulation, Cognitive Applications have built a successful, interactive experience.

These screen shots demonstrate the careful planning necessary to produce an involved project such as the Woodward Portrait Explorer. The aim of any ambitious site-specific multimedia installation is to complement the museum's collection and enrich the visitor's experience. The Woodward Portrait Explorer succeeded in this by offering a varied mix of educational, informative and entertaining stimuli with which the viewer can interact.

Computer and video game graphics have come a long way since 'Pong'. Visually, the 1972 gaming pioneer made do with two white rectangular 'bats' and a square white 'ball', on a plain black background. Created in the days before microprocessors, its graphics were hardwired by an engineer.

Today, however, game development is a global creative industry employing tens of thousands of writers, musicians, game designers and artists. User-friendly professional tools have enabled non-engineers to create the vast amount of visual content required for a state-of-the-art title, in high-resolution colour – using many of the same techniques as conventional non-interactive graphic designers and fine artists.

Game development is a highly team-orientated industry. In total, between 13 and 40 people will work closely together during the 14 month to two year period which will see a game grow from concept to final production. Typically, a team will be split evenly between the three departments of art, programming and game design, with a single producer in overall charge.

Each individual department within the team will function as a tightly-knit unit, with individuals assigned their own areas of focus or specialization.

A single artist famed in a different field – comic-book art, for example, or film design – is very occasionally brought in to a game project as a 'star' attraction, and will probably contribute their work independently of the development team; but it is extremely rare to see one person given any sort of headline credit for a game, especially on the art side.

There are some basic technical specializations within most game development art departments – but it is important for any artist to be flexible, and to at least have an understanding of the other elements which together make up the finished graphics. Broadly, there are four areas of game art: conceptual, 2D, 3D and animation.

Conceptual artwork will be sketched in the earliest stages of a game's development to establish the basic look of characters or environments and, in detail, to storyboard in-game sequences or cinematic style

PART 03. DESIGN FOR SCREEN

CHAPTER THREE

# DESIGN FOR GAMES

Left and above: **3D game environments and graphic objects are typically constructed from polygon mesh frames to which 2D 'skins' are applied. The frames are kept relatively simple in order that a typical player's computer is able to** animate them in a naturalistic way. The demand for more and more impressive graphics is one of the main driving forces behind the ever-increasing processing speed of consumer computers.
Design by Shane Caudle, USA

Below: **Myst III**
Games development is a field in which unrestricted imagination and digital technology can come together. While it is true that most games graphics are rather formulaic, titles such as the hugely popular Myst series have proved that there is a demand for computer games with a high degree of artistry.
Design by Presto Studios, USA

Above: **MechWarrior 4**
Players must visit this complex interface before the main game can begin. It could have been boring but the agressive font and brooding lighting work to build excitement.
Design by Microsoft, USA

'cutscenes'.

'Finished' 2D work is required for the creation of on-screen display elements (scores, meters, indicators and icons), or menu-based interface screens. Very recently, Flash has become a viable cross-platform development environment for this kind of 'front end' work. Generally, though, 2D images are created and manipulated in a graphics editing package such as Adobe Photoshop. This is certainly the tool most often used for the creation of the fundamental building-blocks of contemporary game graphics: 2D textures, which will be overlaid onto flat polygons in the game's 3D-rendered world.

Although there are a small number of popular modern titles which don't create a fully-3D game space, they are very much in the minority. Hardware advances over the past seven or eight years have resulted in the normalization of this once-revolutionary approach.

Technical challenges still abound, however, and any 3D artist has to work strictly within the confines established by the game 'engine' written by the programming team. This will determine, for example, how many individual polygons can be used to build any particular character or object, without affecting the game's performance.

The most prevalent professional tools for 3D and animation work are Discreet's 3D Studio Max and Alias|Wavefront's Maya. Using either of these packages, artists have total modelling control over every detail of the landscapes, architecture, objects and characters which populate today's interactive 3D worlds – totally immersive 'virtual realities' undreamed-of by those first 'Pong' players a few short decades ago.

Left: **Discreet's 3D Studio Max** is the world's best-selling 3D animation and modelling software package. It is used by a wide variety of users, from game developers and film animators to architectural designers.

Left: **Alias|Wavefront's Maya** is perhaps the industry standard software for games development, and is also widely used in the fields of film and broadcast television. The program's power, speed and flexibility, however, are reflected in a very hefty price tag.

# TYPE
# COLOUR
# IMAGE

Type is one of the graphic designer's core tools. With attention to detail, the designer can use type to communicate appropriately, to suggest mood and character and to contribute to page or surface layout dynamics. However, type does need to be handled with care and understanding.

Designers should not only have an appreciation of the aesthetic values of type, (see Design Basics), but also know how type is stored, controlled and output digitally. All these have a direct bearing on how type is printed or displayed on screen.

A typeface is an alphabet (along with numerals and punctuation) considered as a designed or aesthetic visual entity. A font is the collection of characters that is held in one file. One font may contain the alphabet in upper and lower case, with related numerals and punctuation, while an additional font (with the same typeface name) may contain old style numerals, small capital letters, alternate swash characters and an extensive range of ligatures and foreign accents. These additional fonts are often called 'expert sets'. If special characters normally contained in an expert set are included in the basic font, that font may be described as having an extended character set.

Font-related issues have probably been the cause of most design-to-print headaches, and the following short explanation is intended to help designers avoid them.

**PART 04. TYPE/COLOUR/IMAGE**

**CHAPTER ONE**

# TYPE

áéèüöçôåñ˘

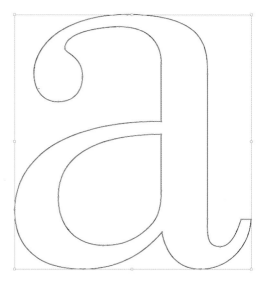

Above: **These are some of the most common accents used in Latin languages. Most can be found by depressing the Option key while typing a character. For example, to obtain an acute accent over an e (é), hold down Option and type e, let go of Option and type e again.**

Left: **Every character in a font is decribed by a set of vectors (its outline description). It is this information that monitors and printers draw upon in order to display and print type respectively.**

Gill Sans
Suitcase

Fonts
Folder

Below: Key Caps is a desktop accessory found under the Apple Menu, which displays a keyboard layout. By depressing Shift, Option or Shift/Option a further three sets of characters are revealed. There are up to four characters held under each key. A useful piece of software called Keyfinder will display the entire character set available and indicate what key or combination of keys are required.

## BITMAPS AND VECTORS

Letterform information is stored digitally in both bitmap and vector forms. Bitmap data provides adequate information for screen display at a fixed size but gives a 'pixelated' appearance when scaled up. Vector (outline) descriptions of each character provide better information from which to print. Because vectors are straight lines and curves recorded in a font as mathematical formula, the resulting shapes, when filled with pixels, improve the quality of the scaling.

Monitors cannot be relied on to show fine typographic detailing, so character shape and spacing intended for a printed job may not be accurately represented on screen. This is less of a problem for screen presentations, since other monitors will display your work in a similar way. PC and Macintosh monitors can, however, vary quite markedly in their display (see Web Design and Multimedia).

## POSTSCRIPT TYPE 1 FONTS

PostScript is Adobe's page description software that among other functions, instructs the printing device to produce letterforms and graphics to a high degree of accuracy at any required size. Documents containing this outline information for printing are called PostScript files. Fonts containing this outline information are called PostScript fonts, and there are two kinds, of which Type 1 is by far the most common. PostScript fonts consist of two parts: a bitmap file for screen display and an outline file, which is the PostScript description of character shapes. The operating system can use bitmap information to draw characters on screen and the PostScript font file for outputting from the printer. A separate PostScript font file is required for each style in a typeface, e.g. regular (plain), italic, bold, bold italic.

Times

The latest editions of the Windows operating system as well as Mac OS X have built-in rasterizers that pick up the outline (vector) information from the font file and create better looking, more accurate letterforms on screen. Older editions of Windows and the Macintosh operating system need to have Adobe Type Manager (ATM) installed to do the same job. Both operating systems must have at least one size of bitmap font installed to enable them to work and also to display the fonts in program menus.

## TRUETYPE

TrueType fonts have become very popular, despite the apparent domination of Type 1 fonts in the design field. TrueType fonts combine vector and bitmap fonts, which allows them to be infinitely and accurately scaled. A TrueType rasterizer is built into both Macintosh and Windows operating systems to provide information for both screen drawing and print output. TrueType fonts are held in a single file (a suitcase on the Macintosh) that can contain sufficient information for constructing regular, regular italic, bold, and bold italic versions of the same typeface.

## MULTIPLE MASTER FONTS

Multiple Masters are Type 1 fonts developed by Adobe, which unlike ordinary fonts, contain several outlines that represent the extremes of variables on a design axis such as weight, width, style or optical size (from small print to display). The designer is able to create custom fonts by choosing points between the extremes using the Font Creator utility, built into ATM for Windows or as a stand-alone application on the Macintosh. Multiple Master fonts may have axes for weight, width, style or optical size – or (in theory) all four. Potentially, they allow for great flexibility of character shape without the problems of distortion, but are rather uncommon.

~ATM™

**part 04. type/colour/image**

## WHICH FONT FORMAT TO USE

There are potential problems in mixing TrueType font and Type 1 fonts within the same design. To avoid confusion it is a good idea to make sure you don't have fonts of the same name in the different formats.

When using Type 1 fonts, be sure that there is an outline font available to download to the printer and check that no fonts are missing.

On the Macintosh, TrueType fonts and the bitmaps for Type 1 fonts are kept in 'suitcases' in the fonts folder. PostScript files for the printer are kept loose in the font folder and can have various icons according to the font vendor. Under Windows, TrueType and PostScript files are kept in separate folders. Alternative locations are possible if you use a font manager such as Suitcase.

## FONT METRICS

Font metrics are a component of all fonts. They are measurements that govern spacing, kerning, and hinting, and contain the font's kerning tables. They are only used by some software and are generally not required to display or print fonts.

## FONT PROBLEMS

Many font problems are unwittingly self-inflicted, but a little organization and care should keep most designers out of trouble. Understanding font icons can help a lot; examples are shown in the illustration.

One of the most common problems is type that looks horribly jagged on screen. This happens when the relevant PostScript file is missing from your system and needs to be reloaded. It also happens when ATM is switched off. If type prints out incorrectly, the PostScript file for a style of font may be missing or may have been put into the wrong

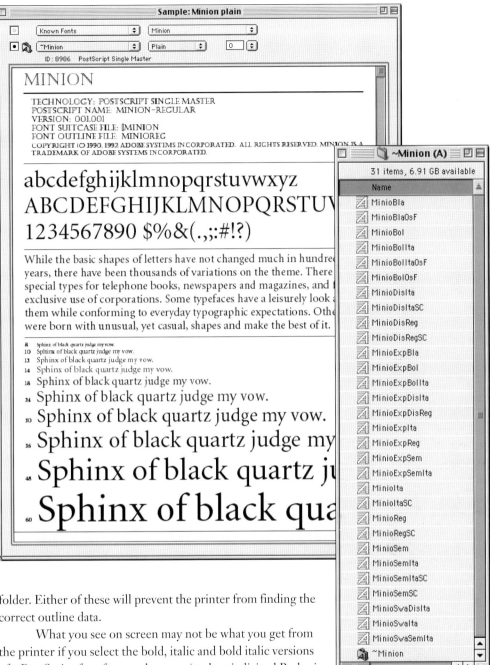

folder. Either of these will prevent the printer from finding the correct outline data.

What you see on screen may not be what you get from the printer if you select the bold, italic and bold italic versions of a PostScript font from style menu (such as italicized Bodoni Regular) rather than from the font menu (for example, Bodoni Italic). If a TrueType file contains regular (plain), bold, regular italic and bold italics, you can select these styles from font menus or by clicking on a floating palette.

Some fonts may not be listed alphabetically where you expect them in the font menu, for example. Bodoni Italic may be listed as 'I Bodoni Italic'. If this confuses you, you can use a utility such as Adobe Type Reunion or Adobe Type Manager to group fonts into typeface families.

If line endings and text flow change unexpectedly, you may have two similarly named versions of the same typeface. Almost certainly, they will have different spacing or kerning,

Above left: Another feature of ATM is a Window that previews chosen typefaces, showing their visual appearance in a variety of sizes and line settings (left).

Above: the open Window of a font folder shows all the PostScript files that accompany the Suitcase for the typeface Minion.

Above: **Many type foundries and type libraries may be found on the Internet. Most sites contain useful information concerning the history of typefaces, their designers and facilities to try typefaces out.**

causing the spacing to differ. It is advisable to keep just one version of a font to avoid mixing them up.

This problem can be most acute when your job goes to the output bureau or print shop. A bureau or printshop may assure you that it has a copy of your font, but you need to be sure that type is rendered using precisely the same outlines and metrics that your font has given you. Make sure to send a copy of your font to the bureau or printshop, but remember that this is only legal if the bureau or printshop also owns a licence for that font (see Font Copyright).

If your bureau or printshop tells you that a font is missing, especially one that you think you have not used, the problem most likely lies in a blank line or invisible character (including spaces and returns), all of which will have font and style settings applied to them. Make a final check of all these in the 'Font usage' dialog before you send the job, rather than wasting time supplying them later.

One way to avoid all such font problems is to supply files in the PDF format (see page 70) with the fonts 'embedded'.

## FONT COPYRIGHT

Fonts are protected by copyright law. When you 'buy' a font, it is in fact usually only the licence to use it that you have acquired.

Typical single-user licences allow one copy of a font to be installed on one computer. You may use the font to print directly to any output device (laser printer, inkjet printer or imagesetter), as fonts are only temporarily uploaded during the process.

Type used on Web pages will display properly only if the person viewing the page has the required font installed on his or her system. However, copyright rules prevent fonts from being supplied or served with the pages. Software is available to allow only the characters you have used to be supplied to a Web page as vector-described glyphs. This will bring infinitely scalable, good-looking type to your website.

# jaggies

# jaggies

Antialiased type       Bitmap type

Above: **Antialiasing,** particularly at small sizes, helps to create a better shaped letter as these enlargements show.

Above: Jaggies is the name given to to the crude pixelated rendering of type on screen which occurs when bitmap fonts are enlarged. Smooth results are obtained when outline information is made available through the use of TrueType fonts or PostScript fonts.

## IMPROVING TYPE ON SCREEN FOR ON-LINE VIEWING

The best rendering of type is achieved through imagesetter output, since resolution is much higher than on screen. Resolution (the number of dots per inch) varies from one printer type to another. Inkjet and laser printers output at 300–600 dots per inch (dpi) or better, producing prints of the quality of a good photocopy, but imagesetters output at up to 3000dpi, producing prints with crisp, sharp edges and very fine detail.

The quality of digital type on screen, however, is constrained by the resolution of the monitor. When a font outline is rasterized on screen, only the pixels that fall within the outline shape will normally be drawn. The relatively low resolution of monitors cannot display fine detail (less than one pixel), causing inconsistencies or loss in features such as serifs and stroke weights and badly formed letters and spaces. Small sizes of type display badly on screen. Since small sizes are those most commonly used for text meant for extended reading, this is unfortunate.

A technique known as hinting can be used to adjust the arrangement of pixels to take account of lost detail. When there are too few pixels to display a small letterform correctly, hinting instructions in the font file can be used to provide a better-looking letterform and maintain optically balanced spacing.

Though it is important for print designers to have a good preview of their work, the quality of screen display becomes all the more urgent for on-line viewing where the screen image is actually the finished product.

To counteract the disappearance of detail at small sizes, larger type is often used for on-line pages than would be appropriate for a comparable printed job. But this doesn't really solve the problem. Improvements are constantly being made to give small type a smoother appearance and make it easier to read on screen. Antialiasing techniques, in particular, are now frequently used to improve the on-screen look of all sizes of type.

Agfa Monotype produces a useful range of Enhanced Screen Quality (ESQ) fonts specially designed for optimum on-screen readability and clarity across a range of point sizes and screen resolutions.

## ANTIALIASING

Antialiasing is the strategic insertion of pixels of various shades around parts of the letterform to create an illusion of relative stroke bulk and smoothness – an exercise that works well by tricking the eye. Adobe products use antialiasing by default for displaying text on screen and Microsoft Windows software automatically smooths fonts above a certain size.

The appropriate and emotive use of colour is integral to the competence of the digital graphic designer. In our consumer-led, information- rich, entertainment-orientated society, the designer must understand thoroughly both the nature of colour and the way in which it works in order to use it effectively.

There are several reasons why the nature and the workings of colour are important (see also Design Basics). First, when designing on screen with colour (and when screen colour is actually used in Web and multimedia projects), that colour is transmitted directly from a white light source. However, when colour is reproduced through the use of printing inks, the colours are not transmitted but reflected. Crucially, the range of colours that can be printed with inks is smaller than and different from the range that can be created from white light on a computer monitor. So the final digital file, particularly one used for print, must contain reliable information about colour output.

**PART 04. TYPE/COLOUR/IMAGE**

**CHAPTER TWO**

# COLOUR

## WHERE DOES COLOUR COME FROM?

All colour comes from pure, white light. Most of us have seen light passed through a glass prism and split into the colours of the spectrum. The colours seen from the prism are transmitted directly onto the retina and are not reflected from any surface. The computer monitor is a source of artificial white light and the colours seen on a monitor are also transmitted directly onto the retina.

Since all the data that constructs computer imagery is digital, monitors need a method whereby all the colours of the spectrum can be quickly simulated. The method used displays only the three primary colours that make up white light, in a grid of pixels. By using up to 256 different intensity levels of each of the primary colours to display each pixel, it is possible to arrive at a total of 6.7 million colours (256 x 256 x 256). The three primary colours used are red, green and blue, known as RGB for short. If we created products only for screen viewing, what we would need to understand about primary colours could stop there. However, most designers also produce for print, so they have to simulate colour through printing inks. Ink colours are perceived by the viewer through the reflection of light from the printed surface. The RGB primaries apply exclusively to transmitted light, and for reflected light we need a second set of three colours. These are cyan, magenta and yellow, or CMY.

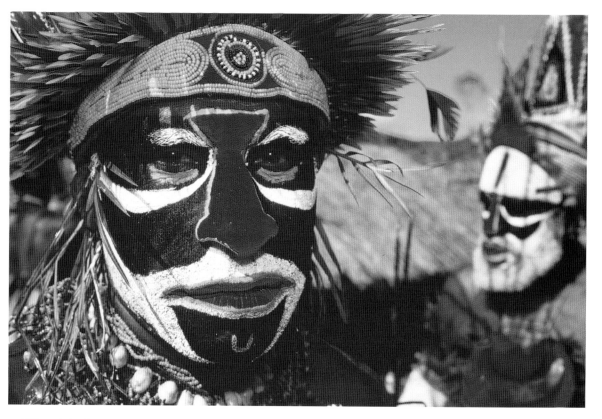

Right: The use of colour for decoration, symbolism and communication is an integral part of every human culture.

Left: This powerful poster by Nicklaus Troxler shows how vibrant colours contribute to the verve of the subject matter and help to delineate the composition.

## Additive colour

This diagram represents Red, Green and Blue light falling onto a white surface. Yellow is formed when Red and Green overlap because there is additional light in that area. When all three colours overlap, we see white since all the components of white light are now present.

## Subtractive colour

Here, three primary subtractive coloured inks have been printed onto paper. Each of these colours has one of the additive primaries subtracted so, where two overlap, two primary colours are subtracted leaving only one of the primaries visible. Once all three subtractive colours overlap then all three components of white light are absorbed; no light escapes and black is perceived. In practice a small amount of light does get relected and a true black is not achievable using only Cyan, Magenta and Yellow. To correct this, printers use a fourth ink, Black, to create deep shadow areas necessary for good colour-image reproduction.

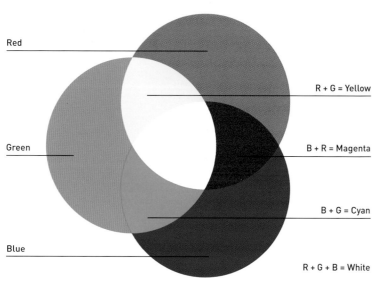

Red

Green

Blue

R + G = Yellow

B + R = Magenta

B + G = Cyan

R + G + B = White

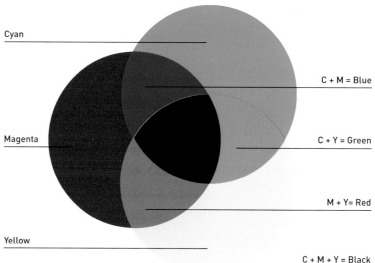

Cyan

Magenta

Yellow

C + M = Blue

C + Y = Green

M + Y= Red

C + M + Y = Black

## TRANSMITTED OR ADDITIVE COLOUR

When one primary transmitted colour is combined with another, more light is perceived than with one colour alone. When combined, red, green and blue add up to white and for this reason are referred to as primary 'additive' colours. Thus, combining red light with green light, for instance, produces a colour that starts to approach white light (in fact, yellow). Similarly, a combination of red and blue produces magenta, and a combination of blue and green produces cyan. It will be seen that each primary additive (or transmitted) colour appears the way it does because each represents white light minus two primaries. Thus, for example, red is white light minus green and blue.

## REFLECTED OR SUBTRACTIVE COLOUR

In our material world, everything we see has a particular colour because most matter absorbs white light (which we get, with varying degrees of purity, from sunlight and artificial light) to a greater or lesser extent. Black objects absorb all the white light that shines on them, whereas white objects reflect all the white light that hits them. What is generally understood to be an object's colour is, in reality, only the reflection of certain amounts of the three primary colours. It is a combination of these that is perceived and interpreted as a particular colour. For example, if an object appears red, it means that the material of which it is made is absorbing all the green and blue light, leaving only the red part of the spectrum to be reflected. Paints, inks and all other kinds of colouring pigment behave in the same way, by subtracting (absorbing) a certain amount of light and reflecting the rest.

Since pigments subtract colour from white light, it should be easy to see why red, green and blue inks cannot be combined to mix colours for printing on white paper (which reflects the red, green and blue that compose white light). Remembering that each primary additive colour is white light

Right: **Photoshop's Channels Palette** shows how an image is composed in RGB or CMYK mode. On the right are the four channels of CMYK, which appear very much like the proofs taken from each lithographic printing plate. The channels displaying RGB (left) are instantly recognizable by the areas of black in each channel which represent the absence of light. Note that the top images in these palettes are not channels themselves but show a view of the combined channels (CMYK or RGB).

minus two other primaries, it should be clear that mixing any two additive primaries as pigments (making them part of the reflective surface rather than transmitted light) will result in all colour being absorbed.

If the goal is to mix a wide range of printing colours from a small number of basic hues (say three), colours that absorb only one primary colour must be identified. You will recall that the secondary colours – cyan, magenta and yellow – are each achieved by absorbing (subtracting) just one primary colour from white light. Similarly, mixing two secondary colours will absorb (subtract) two transmitted colours and leave the third. Thus, mixing cyan pigment with yellow pigment would produce green; mixing cyan with magenta would produce blue; and mixing magenta and yellow would produce red. All printing devices can therefore use cyan, magenta and yellow as printing primary colours.

Light reflected

Light reflected

Light reflected

Light absorbed

Light absorbed

Light absorbed

**RANGE OF ACHIEVABLE COLOUR** Since the computer monitor generates white light, it is able to display virtually all the colours that the eye is capable of seeing. However, it is a fact of physics that (mirrors excepted) all objects absorb some light, even if only a very small amount. Thus the entire spectrum can never be reflected.

You may have noticed that the white of a computer screen is always so much brighter than the whitest of white printing papers. This is because paper does not reflect all the white light that falls on it. None of the many rich and vibrant pigments used in paints and inks can match the brilliance of the computer screen.

It is also impractical to use thousands of different coloured inks to reproduce coloured images. In printing, therefore, the three basic colours of cyan (C), magenta (M) and yellow (Y) are 'mixed' to simulate real-world colour as closely as possible. Black (K) ink is also added to boost shadow areas and make them crisper. Mixing is achieved by printing formations of tiny dots, each of a separate colour, that merge when viewed at reading distance. This method of reproduction is known as four-colour process (CMYK or just 'process'). The use of only cyan, magenta, yellow and black thus produces a restricted range of vibrant colours known as process colours.

Above: **Some of the brighter and subtler shades of colour will be lost when an image goes to CMYK printing. In these illustrations Photoshop's gamut warning is shown in green, revealing the shades that will be lost from the original RGB image when it is printed in CMYK.**

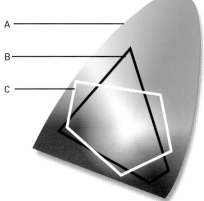

A

B

C

Left: **The human eye is able to see a greater range of colour than either CMYK printing or RGB monitors are able to reproduce. Generally, more vibrant colours are available on screen than can be printed.**

a = The visible spectrum
b = RGB monitor
c = CMYK process

Above: It is absolutely vital that, when selecting colour from a palette in their graphic arts software, it is understood that, (with the exception of pure Cyan), virtually all the PANTONE colours can be displayed on screen accurately but they will not necessarily appear correctly when printed utilizing the CMYK four colour process.

## PANTONE MATCHING SYSTEM

If a job only requires one or two colours, it would be unnecessary to run a four-colour press. A special colour of ink would be much more useful than a mix of cyan, magenta, yellow and black. Many printers once held stocks of inks from a number of different ink manufacturers but, for practical reasons, the range of colours was somewhat limited. The PANTONE Matching System was devised to meet the needs of designers who want to specify a special colour. It is essentially a set of standardized pigments and a recipe book in the form of a colour sampler containing hundreds of colours that can be created by mixing specified amounts of them.

By following these colour recipes, printers across the world can accurately mix and match any PANTONE colour from their basic stock and use it on their presses. The resulting colours are solid ink colours, known as spot colours or specials, and they are quite unlike the colours simulated by halftone dots in the four-colour printing process. Thanks to the stronger and wider range of pigments used, many PANTONE colour mixes can be more vivid and vibrant than those achievable using only cyan, magenta, yellow and black.

To give the digital graphic designer the widest range of colour choice, for print, almost all graphics arts software shows the full range of PANTONE colours as well as providing cyan, magenta, yellow and black (CMYK) controls for mixing process colours. The designer has the option of choosing either a PANTONE colour to be printed as a spot colour, or one to be simulated by cyan, magenta, yellow and black. Simulation can be successful but in many cases a good match cannot be achieved because the PANTONE colour is beyond the range achievable by the four-colour process (out of gamut).

Right: When a PANTONE colour is mixed according to the recipes shown on the swatch, it is *inks* that are being mixed to produce a single coloured ink. This is radically different from the simulation of a colour by the use of small dots of CMYK, which creates the illusion of colour change.

Left: Typical inkjet printer cartridges of black and CMYK. Some printers may have extra cartridges for pale cyan and pale magenta in order to increase the range of printed colour.

**COLOUR ATTRIBUTES**  Whether colour is transmitted directly onto the retina or reflected from different pigments (including cyan, magenta, yellow and black) it still consists of the three primaries – red, green and blue. These primaries are the ingredients of different colours but all colours have three other attributes: hue, saturation and brightness.

Above: **The Saturation level of the top picture is high (thus fully saturated) and the bottom picture is very low (desaturated). A fully saturated image contains maximum values of each colour and can often produce an exaggerated, rather than accurate, representation.**

Above: **The Brightness level of the top picture is optimum and the bottom picture is very high. Towards each extreme the contrast diminishes and thus the optimum brightness level of an image is that where the contrast is greatest.**

Understanding the attributes of hue, saturation and brightness (often referred to as HSB values) is essential to working with colour successfully. They form the basis of colour language and underpin dialogues between users of colour throughout the graphic arts industry.

### HUE

Hue is the easiest term to understand, as it is essentially interchangeable with the word 'colour'. The colours of the spectrum are often displayed in a circle or colour wheel, and we can use basic names to identify each main colour: red, orange, yellow, green, blue, cyan, magenta, blue, violet and indigo. Many hundreds of names are possible for the colours in between. When we refer to a colour as being 'orange' we are identifying its hue. It doesn't matter, for instance, whether it is a vibrant, dull or very dark orange: orange remains the common hue.

### SATURATION

Saturation refers to the vibrancy and purity of a colour. To understand saturation it is often helpful to look at its opposite, 'desaturation'. Since colours are made up from the three primary colours a total absence of light (i.e. no red, green or blue) will lead us to perceive black. If there is equal, full-strength red, green and blue, white is perceived (so it follows that white is, in fact, full colour). As grey lies somewhere between black and white, grey is made up of equal amounts of less-than-total red, green and blue. The three amounts of colour are in perfect balance, and the result is described as a totally 'desaturated' colour. If we now, for example, gradually increase the red element in our grey, while decreasing the blue and green in proportion, the grey will turn redder and eventually become a totally saturated, vibrant red. The nearer the amounts of red, green and blue are to being equally balanced, the less saturated a colour will appear. Conversely, the more difference there is in individual amounts of red, green and blue, the greater is the saturation. Saturation levels can be described as the tendency of a colour to move towards or away from being grey.

## BRIGHTNESS

Brightness (sometimes referred to as lightness or tone) refers to how much light has been used to produce the colour in question. Saturation or desaturation of a colour depends on the ratios of red to green to blue but not necessarily the overall quantity of light used to create it. If a large amount of light is used to create a colour (irrespective of the relative ratios of red, green and blue) the colour will be bright (or light). If little overall light is used then the colour is perceived as being dark.

## COLOUR MANAGEMENT

The accurate management of colour from screen to printing press is complex and difficult. Much work has gone into the production of colour 'profiles', which are software modules designed to simulate printed colours accurately on screen while taking account of known variables affecting hardware and design programs. Colour profiles are truly effective only if all programs and related hardware are catered for and are regularly calibrated. The best advice for achieving predictable colour output is to make test prints on the same printer that is used for the final work from files generated on your own workstation and look at them against your screen.

Gamma represents the level of brightness emitted by the midtone colour values of a monitor. Difficulties with gamma sometimes arise, for example, when working on an image that will be viewed on both Macintosh and Windows platforms, because while the Mac OS gamma value is 1.8, that of the Windows platform is 2.2. The higher the number, the darker the image; thus, an image created on the Mac OS using Mac gamma will appear darker when viewed on the Windows system.

Above: Understanding colour is made simple when viewing Photoshop's Colour Palette. In the examples on the left hue and brightness values have been kept the same and it is purely the change of saturation (indicated by the slider) that changes the colour applied to the image.

The examples in the centre have been modified purely by hue and those on the right by the value of brightness. Often hue, saturation and brightness controls are used in conjunction with one another but to get a better understanding of what is happening it is useful to refer to and experiment with

this palette, using one slider at a time. This method of mixing colours (found in other graphics arts applications) is invaluable for mixing controlled ranges, or sets, of colours allowing the user to maintain some attributes of colour while altering others.

Images created on the computer can range from a simple icon printed in one colour to a multi-layered photographic montage using all the colours of the spectrum. Different types of image include diagrams, charts, graphs, maps, technical illustrations, logos, icons, symbols, photographs, collages, montages and photomontages, any of which might be incorporated into a design to inform or entertain, or both.

Images are designed in different styles, for aesthetic reasons and to meet production limitations. What images are, what they do, and how they are created is of considerable importance to the graphic designer. Image-making requires care, a rich visual language, a sense of purpose and sensitivity to the way in which the outcome can affect the viewer.

Many graphic designers concerned with image-making are, or become, photographers and illustrators, with much of what they create being integral to their own designs. The graphic designer's motivation often springs from a client-generated brief, the parameters of which will often dictate the use of type and image.

## WHERE TO OBTAIN IMAGES

Rich sources of copyright and copyright-free art are available on CD and the Internet, which, together with images generated by the designer, can provide a springboard for inventive, image-based design solutions. Collections of imagery can inspire the designer into developing, simplifying or synthesizing them to support a project. This can often be detected in logo design, where several visual references may have been modified and fused into a single graphic symbol.

Much of the time, however, the graphic designer is the creative manager of visual components and uses images created by illustrators and photographers. A balance has to be maintained between giving the illustrator or photographer

**PART 04. TYPE/COLOUR/IMAGE**

**CHAPTER THREE**

# IMAGE CREATION

creative freedom and ensuring that the commissioned work complements the project. Building a good working relationship and establishing a rapport with other artists is essential to professional working practice and to getting the right results.

The advent of digital control over images has almost immeasurably expanded the creative scope of illustrators and photographers. With accessible, powerful software for creating and manipulating images at their finger tips, digital graphic designers can produce a wide range of graphic effects to incorporate into existing or newly created images. Respect for the integrity of other image-making professionals is, of course, extremely important. It is not ethical either to alter another professionals' work or to manipulate it gratuitously. However, by agreement or in collaboration, it is possible to modify the original dimensions, mood and meaning of an image.

Opposite and above: **Mood and atmosphere can be generated from creative image manipulation in a bitmap editing application. Qualities of layering, transparency and depth are obtained by the inventive use of Photshop functions.**
Designed for MacUser magazine by Tom Hingston Studio, UK

# UNDERSTANDING DIGITAL IMAGE-MAKING The development of software for easy and creative image-making continues in leaps and bounds. Just when the designer exhausts all the tools of one program, an updated version hits the market adding a plethora of new features.

As programs become feature-rich, they attempt to be all things to all people, and in doing so may mask the fact that the behaviour of some aspects of image creation is not entirely compatible with others. It is easy to be overwhelmed by the multitude of features available, so it helps to have an appreciation of some of the underlying principles.

There are essentially two different types of image-making program – painting (or image-manipulation) and drawing, also referred to as bitmap and vector (vector programs are sometimes also called 'object-orientated' software). Bitmap images do not mix readily with vector images, but they can be made to integrate and work together.

Above: **Libraries of images on CDs are popular and readily available.** Usually images are scanned at varying resolutions to meet different requirements. For example, low resolution scans provide economic file sizes for screen-based work; very high resolution is suitable for commercial print quality. Some CDs contain royalty-free images but the better images available are subject to a fee when used commercially. Be aware that altering an image digitally does not alter the laws of copyright.

Right: **Bitmap images (above right)** may be available in full colour or as 'greyscales' printed in a single colour. Images with no gradations between black and white are called line art, often refered to as 'bitmap' images (below right). (Note: bitmap is a generic term and strictly speaking can refer to any image composed of pixels.)

## BITMAP PROGRAMS

The industry-standard bitmap program, used by digital graphic designers, photographers, Web designers and the printing industry, is Adobe Photoshop. There are other bitmap programs used by artists and illustrators, such as Painter. CorelDraw also has a bitmap component called Corel PhotoPAINT, while Deneba Canvas combines drawing and bitmap editing fairly well.

Bitmap programs are used for creating single images and are not used for creating multipage documents. The principle on which the program works is that of a fine grid of pixels. Each pixel can be coloured separately and the arrangement of these pixels produces the effect of an image. This method of image-making can be likened to taking a piece of finely divided graph paper and colouring each individual square with its own colour. From a distance, the squares disappear and the overall impression of a complete image emerges. Because images are constructed purely with pixels, it is possible to use tools that modify them individually or as large groups. Because the program's tools can be made to

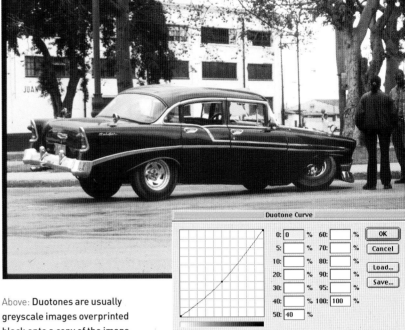

travel across these pixels to create colour changes, the term 'painting program' is often used. Tools with a variety of functions do, in effect, sweep across an image, altering the underlying pixels.

## BITMAP ADVANTAGES

Bitmap software lends itself particularly well to photographic and other 'continuous tone' images, such as paintings or illustrations. A photograph captures a realistic view of what we can see around us. In the environment, hues and shades merge imperceptibly with each other in every direction. This 'continuous tone' effect would be impossible to reproduce realistically using drawn shapes. Scanners read a photograph by recording colour values at thousands or millions of points from side to side and from top to bottom. When these colours are displayed on the computer's monitor as pixels, they are too small to see individually but give the viewer an impression of continuously changing tones. Software tools can alter pixel values in a gradual way, so maintaining realism.

The amount of detail that can been seen in a scanned picture depends entirely on how many times per inch the scanner is made to record the colour values. This figure is called the resolution. High resolution is obtained when pixel information is recorded at say 300 times per inch (300ppi); low resolution may record as few as 72 pixels per inch (72ppi).

Above: **Duotones are usually greyscale images overprinted black onto a copy of the image, which has been printed in spot colour to provide depth and interest. Generally the angle of screen for the black is set at zero and the angle of screen for the spot colour is set at 45⁰, which allows the colour to more visible. Digitization of the image allows for considerable control of the tonal range across the black and spot-colour versions of the image.**
Photo / Ed Seabourne

Below: **These images have been scanned at 300ppi, 150ppi, 72ppi and 36ppi. The lower the scan resolution the less information captured and therefore a coarser image. In order to display these images the same size, on screen or in print, we have had to the enlarge or reduce the view.**

Above: **The essence of a bitmap image is that shapes and images are made up entirely from the uniform arrangement of varying coloured pixels. There is no underlying structure to describe this shape.**

## BITMAP DISADVANTAGES

Bitmap images have two disadvantages. First, in terms of digital storage, bitmap files are very memory-intensive. The values of every pixel that makes up the image must be identified and recorded digitally. This information can be compressed to some degree by using special compression techniques such as LZW or JPEG but bitmap images are still enormous compared to text files. Second, because a bitmap image has no structure other than a sequence of pixels arranged in a grid, the only way to enlarge it is to make every pixel bigger. The viewer will soon lose the illusion of a smooth image and become aware of the individual coloured squares. This 'pixelation' makes the image appear coarse. The best way to remedy it is to re-scan the image at a sufficiently high resolution to allow for the enlargement, but this is not always practical at a late stage in production.

Left: Even apparently rough-edged images can benefit from being created by vectors. Though this logo for Chronicle Books has been enlarged greatly from the same small-scale 'Illustrator' file, it still maintains a sharp edge. This would have been impossible from a small-scale bitmap file.

Below: Bitmap applications provide photo-realism and are useful for applying graphics such as logos or advertising into real life situations. Here a corporate identity has been digitally applied to a rough image of a vehicle so the look can be tested before implementing the design.

## VECTOR-BASED PROGRAMS

Vector-based programs describe the shape of an object as a series of strategically placed points connected by lines controlled by mathematical formulas – rather like a 'join-the-dots' picture with the added benefit that the connections between points can be precisely described as straight or curved lines. The line is called a path or a vector. Paths can have thickness (stroke) and colour, and the shapes or objects they create can also be filled with a colour, gradient, texture and so forth. Each object can be moved around a page independently which allows them to be arranged and rearranged, overlaying or underlying each other as appropriate. By altering the position of the points and the ways in which the paths connect them, the vectors and the resulting shapes they make can be re-formulated.

Vectors are an ideal way of describing the outline shape of letterforms, and in fact printer font files are essentially a collection of outline vectors.

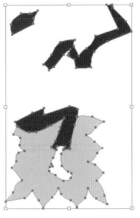

Above: Pamela Geismar of San Francisco's Chronicle Books was able to colour up the humourous illustrations of Thorina Rose, taking advantage of Illustrator 9's transparent colours for the book 'Office Kama Sutra'. It was essential to be able to lay transparent colours in Multiply mode to allow the grey tones to show through.

Above right: The fundamentals of vector shapes are points joined by straight or curved lines controlled either by moving these points or adjusting the curves between them by means of curve levers. All drawing applications use this method of creating simple or complex paths and shapes. It is well worth taking the trouble to master how to use the 'Path' or 'Pen' tools as they are absolutely essential to digital image creation.

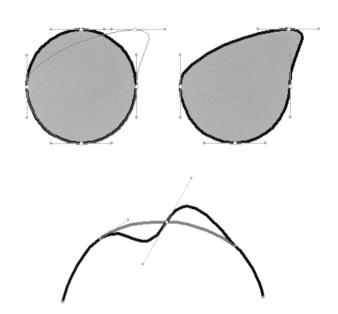

Vector images allow for good-quality scaling both on screen and when output from a printer's RIP (see p. xxx). When a vector image is re-sized, the mathematical formulae ensure that all the points and paths are repositioned so as to maintain their original relationships. Since colouring is simply the filling-in of a defined shape, the scaled shape is automatically refilled. Objects described by outline information are memory-efficient, since a relatively compact set of numbers can describe quite complex shapes and colour fills. Vectors, however, cannot produce photo-realistic images, since realism needs a constantly shifting description of tone and colour that can be satisfactorily carried out only by the subtle changes in pixel colour achievable by bitmap techniques.

Above: Here, in a bitmap editing application (Photoshop) vectors are used purely as an aid for the user to create smooth shapes to which images may be selected, cropped or painted. Once the vector has been used to carry out a function the resulting images are recorded in bitmap form.

Right: 'FreeHand', as with other drawing applications, will create non-printing guides from user-drawn shapes. This is very useful when setting up perpectives and/or plans.

## VECTORS AND BITMAPS TOGETHER

Most major graphic arts programs can handle both vectors and bitmaps, although they represent different imaging technologies. However, one or other technology generally dominates each program. For example, all page-layout and drawing programs are essentially vector-based, but they also have the ability to import bitmap pictures. The bitmap is usually contained within a placement holder, such as a 'picture box', that may or may not have a visible frame. Vectored objects such as typographic elements, graphic shapes, rules, drawn logos and technical illustrations may lie over or under imported images.

Unless it is appreciated that an image composed of a grid of pixels is fundamentally different from a vector image, whose component parts are described as outlines and filled shapes, much confusion may occur. The designer may be left wondering why certain tools and functions do not work for both kinds of image.

Page-layout programs such as QuarkXPress, Adobe PageMaker and Adobe InDesign have features that allow for a certain amount of control over the imported bitmapped

Above: A cube drawn in a vector application (right) has been 'rasterized' when opened in photoshop (left). The process converts the vector image to a bitmap (pixel-based) image.
Above left: A series of circles of increasing size produced from a single bitmap file compared to those produced from a single vector file. It is not difficult to see which are which.

Below: Adobe Streamline is a useful application which can turn bitmap images into vector files. It places points and vectors to create outlines around significant bitmap areas of tone and/or colour. The resultant outlines can then be filled with colour using a drawing application like Illustrator.

images, including scale and shape changes, and the colouring of black-and-white or greyscale pictures. The features vary slightly from one program to another. Adobe Illustrator and Macromedia FreeHand, both of which are drawing programs, have the capability of modifying imported bitmapped images through various special-effect filters, and are also able to convert (rasterize) vector objects into bitmaps. Once rasterization has taken place, the vector information is lost and the result is simply a collection of pixels.

By contrast Photoshop, a bitmap program, has some vector-based tools included to enable the user to make very accurate and smooth selections with the aid of paths. Additionally, text can be created using the outline (vector) information from the font files and still remain editable. In the end, however, vectors and editable text will need to be converted into bitmap before they can be properly integrated into the image.

Working in the opposite direction, Adobe Streamline is a useful program that can process bitmap images and produce outlines (vectors) where colours and tone change. The trace or auto-trace facility in some vector-based software can be used in the same way, especially on selected areas.

Left: When images are imported to a layout or drawing document, it is usual for only low resolution copies to be placed on the page as visual guides. When a printing device comes across a picture imported into a document it searches for the orginal, high quality file. Seen here is Quark's Usage dialog box which keeps track of where the originals of imported images are stored. One of the most common print 'problems' is when designers forget to send their original good quality scans together with their document files.

Right: Seen here is a vector (left) and bitmap (right) version of the same image. In order to maintain a similar quality of reproduction when enlarged to 200% the bitmap image must be re-scanned at a much higher resolution than before, resulting in a much larger file size. By comparison, the same vector file may be used at any size without compromise to quality. Note, though, how bitmap images create smooth transitions throughout all the subtle tonal changes whereas vector images shows well defined, hard edged, shapes.

Native Adobe Illustrator File enlarged 200% – 2.6MB

Original Native Adobe Illustrator File – 2.6MB

Native Adobe Photoshop File enlarged 200% – 11.9MB

Original Native Adobe Photoshop File – 3MB

## SCANNING AND RESOLUTION To work successfully with bitmap pictures, the impact of several different but interrelated technologies must be considered. In planning graphic reproduction the intended result needs to be established before the appropriate preparatory steps can be decided upon. In other words it is usually advisable to start from the output end and work backwards to the beginning.

### SCANNING FOR PRINT

The Print section in Part II of this book explains how a printing plate must be made for each colour in order to transfer the colour-filtered components of the image onto paper. In four- or six-colour process, the coloured areas of an original image are analysed for how much of each printing ink is required to simulate the colour at any given point. Then the location of each required ink colour is transferred to the appropriate plate as tiny, close-printing dots in a conversion procedure called halftoning. The dots in a full-colour halftone vary in size according to how much of their ink colour is required at a given spot, but even the biggest of dots is so small that it merges almost imperceptibly with the surrounding dots to create the illusion of a visually smooth change of colour, tone and intensity.

Imagesetters (output devices used to generate reproduction-quality copy for printing) have a device resolution of up to 3000 dots per inch (dpi). For most printing work, halftone dots are required at a rate or output resolution of 150 halftone dots per inch. Dividing the imagesetter resolution by the output resolution, we find that a 3000-dpi imagesetter has 20 dots with which to construct the largest halftone dot required. Since these rates per inch are linear, the largest (100 per cent) halftone dot would be 400 dots in area (20 dots square) and a 10 per cent dot would be around 40 dots in area. That is more than ample to ensure fine reproduction.

The designer's file must obviously contain all the image detail to produce all the tiny halftone dots that represent how much ink falls where. In fully digital printing and direct-to-plate (DTP) imagesetting, the dots transferred to the plate come directly from the designer's file. More conventionally, there is an intermediate stage in which the imagesetter produces prepared photographic film, through which the plate's light-sensitive, emulsion-covered surface is then exposed to light. In this case, it is the film that comes directly from the designer's file.

In order to produce output at 150dpi (output resolution), the imagesetter must receive information at a minimum of 150 pixels per inch, or ppi (input resolution). If a picture file has been scanned at a lower resolution, there will be insufficient information to satisfy the imagesetter. In the absence of such information, it will make identically sized halftone dots until new information reaches it. For instance, if a file can only provide 50ppi (one-third of the necessary linear resolution), an imagesetter set to output at 150dpi must create three identical dots in a row both across and down. This results in a group of 9 identical dots which, when printed, will look like a little square to the naked eye. Worse, the whole image will be made up of these little squares. The way to avoid this is to scan at a high enough resolution to provide at least 150 unique pieces of information for the 150 demands made by the imagesetter.

That is the theory – but there is one small, added complication. Halftone dots are arranged at angles to each other, with a unique angle for each process colour. The objective is to ensure that any pattern in the dots does not distract the human eye, so that the image appears smoother and more realistic. Since images are scanned horizontally and vertically rather than at an angle, and since imagesetters lay down the dots from left to right, the requirement to work at an angle increases the demand for accurate information across the inch. For this reason, it is recommend that images should be scanned at between one-and-a-half times and twice the intended output resolution.

There is much confusion about the terminology regarding resolution. Dpi, ppi, lpi - what's the difference? It is quite common for lay persons and professionals alike to use dpi (dots per inch ) to decribe any type of resolution. Strictly speaking we use the term samples per inch (spi) when refering to scanned bitmaps – but now ppi is usually used. Pixels per inch (ppi) refers to monitor displays and dots per inch (dpi) refers to particles of ink, toner or light that are used by printing devices to create images. Halftone dots, created from the smaller printer dots (dpi) are arranged in lines to form a mesh, or screen, and so halftone screens are expressed in lines per inch (lpi).

Above: One of the most important concepts to grasp when working with Photoshop is that when the application shows 100% in the bottom left of the picture Window, it does not mean the picture is being viewed at actual size! It means that the screen is displaying each scanned pixel with one monitor pixel (pixel for pixel). It can be seen that if an image is scanned at 72ppi (the same resolution as the monitor, which is fixed) then it will appear the correct size. If an image is scanned at, say, 300ppi, then the monitor will require 4.16 inches to show 300 pixels resulting

in a bigger looking picture. It is not possible to mix pixel resolutions in the one image so when images of variable resolutions are copied and pasted, they will appear to shrink or expand in order to fit the pixel grid of the host image.

Right: The ideal resolution for print work is 300ppi (top). If the resolution is too low or the image is enlarged too much – thereby reducing the effective resolution – then unwanted pixelation occurs (centre). If no halftone dots need to be created, as in lineart images – one may scan at the maximum resolution of the output device which could be as much as 3,000dpi. However a scan at 600ppi will normally be sufficient to obtain a visually sharp edge (bottom).

Left: When an area is enlarged on screen for a zoomed-in view, the application's software creates squares of identically coloured pixels to give the illusion of enlargement. Pixels are still displayed at the rate of 72ppi but the illusion is that they have 'grown'. A similar effect is seen when an image scanned at low resolution is printed and there are not enough pixels per inch for every halftone dot required. So a few neighbouring halftone dots will use the same information and therefore appear identical, vertically and horizontally. This results in visible squares and the picture appearing 'pixelated'.

Above and right: **Image size and resolution are interlinked.** When an image is scanned its size may be expressed in two ways. Firstly, by how many pixels it measures horizontally and vertically: this need not dictate how big it will print, just how many bits of information record the picture. Secondly, we are able to give the picture a physical size so that when sent to a printer there is some reference as to how big the picture should be reproduced. Above left are two versions of a picture that has been scanned once - its pixel size is 148pixels x 118pixels. The top picture is described physically 2.5cm x 2cm at a resolution of 150ppi whereas the lower picture is described 5cm x 4cm at a resolution of 75ppi. This is very similar to looking at a mosaic on a wall close to or from a distance - the number of squares that make up the picture do not change, it is the viewing distance that makes the picture appear biggger or smaller and coarser or smoother respectively.

By contrast the picture on the right has been given the same physical dimensions as the one at lower left but has been scanned at a far higher resolution (300ppi) so that the pixel size is 591pixels x 472pixels.

Most designers tend to err on the side of caution and stick to scanning at double the halftone rate. So, for most general commercial offset litho printing, pictures are scanned at 300ppi at the final output size. There will be no quality problems if a picture is scanned at higher resolution, but equally there will be no quality improvement. However, there will be an enormous increase in file size and processing time, which will slow all processes down.

If an image is to be printed in solid process colour, requiring no halftone dots, it is known as line art. Theoretically, for the best results you could scan that image at 3000ppi to match every imagesetter dot. However this is impractical for file size reasons. For crisp results, line work should be scanned at 600ppi. Any extra quality obtained from scanning at much above this level of resolution is imperceptible.

The resolution of an image must be correct for the size at which it will be printed. It is no good scanning a picture at 300ppi and then enlarging it dramatically in a page-layout program. Your original picture file will still contain the same information, but it will now be stretched two or three times beyond its original dimensions. This has the effect of substantially lowering the resolution relative to its new size. A small amount of scaling up or down may not result in print quality problems, but it is always best to scan a picture at the correct resolution for the intended output size. Fortunately, most scanning software allows the user to set a resolution and a scaling ratio. The scanner then ensures that the picture is scanned so that the resolution is correct at the new image size.

When buying a scanner, it is important to ascertain the highest resolution actually achievable. Some manufacturers claim a very high output, but this is sometimes achieved by interpolation – the software recalculates its best actual result to add more pixels per inch. Although interpolation will smooth out an image, it will capture no more detail, so always judge by 'optical' not 'interpolated' resolution. Interpolation also takes place when an image or parts of it are rotated or transformed in some way. Sometimes, owing to looming deadlines or unavailability of the original image, a designer will need to increase a picture's resolution directly in the file. PhotoShop can interpolate and increase the number of pixels in an image; if this proves necessary, the bicubic method should always be used for the best results.

## FOR SCREEN PRODUCTS

Resolution issues for image use in Web pages or multimedia production are much more straight-forward than for print, since the designer knows that the audience will be viewing images on a monitor not dissimilar to the one on which the design was created. There is a lot of confusion over the difference between Macintosh and Windows screen resolution. Text in Windows is drawn using a 96ppi model, but you can safely stick to 72ppi for your bitmap design work. The good news is that 72ppi images contain just 5184 pixels per square inch, less than one fifteenth of the size of a 300ppi file. This makes for quick transmission over the Internet.

## FILE FORMATS FOR BITMAPPED IMAGES

Digital images can be saved in a variety of file formats, each of which has its own unique way of storing information and of handling digital data. Choice of file format is important to the digital graphic designer, since the one selected will have a bearing on the efficiency and performance of the stored image.

**PICT** (Macintosh picture file) is the Macintosh operating system standard format for saving bitmap information. It cannot store CMYK information.

**BMP** (Windows bitmap) is the Windows operating system standard format for saving bitmap information. It cannot store CMYK information.

**TIFF** (Tagged Image File Format) is the most widely used file format for print. It can store bitmap (black and white), greyscale and colour information (RGB, CMYK or indexed colour) and include masking information. Furthermore, TIFF files can be compressed without losing data. Most programs can read TIFF files. The Macintosh and the PC use different versions of the TIFF format, but both versions can be read by Photoshop and re-saved for the platform required. Clipping paths cannot be saved in the TIFF format.

**JPEG** (Joint Photographic Experts Group) is favoured for photographic images, especially on the Internet. It can offer high compression of file sizes, reducing them to a fraction of their original size. The drawback is the loss of information in the compression process: the greater the compression, the greater the loss. The user, who can make a trade-off between file size and quality, can control the amount of compression. Repeated compression and decompression will make the quality worse.

**EPS** (Encapsulated PostScript) is a PostScript image file, with an encapsulated screen preview, most often produced by vector image programs. It may be re-sized or cropped but usually no alteration to the content can be made other than by the program in which it was created. Photoshop can open and save EPS files, and can also compress them to JPEG. If a clipping path (cutout instruction) has been created in Photoshop, saving in EPS format ensures that when the file is opened in another program, it can appear in the shape to which it was clipped. EPS files are also able to hold information about the appearance and output of duotones.

**GIF** (Graphics Interchange Format) is a format normally only used for Web work. It supports only 256 indexed colours. A useful feature is that, on saving, it is possible to select a colour to appear as transparent for cutout effects.

Below: **In Photoshop, file formats may be selected from the Save or Save As menu. Some file formats, such as Pixar or Amiga, are for more specialised computing systems and for most users may be ignored. Often, some file formats are 'greyed out' on the popup menu. This is because some work only with RGB images and some only with CMYK images. When all of the file formats are 'greyed out', except Photoshop format, this indicates that the picture contains layers that will have to be flattened before the image can be recorded in any other file format. To create GIFs the Export menu (under File) needs to be selected unless the image colour has been indexed.**

Far left: **Picture files, when saved, have mini previews displayed in their relevant folder Windows, which is useful for quick selection.**

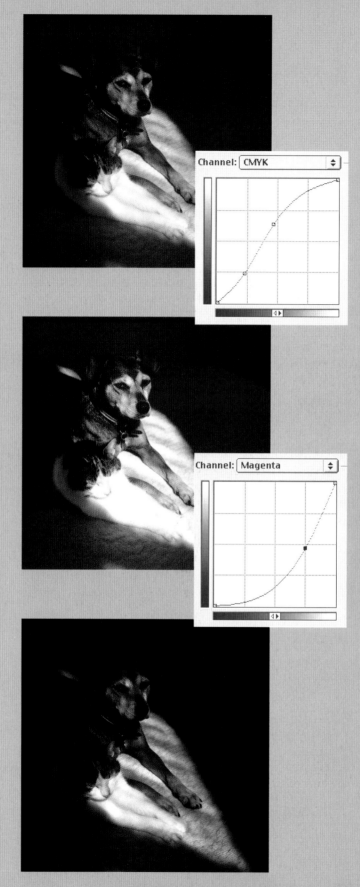

Above: **Transformations in Photoshop include scaling, rotating, distorting and perspective. The History palette shows each move taken and allows the user to go back several stages if desired.**

Right: **The Curves control in Photoshop provides a very sensitive method of picture control by allowing the alteration of pixel brightness across all of the colour channels. Each channel may be controlled separately facilitating the inrease or decrease of that colour in any part of the the image between shadows, at one extreme, and highlights at the other.**

## WORKING WITH BITMAP IMAGES IN PAINTING PROGRAMS

Working on a bitmap image is much more flexible than working with the object-oriented, structured nature of vector shapes. Tools, generically termed 'painting tools', can be drawn across a field of tiny pixels to alter them in various ways.

Whether you have selected the eraser, pencil tool or airbrush, you are able to assign a 'brush' size to it. This is measured in pixels (e.g. 1-pixel brush, 10-pixel brush, 35-pixel brush and so on) to describe the area that brush will have effect on. Painting tools can also be assigned an opacity level to determine the strength of 'painting' that the particular tool will have. A colour selected from a range of sources may also be chosen for the tool in use.

Photoshop (the industry standard image manipulation program) has become an extremely powerful, and sometimes bewilderingly complex tool – yet, at its simplest, it is a number-crunching factory. The whole of an image is comprised of millions of regimented pixels, each with a 24-bit binary number dictating the colour it represents. As painting tools are passed over these pixels, their numerical values are changed. To get a clearer idea of how this is achieved, it is useful to breakdown Photoshop's functions into basic operations. Then we shall look at transformations and other image-manipulation features.

### PAINTING WITH TOOLS

Images can be modified by using painting tools, either at full strength or with the opacity level turned down. Changes are carried out in a painterly fashion with the tools responding to hand and mouse control. The rubber-stamp tool is probably the most useful painting tool, allowing a point on an image to be selected and information to be copied from that point to the brush. The information is then used as the painting medium – a form of image-cloning.

Above: **The three fundamental painting tools of Photoshop - Brush, Pencil and Airbrush. Most significant is the default antialiasing of the Brush and Airbrush compared to the pencil. Antialiasing is a technique used by software to place intermediate pixels of lighter tone between one colour and another to create an impression of smoothness. Antialiasing replicates the way the eye sees and helps create photo-realistic imagery.**

Right: **Probably the most useful painting tool in all of Photoshop's armoury, the Rubber Stamp Tool (Cloning Tool) allows one part of an image to be painted across to another part. Combining subtlety of brush size and strength of opacity it is possible to eradicate unwanted material and replace it with other image-forming pixels. In the Window to the right can be seen a circle, which is the Rubber Stamp brush and the cross hair, which indicates the place from where the information is being copied.**

### GLOBAL PAINTING

Large areas, or selected areas of the image, may be filled using instructions from a popup menu. The same colours and opacities as used by the brushes are available.

### SELECTING

If only an identified area within a picture is to be painted, a number of tools can be used to select and isolate accurately the area required. It can be done with rectangular, oval or freehand tools, as well as a magic wand that selects areas of like colour.

### TRANSFORMATIONS

Photoshop menus allow for either the whole image or a selected part of it to be rotated, inverted, distorted, or inverted (colours reversed). Other transformations are also possible.

## GLOBAL COLOUR ADJUSTMENT

Global colour adjustment allows the designer to modify either the entire image or a selected area for colour balance, brightness and contrast, saturation levels, colour replacement and general fine-tuning. The controls are available on a menu, and calculations are carried out and implemented throughout the selection according to the type of adjustment selected.

Right and below: Layer Masks are used to control the amount of image on one layer being viewed. Seen here is a Layer Mask, attached to Layer 1, which is controlling the amount of image appearing thus permitting some of the image in the background layer to show through.

Below: The beauty of masks is that they can be saved and called up any time to select a particular area of an image. Furthermore, a mask can be added to and subtracted from, using any of the painting tools, brush sizes and/or opacities, providing a highly detailed and subtle method of selecting areas for modification as and when required.

Original image

Quickmask

Mask applied

## LAYERS

Layers exist to help the graphic designer create montage work as well as to facilitate making changes to a picture without damaging existing work. Photoshop's layer feature works just like putting a sheet of clear film over your image and painting onto it. The original image can be seen through the layer and, if you do not like what you have created on the layer, parts of it can be erased or thrown away. The important thing is that the original remains intact. Photoshop is cleverly able to apply varying opacities (and many other properties) to each layer to controllable degrees, giving the impression of images fusing into one another.

## ALPHA CHANNELS AND MASKS

A colour file has, by default, a channel dedicated to each primary colour – red, green and blue. In the case of CMYK files, there are four channels. Extra channels (alpha channels) are used for masking information. A mask can be thought of simply as a stencil, a tool that

Above: **Colour Modes** are the way in which colours may be painted onto an image, taking into account the value of the pixels over which they are being painted. The colour blue has been painted across half of the above pictures but the colour 'Mode' selected has been changed for each. From left to right: Colour, Overlay, Multiply, Saturation and Luminosity. The last two are interesting in that only one attribute of blue is being used to change the picture, that is to say the pixels have been changed to match only the value of blue's saturation in one picture and only the value of blue's luminousity in the other.

prevents you from painting over a certain area. This is exactly what Photoshop masks do: you can create your own mask in an alpha channel and bring it into play to paint the shape created by the mask. If you have spent a considerable time in making a selection using some or all of the selection tools, it is usually worth using that selection to make and save a mask. If that selection is needed again, you have only to call up the mask. Masks that are saved with files can be used by layout programs to create cutout images.

## WORKING WITH COLOUR ATTRIBUTES AND COLOUR MODES

In applying colour using brushes or global fills, it is possible to paint with attributes of colour rather than with the colour itself. For instance, if a vibrant red is selected from the palette and a brush set to the colour mode called 'luminosity', the underlying pixels will not change to red when painting starts but will simply be altered to match the luminosity value of the red. Using the colour mode menu allows the designer to colour intelligently. If colour is applied with the 'colour' mode selected, the underlying pixels will change colour but the light and shade qualities will remain unchanged. There are many different colour modes with which to paint, each one affecting the underlying pixels in its unique way.

## FILTERS

Filters apply special effects to images or parts of images enabling many interesting and novel effects to be created quickly. Photoshop is supplied with many interesting standard filters, but dozens of other filters are available from third-party manufacturers, including EyeCandy and Kai's Power Tools.

Left: Just some of the many filters and effects available to modify images. Combinations of filters and the use of a filter several times over provide interesting and more extensive results. From top left clockwise – original picture, frosted glass, find edges, emboss, feather edges, wind blast, colour halftone, pinch.

## WORKING WITH DRAWING (VECTOR) PROGRAMS The vectors used in drawing programs are called Bézier curves. All drawing programs handle Bézier curves in a similar fashion: a pen tool allows the user to set a series of points on the page, and these will automatically be joined by lines.

The shape of these lines is dictated by the way in which the pen is manipulated by dragging and clicking the mouse. Each point, when selected, will display one or two non-printing 'curve handles'. A given point may be selected later and the handles manipulated to modify the curves. The points themselves can be repositioned to create revised shapes.

Drawing programs give the digital graphic designer many powerful tools with which to create complex shapes, to apply special effects and to speed up many otherwise laborious tasks. Not all drawing programs offer identical tools, although most of them do share a core set of features. The menus and terminology employed may also differ, as may the graphical presentation of tools. For example, both Illustrator and FreeHand can convert type into points and vectors; the operation is called 'Create Outlines' in Illustrator but 'Convert to Paths' in FreeHand.

Left: Just a few ways of using type in a drawing program. The type may be converted to paths in order to make adjustments to the letterforms. The shape of type converted to paths may be used as a picture mask and drawn shapes (in this case type) may be rasterised into a bitmap image so that bitmap filters can be used. Of course, once an image has been rasterised it will no longer have any vector structure.

### SOME OF THE FEATURES OFFERED BY DRAWING PROGRAMS

✳ Typographic functions are comparable with those found in leading page-layout programs, so that all character and paragraph formatting and spacing can be applied, together with layout functions such as multiple columns and text flow.

✳ Text can be converted to paths so that letterforms can be used in the same way as any other hand-drawn object.

✳ Shapes may be stroked (given a coloured outline), filled, cut, rotated, skewed, distorted, duplicated, mirrored, scaled and added to. They may also be grouped, fused, cropped or used to crop others, used as a mask, used to contain a picture and used to make patterns.

✳ User-defined colour palettes can be made up from RGB, CMYK and HSB models as well as from colour libraries such as PANTONE.

✳ Many guides, grids and views are available to support image construction. Views such as 'artwork' mode show only points and paths, without colour or fills, to help to clarify highly complex pictures and speed up screen rendering.

✳ Layers can be used to build up images in coherent groupings. These may be locked against accidental deletion and may also be hidden while other layers are being worked on.

✳ Numerous filters are available to create special alterations and effects with shapes or groups of shapes.

✳ Shapes or groups of shapes can be rasterized, which enables them to be used with an imported bitmap image.

✳ A range of bitmap-only filters may be applied to any imported bitmap or rasterized image.

✳ Multiple blends may be used between two shapes to act as a morphing technique.

✳ Space and align tools allow for swift arrangement of disparate elements.

Page-layout applications are also vector based, but generally have fewer drawing tools than dedicated drawing programs. All these features contain additional sub-features of their own, allowing many permutations. The powerful software that drives these programs demands determination to master some of the techniques.

In almost every case your finished drawings should be saved in EPS format, since only the Postscript language is able to make sense of vector information and is capable of converting it for print. A few applications, notably Photoshop Freeway, FreeHand and After Effects, can read Illustrator files directly, in some cases making better use of that format.

As with bitmap programs, the major vector-based applications have many features for preparing artwork for further dedicated animation and Web authoring software.

Above and right:
Illustrator Lawrence Zeegen uses FreeHand to assemble and manipulate a combination of bitmap and drawn images. When displayed in 'artwork' form it is easy to see the entire structure and layout of object-oriented components.
Design by Lawrence Zeegen, UK

# GLOSSARY

**animation** The process of creating a moving image by rapidly moving from one still image to the next. Traditionally achieved through a laborious process of drawing or painting each frame, animations are now created with specialist software *(qv)* that renders sequences in a variety of formats.

**antialiasing** The strategic insertion of pixels *(qv)* of various shades around parts of the letterform to create an illusion of relative stroke bulk and smoothness. Used by default in certain programs, for example Adobe products.

**Apple Macintosh** The brand name of Apple Computer's range of PCs *(qv)*. The Macintosh (or 'Mac') was the first personal computer to make use of the graphical user interface that had been pioneered by Xerox at the Palo Alto Research Center. The use of this interface provided the platform for the software *(qv)* applications that gave rise to desktop publishing, revolutionizing graphic design.

**authoring tool** Software *(qv)* for creating interactive presentations or websites. Such programs typically include text, drawing, painting, animation *(qv)* and audio features. These are combined with a scripting language that is used to determine how each element of the page or screen behaves – for example, it may be used to ensure that a movie is played when a certain button *(qv)* is pressed.

**bandwidth** The measure of the speed at which information is passed between two points (for example, between two modems *(qv)* or from memory to disk). The broader the bandwidth, the faster the data flow. Bandwidth is usually measured in cycles per second (hertz) or bits per second (bps).

**Bézier tools** Vector-based *(qv)* drawing tools, employed by many drawing programs. A pen tool allows the user to place a series of points on the page; the points are then automatically joined by a line. The points may be moved or otherwise edited to create new shapes.

**bit** A contraction of 'binary digit', the smallest unit of information that a computer can use. A bit may have one of two potential values: on or off, positive or negative, 1 or 0, something or nothing. Eight bits form a byte, the unit that is required to store an alphabet character.

**bitmap** Any text character or image that is composed of dots. A bitmap is a 'map' of bits *(qv)* that correspond with the items – pixels *(qv)*, for example – that are required to represent the image. 'Bitmapped fonts' are composed of dots or pixels (as opposed to 'outline fonts', which are composed of vectors*(qv)*), and are often used to render PostScript *(qv)* Type I fonts onscreen (and thus are also known as 'screen fonts'). To draw the character shapes accurately, the computer must have a bitmap installed for each character size; if this is not present, the character will take on a jagged appearance. TrueType *(qv)* fonts are outline fonts, and thus do not require bitmapped versions. The use of Adobe Type Manager also means that bitmapped fonts can be avoided. Similarly, bitmapped graphics are those that employ pixels rather than vectors, and these may also take on a jagged appearance when viewed at an enlarged size.

**bleed** The margin outside the trimmed area of a sheet, which allows for tints, images and other matter to print beyond the edge of the page. If sheets are printed without bleed, it is generally not possible to print matter right up to the edge of the page.

**body text** The matter that forms the main text of a printed book, excluding captions *(qv)*, headings *(qv)*, page numbers and so on.

**brand guardian** A person who is employed, usually by the client of a design or advertising agency, to ensure that the corporate brand identity of the client company is consistently presented.

**broadband** Telecommunications that employ a high bandwidth (qv), enabling a faster rate of data flow.

**browser** An application that enables the user to view (or 'browse') Web *(qv)* pages across the Internet *(qv)*. The most widely used browsers are Netscape Navigator and Microsoft Internet Explorer. Version numbers are particularly important in the use of browsers, as they indicate the level of HTML *(qv)* that can be supported.

**button** An interface control, usually in a dialog box, that is clicked by the user to designate, confirm or cancel an action. Default buttons are usually emphasized by a heavy border and can be activated using the Return or Enter keys.

**CAD** Acronym for 'computer-aided design'. May be used to refer to any design carried out using a computer, but is usually used for three-dimensional *(qv)* design, such as product design or architecture, in which software *(qv)* is used to control the entire process from concept to finished product.

**caption** Strictly speaking, a caption is a headline printed above an illustration, identifying the contents of the image. However, the word is now used to describe any descriptive text that accompanies illustrative matter.

**CD-ROM** Acronym for compact disk, read-only memory'. A CD technology that was originally developed for the storage and distribution of digital data. Based on audio CD technology, CD-ROMs come in two formats: 74 minutes (650 megabytes of data) and 63 minutes (550 megabytes).

**client-side image map** An image map *(qv)* that holds everything to do with the map, including URL *(qv)* addresses, within HTML *(qv)* code.

**CMYK** In four-colour process *(qv)* printing, an abbreviation for cyan, magenta, yellow and black (black being denoted by 'K' for 'key plate').

**compression** The technique of rearranging data so that it either occupies less space on disk, or transfers more quickly between devices or along communication lines. Different kinds of compression are used for different kinds of data: applications, for example, must not lose any data when compressed, whereas images and movies can tolerate a certain amount of data loss.

**contrast** The degree of difference between tones in an image (or computer monitor) from the lightest to the darkest. 'High contrast' describes an image with light highlights and dark shadows but few shades in between, whereas a 'low contrast' image is one with even tones and few dark areas or light highlights.

**corporate identity** A design or set of designs for use on corporate stationery, livery, etc.

**CSS** Abbreviation for 'cascading style sheets'. These allow the Web *(qv)* designer to exercise control over typography and layout in much the same way as an ordinary page-layout program, enabling him or her to apply preset formats *(qv)* to paragraphs, individual page elements or entire pages. Several style sheets can be applied to a single page, thus 'cascading'.

the complete guide to digital graphic design

**default settings** The settings of a hardware device or software *(qv)* program that are determined at the time of manufacture. These settings remain in effect until the user changes them; such changes will be stored in a 'preferences' file. Default settings are otherwise known as 'factory' settings.

**Director** Macromedia's CD-ROM *(qv)* authoring software *(qv)*.

**display type** Text that employs large-size fonts *(qv)* – usually 14pt or more – for headings *(qv)*, or any matter that is intended to stand out or be highlighted on the page.

**download** The transfer of data from a remote computer – such as an Internet *(qv)* server – to a PC *(qv)*.

**dpi** Abbreviation for 'dots per inch'. A unit of measurement used to represent the resolution *(qv)* of devices such as printers and image setters. The closer the dots (ie, the higher the value), the better the quality. Typical values include 300dpi for a laser printer, and 2450dpi+ for an image setter. Dots per inch is sometimes erroneously used as a value when discussing monitors or images; the correct unit in these cases is ppi (pixels *(qv)* per inch).

**DVD** Abbreviation for 'digital versatile (or video) disk'. A storage disk similar to a CD-ROM *(qv)*, but distinguished by its greater capacity (up to 17.08 gigabytes).

**embedded fonts** Fonts *(qv)* that are fixed within files, meaning that the original font folder does not need to be provided in order for the file to be printed or set.

**embossing** Relief printing or stamping in which dies are used to impress a design into the surface or paper, leather or cloth so that the letters or images are raised above the surface of the paper.

**EPS** Abbreviation for 'encapsulated PostScript'. A graphics file format used primarily for storing object-oriented or vector *(qv)* graphics. An EPS file consists of two parts: PostScript *(qv)* code, which tells the printer how to print the image; and an onscreen preview, usually in JPEG *(qv)*, TIFF *(qv)* or PICT format.

**film** The material that provides the template for printing plates. A cellulose acetate-based material, coated with light-sensitive emulsion so that images and text can be recorded photographically.

**finishing** As the name implies, the final part of the print production process. It encompasses various processes, including collating, trimming, folding, binding, embossing *(qv)*, laminating *(qv)*, varnishing *(qv)* and so on.

**Fireworks** A Web-specific graphics production tool by Macromedia.

**Flash** Macromedia software *(qv)* for producing vector *(qv)* graphics and animations for Web *(qv)* presentations. Flash generates small files that are quick to download *(qv)* and, being vector-based, the graphics may be scaled to any dimension without an increase in file size.

**font** A complete set of type characters of the same size, style and design.

**format** In printing, the size or orientation of a book or page.

**four-colour process** Any printing process that reproduces full-colour images which have been separated into three basic 'process' colours – cyan, magenta and yellow – with a fourth colour, black, added for greater contrast. *See also CMYK.*

**frames (1)** Decorative designs or rules surrounding items of matter on a page.

**frames (2)** On the Web *(qv)*, a means of displaying more than one page at a time within the same window: the window is divided into separate areas, known as frames, each one displaying different content.

**Freehand** Vector-based *(qv)* drawing software by Macromedia.

**Freeway** A website layout program produced by SoftPress.

**GIF** Acronym for 'graphic interchange format'. A bitmapped *(qv)* graphics file format that compresses *(qv)* data without losing any, as opposed to JPEGs *(qv)*, which tend to lose data.

**gobos** Small metal or glass disks with designs printed onto them or cut into them.

**GoLive** A website layout program produced by Adobe.

**graphic** A general term that is used to describe any illustration or drawn design. May also be used for a type design based on drawn letters.

**grid** A template *(qv)* – usually showing such things as column widths, picture areas and trim sizes – used to design publications with multiple pages, to ensure that the basic design remains consistent.

**hairline rule** The thinnest line it is possible to print. It usually has a width of 0.25pt.

**halftone (1)** The technique of reproducing a continuous tone image on a printing press by breaking it up into a pattern of equally spaced dots of varying sizes. The dot size determines tones and shades: the larger the dot, the darker the shade.

**halftone (2)** An image reproduced using the halftone process.

**heading** A title that appears at the top of a chapter, or at the beginning of a subdivision within the text.

**hierarchy of information** The technique of arranging information in a graded order, which establishes priorities and helps users to find what they want.

**hinting** In typography, information contained within outline fonts *(qv)* that modifies character shapes to enhance them when they are displayed or printed at low resolutions *(qv)*.

**HSB** Abbreviation for 'hue, saturation and brightness'.

**HTML** Abbreviation for 'hypertext mark-up language'. A text-based page-description language used to format documents published on the Web *(qv)* and viewed on Web browsers.

**hue** Pure spectral colour that distinguishes a colour from other colours. For example, red is a different hue from blue. Light red and dark red may contain varying amounts of white and black, but they are the same hue.

**hyperlink** A contraction of 'hypertext link', a link to other documents that is embedded within the original document. It may be underlined or highlighted in a different colour. Clicking on a hyperlink will take the user to another document or website.

**Illustrator** Vector-based *(qv)* drawing software by Adobe.

**image map** An image that contains embedded links to other documents or websites. These links are activated when the appropriate area of the image is clicked on.

**ImageReady** Software *(qv)* for the production of Web-ready images, produced by Adobe.

**imposition** The arrangement of pages in the sequence and position in which they will appear on the printed sheet, with appropriate margins for folding and trimming, before platemaking and printing.

**InDesign** Desktop publishing software *(qv)* produced by Adobe.

**ink** A fluid comprising solvents and oils in which is suspended a finely-ground pigment of dyes, minerals or synthetic dyes, which provide colour. There are many different types of ink for the various printing processes.

# GLOSSARY

**inkjet printer** A printing device that creates an image by spraying tiny jets of ink on to the paper surface at high speed.

**Internet** The entire collection of connected worldwide networks, including those used solely for the Web (qv).

**Internet Explorer** Web browsing software (qv) from Microsoft.

**intranet** A network of computers similar to the Internet (qv), but to which the general public does not have access. Mainly used by large corporations or governmental institutions.

**ISDN** Abbreviation for 'integrated services digital network'. A telecommunications technology that transmits data on special digital lines rather than on old-fashioned analogue lines, and is thus much faster.

**ISP** Abbreviation for 'Internet (qv) service provider'. Any organization that provides access to the Internet. Most ISPs also provide other services, such as email addresses.

**JavaScript** Netscape's Java-like scripting language, which provides a simplified method of adding dynamic effects to Web (qv) pages.

**JPEG** Abbreviation for 'Joint Photographic Experts Group'. This International Standards Organization group defines compression standards for bitmapped (qv) colour images, and it has given its name to this popular compressed (qv) file format. JPEG files are 'lossy' (ie, they lose data during compression), but they are suitable for graduated tone images.

**kerning** The adjustment of the space between adjacent type characters to optimize their appearance. Kerning should not be confused with tracking (qv), which involves the adjustment of space over a number of adjacent characters.

**lamination** The application of transparent or coloured, shiny, plastic films to printed matter to protect or enhance it.

**layers** In some applications, a level to which the user can consign an element of the design being worked on. Individual layers can be active (meaning that they can be worked on) or non-active.

**layout** The placement of various elements – text, headings (qv), images – on a printed page.

**leading** The spacing between lines of type.

**Lingo** A powerful scripting language contained within Macromedia's Director (qv) software (qv).

**Mac OS** The operating system used on Apple's 'Macintosh' computers.

**master page** In some applications, a template (qv) that includes attributes that will be common to all pages, such as the number of text columns, page numbers and so on.

**Media Player** The most widely used multimedia player application. Part of the Microsoft Windows suite.

**modem** Contraction of 'modulator–demodulator'. A device that converts digital data to analogue for transfer from one computer to another via standard telephone lines.

**mounting** The process of sticking artwork on to a thick piece of board, usually for display or presentation purposes.

**MP3** Abbreviation for 'MPEG audio layer 3'. A compressed (qv) audio file format.

**offset lithography** A common bulk printing method involving the use of photographic plates.

**PageMaker** Vector-based (qv) page make-up software from Adobe.

**PANTONE** The proprietary trademark for Pantone's system of colour standards, control and quality requirements, in which each

colour bears a description of its formulation (in percentages) for subsequent printing.

**PC** Abbreviation for 'personal computer'. The term is generally used to denote any computer that is IBM-compatible and runs the Windows (qv) operating system (as opposed to the Mac OS (qv), for example).

**PDF** Abbreviation for 'portable document format'. A cross-platform format that allows complex, multi-featured documents to be created, retaining all text and picture formatting, then viewed and printed on any computer with an appropriate 'reader', particularly Adobe Acrobat Reader.

**Photoshop** Powerful, industry-standard image manipulation software from Adobe.

**pictogram** A simplified, pictorial symbol distilled to its salient features to represent an object or concept.

**pixel** Contraction of 'picture element'. The smallest component of a digitally-generated image, such as a single dot of light on a computer monitor. In its most simple form, one pixel corresponds to a single bit (qv): 0 = off, or white; 1 = on, or black. In colour and greyscale images (or monitors), one pixel may correspond to several bits: an 8-bit pixel, for example, can be displayed in any of 256 colours (the total number of different configurations that can be achieved by eight 0s and 1s).

**plug-in** Software (qv), usually developed by a third party, that extends the capabilities of a program. Plug-ins are common in image editing and page layout software for such things as special effects filters. They are also common in Web (qv) browsers for playing such things as movies and audio files.

**PNG** Abbreviation for 'portable network graphics'. A file format for images used on the Web (qv) that provides 10 to 30 per cent 'lossless' compression (qv) (meaning that no data is lost, as opposed to JPEG files (qv).

**point** The basic unit of Anglo-American type measurement in which the inch is divided into 72 points.

**PostScript** Adobe's proprietary page description language for image output to laser printers and high-resolution (qv) image setters.

**pre-press** Any or all of the reproduction processes that occur between design and printing, especially colour separation.

**proof** A prototype of a job, taken at various stages from laser printers, image setters, inked plates, screens and so on, in order to check the progress, quality and accuracy of the work. *See also* soft proof p. 70.

**QuarkWrapture** Powerful packaging design application from Quark.

**QuarkXPress** Industry standard page layout program.

**QuickTime** Apple Computer's software (qv) program and system extension, which enables computers running either Windows (qv) or the Mac OS (qv) to play digital movies and audio files, particularly over the Internet (qv) and in multimedia applications.

**rasterize/rasterization** Deriving from the latin 'rastrum' (rake), a 'raster image' is any image defined as rows of pixels, dots or lines created in a 'raking' sequence, i.e. from top to bottom of an image area, monitor, etc. On a monitor, the screen image is made up from a pattern of several hundred parallel lines created by an electron beam that 'rakes' the screen from top to bottom in about one-sixtieth of a second. An image is created by the varying intensity of the beam's

the complete guide to digital graphic design

brightness at different points. The speed at which the image or frame is created is the 'refresh' rate.

**Real Audio** An audio-file player from Real Networks. Highly compressed *(qv)* for optimum playback performance.

**reprographic printing** Individual or short-run or copying printing, typically using photocopiers rather than commerical printing presses.

**resolution** The degree of quality, definition or clarity with which an image is scanned *(qv)* or displayed. The concept is used in connection with monitors, printers and other output devices.

**RGB** Abbreviation for 'red, green, blue'. The primary colours of the 'additive' colour model, used in video technology, and therefore in colour monitors. Employed for Web *(qv)* and multimedia products that will not be printed using the traditional CMYK *(qv)* model.

**RIP** Acronym for 'raster image process'. The conversion of data that has been generated in a page-description language, such as PostScript *(qv)* (in other words, a page that has been put together by a designer), into a rasterized (qv) form that can be output by a high-resolution *(qv)* imagesetter for use in commercial printing.

**rollover** The rapid substitution of one or more images when a mouse pointer is rolled over the original image. Used for navigation buttons on Web *(qv)* pages.

**rule** A printed line.

**sans serif** The generic name for type designs that lack the small extensions (serifs, *qv*) at the ends of the main strokes of the letters. Sometimes called 'lineal type'.

**saturation** The variation in colour of the same tonal brightness from none (grey) through pastel shades (low saturation) to pure colour with no grey (high or 'full' saturation).

**scamp** A preliminary drawing showing a proposed design.

**scan, scanner** A scanner is an electronic device that uses a (sequentially) moving light beam to convert artworks or photographs into digital forms (scans), so that they can be manipulated by a computer or be output to separated film. Some scanners are simple, flatbed, desktop models that are generally used for creating positional pictures; others are sophisticated devices ('drum scanners') that are used for high-quality reproductions.

**serif** The short counterstroke or finishing stroke at the end of the main stroke of a type character.

**ShockWave** A Macromedia technology used for making Director *(qv)* presentations that can be delivered across the Web *(qv)* and viewed with a browser *(qv)*.

**silkscreen printing** ('screen printing') A method of printing in which ink *(qv)* is forced through a stencil fixed to a screen made of silk. Modern printers more commonly use a screen made of synthetic material .

**software** Specially written 'programs', that make it possible for computers and computer-based machines ('hardware') to perform their tasks.

**spot colours** A printing colour that has been specifically mixed for the job, as opposed to using the four-colour process *(qv)* colours.

**strapline** A sub-heading adjacent to the heading *(qv)* in a piece of text. Straplines are used to give extra information about the subject matter of text pieces.

**streaming** A method of transmitting audio or video files, allowing them to be played continuously.

**tagging** Mark-up language formatting comands. A tag is switched on by placing a command inside angle brackets (<command>), and turned off by typing the same command again, with a forwards slash before it (</command>).

**template** A document created with pre-positioned areas, used as a basis for repeatedly creating other documents that follow the same format and style.

**three-dimensional (3D)** The effect of creating an illusion of depth on a page or monitor.

**TIFF** Acronym for 'tagged image file format'. A standard and popular graphics file format originally developed by Aldus (now merged with Adobe) and Microsoft. TIFFs are used for scanned *(qv)*, bitmapped *(qv)* images, and for colour separations. They can be used to transmit black-and-white, greyscale or colour images that have been generated on all the most popular platforms.

**touch screen** A computer screen that responds to touch, side-stepping the need for a computer mouse. Large touch screens respond to finger touches, while small versions are usually navigated using a round-nibbed plastic pen ('stylus').

**tracking** The adjustment of space between characters in a seleced piece of text. See also *kerning*.

**traffic** In an advertising context, elements of client business that an agency is handling.

**trapping** Settings in DTP programs which determine the interaction of overlapping colours. Also refers to printing problems when one solid colour completely overprints another. Trapping preferences are complex and best left to the service bureau or printer.

**TrueType** Apple Computer's digital font *(qv)* technology, developed as an alternative to PostScript *(qv)* and now used by both Apple and Microsoft for their respective operating systems. A single TrueType file is used for both printing and screen rendering, while PostScript fonts require two separate files for these functions.

**typography** The art of type *(qv)* design and its arrangement on a designed page.

**URL** Abbreviation for 'uniform resource locator'. The unique address of any page on the Web *(qv)*. A URL is usually composed of three elements: the protocol (such as 'http'), the domain name and the directory name.

**varnish** A liquid that dries to form a hard surface, which does not dissolve in water. Varnish is used in the manufacture of printing inks *(qv)* and as a surface protector for printed matter, especially covers.

**vector** A miniature database that stores information about the magnitude and direction of a line or shape. Sometimes used to refer to the lines themselves.

**Windows** The PC *(qv)* operating system devised by Microsoft. Windows uses a graphical user interface that is similar to the Mac OS *(qv)*. In some circumstances Windows can be run on a Macintosh *(qv)* computer, but the Mac OS cannot run on a PC that is designed to run Windows.

**Web** Also known as 'World Wide Web' (WWW). The entire population of Web servers that are connected to the Internet *(qv)*. The term is also used to describe a particular kind of Internet access architecture that uses a combination of HTML *(qv)* and various graphic formats such as JPEG *(qv)* to publish formatted text and pictures that can be read by Web browsers *(qv)*.

# BIBLIOGRAPHY

**ART & DESIGN**
**Books**
*The Design Annual*, Graphis International, New York
Albrecht, Donald, Holt, Steven, Lupton, Ellen, *Design Culture Now: The National Design Triennial*, Princeton Architectural Press, New Jersey, 2000
Berger, John, *Ways of Seeing*, Viking Penguin, London, 1991
Heller, Stephen, *Icons of Graphic Design*, Thames & Hudson, London, 2001
Hollis, Richard, *Graphic Design: A Concise History*, Thames & Hudson, London, 2001
Hughes, Robert, *The Shock of the New*, Thames & Hudson, London, 1991
Livingston, Alan, Livingston, Isabella, *The Thames & Hudson Dictionary of Graphic Design and Designers*, Thames & Hudson, London, 1992

**Periodicals**
*Blueprint, Computer Arts, Creative Review, Design Weekly, Emigre, Eye, Flash Art, Frieze, Mac User, Wallpaper, Wired*

**PRINT**
**Books**
Fawcett-Tang, Roger, *Experimental Formats*, RotoVision, Hove, 2001
Fishel, Catherine, *Paper Graphics*, Rockport, Gloucester MA, 1999
Foges, Chris, *Magazine Design*, RotoVision, Hove, 1999
Hochuli, Jost, *Designing Books: Practice and Theory*, Hyphen, London, 1997
Hurlburt, Allen, *The Grid*, John Wiley & Sons, New York, 1982
Koren, Leonard, *Graphic Design Cookbook*, Chronicle, San Francisco, 2001
Pipes, Allan, *Production for Graphic Designers*, Laurence King, London, 2001

Sen, Lim Ching, *By Design*, HarperCollins, London, 2001
Zappaterra, Yolanda, *Digital Lab: Editorial, Print and Electronic Design*, RotoVision, Hove, 2001

**ADVERTISING**
**Books**
Aitchison, Jim, *Cutting Edge Advertising*, Prentice Hall, London, 1999
Brierley, Sean, *The Advertising Handbook*, Routledge, London, 1995
Butterfield, Leslie (ed), *Excellence in Advertising*, Butterworth-Heinemann, Boston, 1997
Chaffrey, David, *Internet Marketing*, Prentice Hall, Harrow, 2000
Goddard, Angela, *The Language of Advertising*, Routledge, London, 1998
Williamson, Judith, *Decoding Advertisements*, M Boyars, New York, 1979

**Websites**
www.mediaguardian.co.uk/media lounge; www.ipa.co.uk; www.dan-dad.co.uk; www.adassoc.org.uk; www.eaaa.be; www.aaaa.org; www.americanadagencies.com; www.aaf.org; www.adforum.com

**PACKAGING**
**Books**
Cliff, Stafford, *Fifty Trade Secrets of Great Design Packaging*, Rockport Publishers, Gloucester MA, 1999
Design Week Books, *The Packaging Design Book* (annual), Centaur Publishing, London, 2001
Fishel, Catharine, *The Perfect Package*, Rockport Publishers, Gloucester MA, 2000
Meyers, Herbert and Lubliner, Murray, *The Marketer's Guide to Successful Package Design*, NTC Publishing Group, Chicago, 1998
Phillips, Renee, *Packaging Graphics and Design*, Rockport Publishers, Gloucester MA, 2001

**SIGNAGE**
**Books**
Barker, P, *Sign Design Guide*, JMU Access Partnership & Sign Design Society, London, 2000
Follis, John and Hammer, Dave, *Architectural Signing and Graphics*, Whitney Library of Design, New York, 1979
Grayson, Trulove J, Sprague, C Colony, S, *This Way: Signage Design for Public Spaces*, Rockport Publishers, Gloucester MA, 2000
Wildbur, P and Burke, M, *Information Graphics*, Thames and Hudson, London, 1999

**EXHIBITION**
**Books**
Carter, Rob, Majewski, Jan, et al, *Exhibition and Display Design*, RotoVision, Hove, 2000
Mijksenaar, Paul and Westendorp, Piet, *Open Here*, Stewart, Tabori and Chang, New York, 1999
Miles, R S (ed), *The Design of Educational Exhibits*, George Allen & Unwin, London, 1982
Pegler, Michael, *Contemporary Exhibit Design*, Visual Reference Publications, New York, 2001

**WEB/MULTIMEDIA**
**Books**
Bhangal, Sham, Rey, Patrick, *Foundation Flash 5*, Friends of Ed, Birmingham, 2000
Solente, Antony, *After Effects 5 for Macintosh and Windows*, Peachpit Press, Berkeley, CA, 2001
Davis, Jack, Merritt, Susan, *The Web Design Wow! Book*, Peachpit Press, Berkeley CA, 1998
Dayton, Linnea, *The PhotoShop 6 Wow! Book*, Peachpit Press, Berkeley CA, 2001
Greiman, April, *Hybrid Imagery*, Watson-Guptill Publications, New York, 1990
Haskell, Barry, G et al, *Digital Video*, Chapman & Hall, New York, 1996

Riley, Martyn J, Richardson, Iain, *Digital Video Communications*, Artech House, Norwood MA, 1997
Merritt, Douglas, *Television Graphics*, John Wiley, New York, 1987
Piteru, Amit et al, *New Masters of Flash*, Friends of Ed, Birmingham, 2001
Poyner, Rick (ed), *Typography Now 2*, William Morrow, New York, 1998
Robbins, Christopher, *Director 8.5 Studio*, Friends of Ed, Birmingham, 2001
Rose, Carla, *Teach Yourself Adobe Photoshop 6 in 24 Hours*, SAMS, Indianapolis, 2000
Towers, J Tarin, *Dreamweaver 4 for Windows and Macintosh*, Peachpit Press, Berkeley CA, 2001
Velthoven, Willem (ed), *Multimedia Graphics*, Chronicle Books, San Francisco, 1996

**Websites**
www.adobe.com; www.computer-arts.co.uk; www.absolutecross /tutorials/photoshop.htm; www.deepspaceweb.com; www.design dojo.com; www.designmuseum.org; www.illustrator-resources.com; www.photoshop-central.com; www.photoshop-cafe.com; www.planetphotoshop.com; www.magicpixel.com.au

**FLASH reference sites**
www.nillmancurtis.com; www.wallpaper.com; www.linkdup.com; www.amoebacorp.com; www.design.net.uk; www.traffic-movie.com; www.egomedia.com; www.deepend.co.uk; www.turtleshell.com; www.cool homepages.com

**Commercial sites**
www.hooven.co.uk; www.newbeetle.co.uk; www.vw.com; www.tothepoint.tl; www.yugop.com

# INDEX

# INDEX

the complete guide to digital graphic design

# PICTURE ACKNOWLEDGEMENTS

**Abbreviations:** t **top;** l **left;** r **right;** b **bottom;** c **centre;** m **middle**

**p2-3** Aston Leach / MacUser Magazine; **p12** Studio Myerscough; **p13** t Phil Bicker / DPICT magazine, b Cahan & Associates; **p14** t AMV BBDO Ltd, photography by Paul Zak, art director: Dave Dye, copywriter: Sean Doyle, account director: Oliver Forder, client: Hugh McCahey, b M&C Saatchi, creatives: Tiger Savage and Mark Goodwin, photography by Christopher Griffin; **p15** t Bartle Bogle Hegarty, London br design by Wieden and Kennedy / graphics by VgL, br Peter Stimpson / courtesy of MCV; **p16** t Area, br Summa, br Cahan & Associates; **p17** t Simon & Lars, b Veuve Clicquot; **p18** t Sussman/Prejza & Company Inc., b Ruedi Baur & Associates; **p19** tr commissioned by Edogawa Ward, design unknown, m Sussman/Prejza & Company Inc., b Niklaus Troxler; **p20** l Ralph Applebaum Associates Inc., r Design by IDEO; **p21** top: Pentagram: partner/designer: Peter Harrison (graphics), partner/architect: James Biber, architect: Michael Zweck-Bronner, design by Christina Freyss, photography by Bill Jacobson and Peter Mauss, Esto, b Poulin & Morris: photography by Tim Wilkes, Tim Wilkes Photography; **p22** br NB Studio, Courtesy of Knoll, tr Daniel Althausen, b Donna DiStefano; **p23** t Memphis, b Imagination for Guinness PLC; **p24** l Maddalene Beltrami and the Ospedale Maggiore di Milano, r InterStitch; **p25** l RTKL, tr Blue Byte, br EA Sports; **p28** Lance Wyman; **p29** br Emery Vincent Design, tr: Carol Naughton & Associates Inc., br Niklaus Troxler; **p30** Produced by the Whitechapel Art Gallery to coincide with the exhibition Live In Your Head (Feb-Apr 2000), design by Jo Stockham and Herman Lelie, Concept and Edited by Alistair Raphael; **p31** br Chermayeff & Geismar, tr Alan Fletcher, c Niklaus Troxler; **p32** Barney Pickard; **p33** t RTKL & Jonathan Spiers & Associates, b Tom Graboski Associates; **p34** l Williams Murray Hamm, r Pentagram: design by John Rushworth, design assistants: Vince Frost and Nick Finney; **p35** t Tenazas Design, br Niklaus Troxler, br Chronicle Books, USA; **p38** l Adobe Systems; **p39** Emery Vincent Design; **p40** l Chermayeff & Geismar, br Adobe Systems, tr Swifty @ Swifty Typografix, cr Gensler, b Barney Pickard; **p41** Regina Frank/SDA Creative; **p42** Wink Design; **p43** l Alan Fletcher, r Williams Murray Hamm; **p44** br Bryn Jones, t Chronicle Books **p45** t Cahan & Associates, b RTKL; **p46** Lippa Pearce; **p47** b Brian Coe; **p48** b Mauk Design; **p51** br Lance Wyman, tr Pippo Lionni; **p52** t Agenda, b Cahan & Associates; **p53** t Cahan & Associates, b Chronicle Books; **p54** l Grey Worldwide, r Cahan & Associates; **p55** t MetaDesign, br Alan Fletcher, br Cahan & Associates; **p56** l Alan Fletcher, r graphic and interior design by Ashdown Wood Design for 'Hang Out Laundry and Drycleaning', Sydney, Australia; **p57** br The Partners, br Summa, r design by Holmes Wood at Tate Gallery, London; **p60** l design by Harry Crumb for Durian Publications, r Teeranop Wangsillapakun, Segura Inc., Chicago; **p61** Why Not Associates, photography by Rocco Redondo and Photodisc, courtesy of Royal Academy of Arts; **p75** Bill Douglas, The Bang, photography by Glenda Stuart and Bill Douglas; **p77** Frederico d'Orazio, PlaatsMaken; **p79** t Dom Raban, Eg.G, br Lippa Pearce Design, br Jon Raimes, Foundation Publishing; **p81** t Pollard & Van der Water Golden, l SEA Design, r Epoxy, courtesy of Rolland Motif Paper; **p83** Jon Raimes, Foundation Publishing; **p84** Duckworth Finn Grubb Waters; **p85** t McCann Erickson, b Rainey Kelly Campbell Roalfe; **p86** Tribal DDB, Spain; **p87** t Brook Street, b DDB; **p88** Triangle Communications; **p89** t Impact FCA!, b Duckworth Finn Grubb Waters; **p90** r TBWA/Chiat/Day; **p91** Craik Jones; **p92** Tequila; **p93** c KLP Euro RSCG, b Benetton; **p95** BMP; **p97** Duckworth Finn Grubb Waters; **p98** Kenzo; **p99** t Pentagram, b Paul Smith Ltd; **p104** l SCA Packaging, r Fuji Seal Europe; **p105** tr Lawson Mardon Packaging; **p110-11**: Richard Gooch, John Lewis Partnership; **p112** Pentagram; **P113** The Partners; **p114** t North Design, b Atelier Works; **p115** t MetaDesign, br Pentagram, br CDT Design; **p117** br Pentagram, tr Royal National Institute for the Blind, b architects: Allford Hall Monaghan Morris, design by Atelier Works; **p 118** t Atelier, b photography by Todd Gipstein, Corbis; **p 119** CDT Design; **p 121** Atelier; **p122-23**: CDT Design; **p124** design by Euroculture, courtesy Jean Michel Folon, Sabam 2001, photography by Thiery Renauld; **p125** br Guggenheim Museum, tr Event Communications, b Event Communications; **p 126** Perks Willis Design; **p127** t Philip Miles Graphic Design, b Perks Willis Design; **p128** t Land Design Studios and The Chase, bl & br design by DEGW, courtesy of the Trustees of the Imperial War Museum, photography by Philip Vile; **p129-31** Exhibition Plus and Perks Willis Design; **p132-33** Exhibition Plus and Perks Willis Design, courtesy of the Natural History Museum, London; **p133** t illustration by Debbie Cook and Colin Mier; **p136** Design by Ego Media; **p137** r Yugo Nakamura, l Dennis Interactive; **p138** Atlantic-Records.com; **p139** tr Google.com, b Apple.com; **p142** t Jakob Nielsen, b Typographic.com; **p154** br & ct Powazek Productions, cb & br Biggles; **p162** Nykris Digital Design, courtesy of the Tate Gallery; **p163** t Nykris Digital Design, courtesy of the Tate Gallery, r Core Design; **p164-165** Design by Headprecious Design; **p166** Cognitive Applications; **p167** Tomato Interactive; **p169** InterStitch; **p170** Tomato Interactive; **p175** Phil Taylor and Phil Jackson; **p177** Cognitive Applications; **p188** photography by Bob Krist, Corbis; **p189** Nicklaus Troxler; **p197** Tom Hingston Studio, courtesy of MacUser Magazine; **p200** photograph by Ed Seabourne **p200** RTKL; **p201** t Pamela Geismar, courtesy of Chronicle Books; **p209** Lawrence Zeegen

**Additional Photography by Rob Turner and Bob Gordon**

**Diagrams by bounford.com**